A Brief History of
Oral Sex

A Brief History of Oral Sex

David DePierre

Exposit

Jefferson, North Carolina

An earlier version of this work was published
by the author as *They Stoop to Conquer*

LIBRARY OF CONGRESS CATALOGUING-IN-PUBLICATION DATA

Names: DePierre, David, 1980– author.
Title: A brief history of oral sex / David DePierre.
Description: Jefferson, North Carolina : McFarland & Company, Inc.,
Publishers, 2017 | Includes bibliographical references and index.
Identifiers: LCCN 2017022287 | ISBN 9781476671260
(softcover : acid free paper) ∞
Subjects: LCSH: Oral sex—History.
Classification: LCC HQ31.5.O73 D47 2017 | DDC 306.77/4—dc23
LC record available at https://lccn.loc.gov/2017022287

BRITISH LIBRARY CATALOGUING DATA ARE AVAILABLE

ISBN 978-1-4766-7126-0 (print)
ISBN 978-1-4766-3027-4 (ebook)

Front cover photograph of sculpture in Khajuraho © 2017 iStock

Printed in the United States of America

Exposit is an imprint of McFarland & Company, Inc., Publishers
Jefferson, North Carolina

Exposit

Box 611, Jefferson, North Carolina 28640
www.expositbooks.com

Table of Contents

Preface

Everyone is doing it: kings, queens, farmers, conquerors, artists, and even religious figures. Queen Victoria did it, Gandhi did it, and even Abraham Lincoln. No less than St. Augustine wrote extensively about it. By the late 1960s, the Beatles mused about it in their song "Why Don't We Do It in the Road?" In fact, if they were not doing it, you would not be here today. Everyone is doing it. And while that axiom may hold true for sex in general, its pertinence to oral sex is a much more complicated issue both socially and historically. Writing about any particular sexual practice is always a difficult exercise in history due to the limited number of sources from so many regions and across so many eras. A matter that is so widespread, yet so private, does not often become the subject of historical conversation. Of all these acts, oral sex demands particular academic attention because of the changing perceptions of the practice over the past 4,000 years. While the belief that primitive man was an anarchic hedonist has now been largely disproven, there were certainly fewer restrictions on his sexual practices. As civilization was constructed and ideas of health, religion, and philosophy arose, certain erotic undertakings came to be considered impure, unclean, or simply unnecessary. Oral sex became one of the first sexual activities of man to fall under that category. In keeping with most prohibitions throughout human history, a subculture of resistance developed and slowly, over thousands of years, whittled away at these restrictions until oral sex was once again an acceptable practice. But did the practice ever truly disappear? Were attempts by individuals, governments, philosophies, and religions to eradicate oral sex actually successful or did it simply continue as before, performed in private and not discussed?

Interestingly, these restrictions seem to have been at times geographically contained. Europe, the Middle East, and North Africa all bore historical aversions to the practice of fellatio and cunnilingus. Yet as one traveled further to the east across Asia and eventually the Pacific, the natural migration of man, these taboos became less pronounced until they eventually disappeared altogether in the wilderness of North and South America. While it is true that the Amerindians were at a more primitive stage of development than Eurasians and thus their view of oral sex may reflect that of the Old World before the rise of civilization, the more relaxed attitude of India and China to the practice is more difficult to explain.

This book will examine the general rise, fall, and renaissance of oral sex in world history. Specific attention will be paid to the overall view of the practice by various cultures as well as anecdotes portraying times when fellatio or cunnilingus altered the history of men or nations. Reasons for the decline and rebirth of the practice will also be explored as well as explanations of the different views of oral sex across the globe. History is little more than a collection of individuals, and individuals are simply an assemblage of their traits, desires, and personal practices. Historically, little has been more personal for people than what they have done between sheets, or, in this case, on their knees.

Introduction

Halfway through Shakespeare's *Hamlet*, while the audience attempts to fathom the play within a play offered by the Prince to identify his father's killer, the main character busies himself with thoughts and talk of sex. As the players on the stage ready themselves for the performance, Hamlet cozies up next to Ophelia.

> **Hamlet:** Lady, shall I lie in your lap?
> **Ophelia:** No, my lord.
> **Hamlet:** I mean, my head upon your lap?
> **Ophelia:** Ay, my lord.
> **Hamlet:** Do you think I meant *country* matters?[1]

Though most high school students and even their teachers may miss the subtle reference today, 17th-century audiences would have certainly perceived not only the joke but its larger associations, and Hamlet was not the only one to have "country" matters on his mind. Man's interest in sex is well established, but his love of oral sex in particular is a subject historically both taboo and under-documented. Long before Hamlet attempted to lay his head in Ophelia's lap for unrestful purposes, men and women were partaking in one of the most intimate forms of love, and for just as long they were stopped from doing so. This work traces the history of that activity, highlighting its function, historical importance, and periods of repression and acceptance.

The first question to be answered is whether oral sex is a purely human undertaking. Zoologists have recently discovered several examples of similar activity within the animal kingdom. Research has been limited, but currently, all of these seem to fall within the class Mammalia, and even then only among certain species. As the most primitive of mammals, specifically the monotremes, appear to not participate in oral sex, the inclination to do so seems to have evolved only in the placentalia orders. A potential reason for this may be the presence of a cloaca in monotremes and non-mammalian species. The combination of reproductive, urinary, and defecation functions into one opening may restrict oral sex due the possibility of bacterial infection and the transmission of disease. Non-placental animals, including monotremes, also lack a corpus callosum within the brain. This bundle of nerves which coordinates communication between the right and left hemispheres of the brain may play a role in the desire for, or delivery of, oral sex.

An interesting case of oral sex among mammals has been found in the greater short-nosed fruit bat (*Cynopterus sphinx*) of Southeast Asia. In an action first observed by the Guangdong Entomological Institute in 2009, the female of the species bent forward and licked the male's penis during mating. Out of the 20 copulations observed, fellatio was involved in 14 of them. The sheer number of occurrences would seem to suggest that this is a conscious and coordinated practice that serves an evolutionary need. Those bats that engaged in the act had longer sexual encounters, with each second of oral stimulation adding six seconds of penetration time. The researchers could only speculate as to the benefit of such an arrangement, suggesting that the increased sex time would lead to a higher chance of successful fertilization or that the female's licking helped to prevent the transmission of STDs. Either way, the female's fellatio seems to have benefited her as much as or more than it did the male.[2]

The Indian flying fox, or *Pteropus giganteus*, has also been observed to take part in oral sex, but the activity was cunnilingus rather than fellatio. A 2013 study seems to suggest that by performing oral sex, male flying foxes were more frequently allowed to then have sex with females. In fact, males who performed cunnilingus were able to mount their mates in 57 out of 69 cases. Much like the benefits observed in fruit bats, the practice of oral sex also seems to have lengthened the duration of sex between the partners. Interestingly, once copulation had finished, these same males once again performed oral sex on the females. In almost all cases this second bout seems to have lasted two to three times as long as pre-sex cunnilingus. The reasons behind this behavior may have to do with cleanliness, disease prevention, social bonding, or the ingestion of lost semen.[3] Finally, prolonging sex may help males and females to restrict competitive mating, giving the male's sperm a greater chance of fertilization and reducing the offspring of other females.

Oral sex in hyenas also seems to serve a purely practical rather than pleasurable purpose. As with many other animals, sexual dimorphism can be seen among spotted hyenas. Females tend to be slightly larger and heavier than males and perhaps in part because of this hyena society is a matriarchal system. Yet physical dimensions are not the only area in which female hyenas outdo their male counterparts. For thousands of years, observers were convinced that this animal was either asexual or hermaphroditic. The Greco-Roman writer Oppian suggested as much when he wrote in the 2nd century, "This marvel also I have heard about the spotted Hyenas, to wit that male and female change year by year, and one is now a weak-eyed bridegroom all eager to mate and anon appears as a lady bride, a bearer of children, and a goodly mother."[4] Similar observations were made by Ovid in his *Metamorphosis*. "But, if we wonder at strange things like these, we ought to wonder also, when we learn that a hyena has a change of sex: the female, quitting her embracing male, herself becomes a male."[5] Aelian and many other writers of the ancient Mediterranean world likewise were intrigued by the sexuality of the hyena, both its biological sexuality and its behaviors. Some Roman writers certainly seized upon this discovery as a way to explain the sexual appetites of their own people, particularly the cinaedus subculture that existed within the empire.

The reason behind this misconceived notion of the animal lies in the fact that female hyenas lack a vagina in the normal mammalian sense. Instead these animals possess a seven-inch clitoris that resembles a pseudopenis in look and function. Females use this organ to urinate and have sex; the difficulty of the latter led in part to hyena society becoming extremely female dominated. "Even though the female's organ is flaccid during copulation, its only opening points forward and downward, so the male must hop around behind the female while he squats behind her, thrusting blindly upward and backward, to achieve intromission. It's actually very comical."[6] Once pregnant, the animal delivers its one kilogram cubs through the same clitoris, a process that often results in it tearing. Though a member of the cat family and very closely related to the mongoose, the hyena appears to be the only animal with such a unique sex organ.

A hyena's clitoris has taken on a social function as well. Able to cause it to erect at will, females of the species employ it as a tool in ceremonies of greeting and subordination. Hyenas who have spent time apart will, when reunited, sniff and lick the clitoris of the female, which she will make erect for such an action. Subordinate members of the group are also expected to perform this act regularly on those above them as a sign of respect. As males are always subordinate to females in hyena society, they never receive oral stimulation in turn.

Among the distantly related great cats we see some oral attention paid also, usually during the mating ritual. Cheetahs of both sexes will lick and nuzzle their prospective partners' genitals in order to attract them. Likewise, a female lion will repeatedly lick a male's penis to get him aroused. As lionesses can mate up to 100 times a day, this may be necessary to attract a weary partner.

Another species that exhibits oral sex behavior is the Ugandan kob. A type of antelope, the kob is another example of a female-dominated species. In a similar way to hyenas, female kobs have been observed performing oral sex on each other. A male will likewise nuzzle and lick the female's vulva prior to engaging in intercourse.[7] Again this seems to be a gender-dominated activity.

The widest range of oral sex unsurprisingly can be found in the species most closely related to humans. Siamangs, a type of gibbon that inhabits portions of Sumatra and Malaysia, have been observed performing oral sex on both genders of the species. In an interesting twist, frequent incestuous oral sex has been seen among the Siamang. This occurs between siblings and between parents and children. Even more advanced versions of fellatio and cunnilingus appear among gorillas and chimpanzees. The former has been observed orally and digitally stimulating the female of the species during the mating ritual.[8] Gorillas are also one of the few species to be observed performing simultaneous oral sex on each other. Likewise, male chimpanzees have been known to perform oral sex on females, specifically focusing on the clitoris.[9]

The animal whose sexual practices most closely resemble those of humans happens to be one of our closest relatives, the bonobo. Also known as pygmy chimpanzees, bonobos live in highly social tribes. For this species, sex is used for a variety of functions beyond simply mating. Included among these are problem solving, tension relief, bond building, and simple greeting. Oral sex plays a large part in these activities, with much of it being male-on-female or female-on-female. In fact, female bonobos have a clitoris three times larger than a human, though they themselves are much smaller in size.[10] So accustomed to the practice of oral sex are they that bonobos on reserves have been known to actually approach humans for sex.

Besides these instances of oral sex within the animal kingdom, most recently other, less-than-ordinary sex acts have been recorded among different creatures. In September of 2003, two male bears in a Croatian zoo received international attention when they began engaging in oral sex. While the report was trumpeted in an attempt to buttress various agendas, scientists argued that the practice was actually non-sexual in nature. For three years the same male initiated and performed fellatio on the other, who did nothing in return. It was speculated that the first bear was compensating for missed nursing experience when he was a cub.[11] Apart from this instance, there appears to be no observable oral sex practiced by bears in the wild. At the same time numerous cases of self-fellatio do exist in the animal world. More common examples include thinhorn sheep, dolphins, sea otters, and manatees. While certainly many of these episodes are sexual in nature, some are matters of simple self-cleaning.

The reasons some animals engage in oral sex appear to be varied, including a desire for cleanliness, as a mating ritual, to build social bonds, or to encourage fertilization, but it is evident that there is a biological and evolutionary basis to the act as well. As incidents of oral sex only appear in placental mammals and become more common as one moves through the primate family toward hominids, an argument can be made for a connection between evolution and fellatio and cunnilingus. With all of the above reasons as to perhaps why animals perform oral sex, it is not surprising that a species that undertakes fellatio and cunnilingus as much as humans would have even more reasons for doing so. Numerous biologists, historians, and anthropologists have attempted to explain man's predilection for and interest in the act in social and anatomical ways. Is there an evolutionary and biological basis for oral sex or did it grow from social or cultural roots?

One of the more bizarre reasons promulgated for the abundance of oral sex among humans is as a form of infidelity detection. The argument runs that men are unconsciously looking for sperm and are working toward keeping their mates from cheating. Women also performed fellatio for the same reason. A study by Michael N. Pham on the subject postulated that men with more attractive partners were more willing to give their women oral pleasure most likely because of the increased risk that these women would cheat.[12] In a related theory, oral sex could serve as a means to preemptively discourage cheating as the partner would be able to detect the foreign fluid, yet it would seem that with the development of modern hygiene, the chances of detecting foreign fluids through oral sex would be limited and thus the act would most likely have faded away rather than taken hold.

A second area of focus is that oral sex helps to increase the success of mating. A number of works on the subject argue that fellatio and cunnilingus can be used to demonstrate sexual prowess, physical fitness, or general health and cleanliness to a mate.[13] Still another study suggests that a woman who experiences an orgasm had a better chance of retaining sperm; as oral sex aided a woman's ability to climax it therefore increased a man's chances of passing on his genes.[14] This became a popular belief among some scientists during the Enlightenment and helped to push groups such as the Jesuits toward a more nuanced acceptance of the practice. In a similar way, oral sex is seen as a way to build bonds between partners. This exercise pays dividends in monogamous species that exclusively mate to successfully raise their offspring. Likewise, oral sex is a practice wrapped up in a level of trust between partners. A tremendous amount of faith must be placed in the fellator or cunnilictor that he or she will not cause damage to the valuable reproductive organs of the recipient. While sex itself is by and large lacking in the ability to cause serious, permanent injury to the sex organs, oral sex is much more dangerous. The hands or mouth could seriously harm an individual, threatening not only his or her life but potentially damaging a woman's ability to conceive or carry offspring. Thus, it is a dangerous diversion from regular, reproductive sex which is entered into only with a certain level of personal trust.

A third area of explanation involves human psychology. To Freud and others, dreams of fellatio and the actual act itself were unconscious reminders of and desires for nursing.

> Women, it seems, find no difficulty in producing this kind of wishful phantasy spontaneously. Further investigation informs us that this situation may be traced to an origin of the most innocent kind. It only repeats in a different form a situation [when] we took our mother's nipple into our mouth and sucked at it and when at a later date the child becomes familiar with the cow's udder whose function is that of a nipple, but whose shape and position under the belly make it resemble a penis, the preliminary stage has been reached which will later enable [her] to form the repellent sexual phantasy.[15]

Thus, the practice of oral sex, most notably fellatio, can be explained as an unconscious desire for one's mother. When the great psychoanalyst developed his theory of the stages of sexual development, he placed the oral stage as the lowest level of maturation. This low placement was to be a common view of most Western civilizations from the time of the ancient Greeks to the dawning of the 20th century.

Perhaps in line with Occam's razor, though, the simplest explanation is actually the most correct. The purpose of oral sex could certainly just be the pleasure of the practice. The act evolved and continued exclusively due to the fact that men and women enjoyed it. Physiologically, oral sensation activates a tremendous number of neurons, producing pleasure in the performer and the recipient.[16] In this way fellatio and cunnilingus resembled other non-reproductive related sexual activities. Regardless of the reasons behind the practice, the act itself played an interesting role in numerous cultures and across times, destroying careers, raising kings from the dead, and bringing world leaders to their knees.

Napoleon once opined that there are two things that amateurs often end up doing better than professionals: waging war and having sex. The latter especially requires no formal training, expensive schooling, paid-for degrees, access to expensive equipment, research grants, or government programs. The private individual, in the comfort and anonymity of his or her own life and home, can become quite adept at the practice. Thus, morals, laws, religious dogma, and public scruples can do little to combat it. Whether everyone was doing it, or simply assuming that everyone was, at the very least very few were talking about it.

As a matter of apology, researching a particular sexual act can prove to be a difficult endeavor. Apart from obvious issues of historical censorship, terminology proves to be a more delicate matter. In keeping up with the censors and with societal trends, oral sex has gone through three millennia of names, terms, and slang. Cunnilingus, considered the proper term for the act in the English language, was largely unused in writing before the 1890s except in the works of the Roman poet Martial. Still later the term sodomy became commonly used in Western literature to define a wide series of acts, including oral sex and homosexual intercourse. The history and anecdotes herein represent the author's best attempts at decoding 3,000 years of man's attempts to tell without telling about one of the most interesting and forbidden acts in history.

1

Sex in the Ancient World

Though many primates practiced fellatio or cunnilingus to varying degrees, it appears that the evolution of hominids led to the subsequent evolution of oral sex. Man's sexual proclivities were no more developed from the start than his mental or physical abilities were; all underwent changes and adaptations over the course of tens of thousands of years. It does appear that the adoption of oral sex as a more standard practice probably began at a relatively early stage of hominid evolution. With new studies showing the vast amount of interbreeding between various species of early man, sex was hardly an infrequent affair. Yves Coppens, who headed the Hardar Expedition that discovered the remains of Lucy, has speculated that she and other Australopithecus of her time engaged in fellatio and cunnilingus for a variety of reasons. Besides the lack of a moral code restraining them from such behavior, they now had the upright posture and free hands to partake in such a practice more readily than their immediate ancestors did.[1] One of the reasons for the absence of endemic oral sex in the animal kingdom, even among those mammals who do practice it, may be in the lack of a physical, biological ability to do so. Undoubtedly, the enjoyment of the practice also helped to push in part reproductive choice, thus securing the passing on of physical traits that allowed for it. Oral sex helped man to evolve.

This idea fits in well with recent research done by Jennifer and Laura Berman, among others. The Bermans speculated that there are two personality types in regard to sex, pleasure-oriented and goal-oriented.[2] The former solely focused on themselves and the immediate results of intercourse, with any pleasure being derived from it serving as an end in and of itself. Goal-oriented people, on the other hand, aim at a final climax for themselves and their partners. As many women are only able to achieve orgasm through oral stimulation, goal-oriented partners are more likely to engage in cunnilingus and are the more desirable sexual partner. Furthermore, it can be argued that people who are goal-oriented toward sex are likely to carry this mindset into other fields and endeavors. Overall, goal-oriented people are more likely to reproduce successfully and provide for the survival of their offspring, thus making oral sex an evolutionary advantage.

Other reasons for the rise of oral sex among early man were perhaps more practical. Prostitution has often been referred to as the oldest profession, with many anthropologists assuming that primitive females could trade sexual favors for food, protection, or supplies. Surely this had to involve oral sex as well since it would be counterproductive to risk potential pregnancy in exchange for a little food. Though it is difficult to fathom early man's understanding of the exact components of the reproductive process, perhaps enough knowledge or fear existed to necessarily limit their practice of sexual intercourse. Oral sex could have also been practiced by people in general, however not necessarily just during promiscuous encounters. As with bonobos, the act also helped to build bonds between members of the tribe or factored into early religious or coming of age ceremonies. Clearly much of this is simply necessary speculation, yet such a widespread and recorded behavior among humans, with clear parallels in the animal kingdom, must certainly have had an early origin, one that even predated written records.

As early man progressed further he sought to move beyond the present and express himself to his contemporaries and posterity. The earliest means by which he accomplished this was through oral tales—stories and songs that would deliver a message through the generations. Around 40,000 years ago, though, the preferred method of communication changed dramatically as people instead began to draw on cave walls as a more permanent means of relaying information. The themes that early man included in his art tended to reflect issues important to him. Thus, hunting, fighting, and the physical world became the most commonly drawn subjects for primitive people. Even mundane tasks and daily activities were drawn. Perhaps unsurprisingly, sex and oral sex are also featured in a number of illustrations. In La Marche, France, a 14,000-year-old cave painting depicts some of the earliest known references to oral sex. The clear image of a man can be seen thrusting his face in between a woman's thighs. While the validity of the site itself remains controversial among archaeologists and historians, it is taken for granted that certainly by the Paleolithic Era man practiced oral sex.[3] Art had begun to depict an act that would become standard fare for painters and sculptors on every continent for thousands of years.

While written evidence of the act from the time period is lacking, a certain number of conclusions can be drawn based on comparative studies. Apart from the general practice of the act, the initiation rituals of much later tribes in Oceania and Africa may bear some relation to ritualized oral sex practices among Paleolithic people. Among the Sambia people of New Guinea, young men ingest the semen of older members of the tribe through fellatio in an effort to acquire their strength and virility. Some researchers have suggested a similar practice among early men, connecting it with cannibalism and headhunting.[4] The practice of the tradition among other groups as far afield as Africa implies a certain universality to it.

The onset of the Neolithic Age led early man to begin forming small villages and larger towns in order to accommodate his new agricultural lifestyle. Living in closer quarters, with a greater number of people and in a sedentary manner, allowed for increased non-reproductive sex. A recent study has proposed that it was this dalliance with oral sex around the end of the last Ice Age that led to the emergence of gonorrhea, a disease still ravaging humanity. The bacterium that causes the disease, Neisseria gonorrhea, is itself a mutation of a more harmless bacterium called Neisseria meningitides. The latter normally lives in the throats of humans, but due to chance mutation brought about by an increase in oral sex among early man, began to live in genital areas instead. The protein that it produced to bind itself to this new location produces the inflammation associated with the condition.[5] Undoubtedly the creation of trade connections between these new towns and the constant migration of man helped to spread the disease further until it touched practically every corner of the globe. Some in the 19th century blamed cunnilingus for the evolution and spread of syphilis as well. "They had no shame in serving women and girls during their menses; and this is a fact that has great importance from the standpoint of viewing the genesis of syphilis."[6] The hedonistic, consequence-free world of primitive man, if it ever had existed, was already beginning to crumble.

In fact, several recent studies have suggested that the increased prevalence of sexually transmitted diseases led to the invention and spread of marriage. The population growth associated with the Neolithic Revolution, when combined with the rise of genital herpes and genital gonorrhea from increased oral sex, resulted in an explosion of sexually transmitted infections. Monogamy became a necessary alternative to the polygamy that seems to have characterized early man. Tribes and bands who failed to adopt this new practice soon dwindled and died out because of the damaging effects on fertility from sexually transmitted diseases. Thus, monogamy was strongly encouraged, with those living outside of this norm ostracized. As the chief deities became associated with farming or weather, their wives were more often than not the goddesses of marriage and fertility showing the importance of the practice.

Another 10,000 years would elapse before the sex lives of the ancients made their way into written history. The oldest recorded tale involving the practice comes from the ancient Egyptians. Appearing in the myth of Osiris and Isis, the story is documented from at least the time of the Pyramid Texts. Traditionally dated to around 2400 BC, this collection of stories and hymns is regarded as one of the oldest pieces of religious literature on the planet. Among the chants and spells in the collection is the story of the death and resurrection of the god-king Osiris. The myth was an archetype common to many ancient societies and in this particular manifestation concerned Osiris's murder at the hands of his brother Set, whom he had recently cuckolded by impregnating his wife. In a jealous attempt to seize power for himself, Set sealed Osiris into a box and later dismembered him into countless pieces. The dead god's wife and sister, Isis, wandered the length of Egypt collecting parts of her deceased husband. He was eventually pieced back together, but according to Plutarch's retelling of the tale, "notwithstanding all her efforts, Isis was never able to discover the phallus of Osiris, which, having been thrown into the Nile immediately upon its separation from the rest of the body, had been devoured by the Lepidotus, the Phagrus, and the Oxyrhynchus, fish which above all others, for this reason, the Egyptians have in more especial avoidance."[7] Isis then constructed a golden phallus to replace the missing part, and in a scene repeated time and again in Egyptian art, proceeded to sink to her knees and blow life back into Osiris. Having performed this resurrecting fellatio on the god she then mounted him and conceived a child, Horus. The later Cult of Isis incorporated her role in this myth into their initiation and worship of the goddess, with its priestesses becoming renowned either truthfully or derisively for their skill at fellatio.

The story of Osiris's death and resurrection bore important meaning for the ancient Egyptians. The dropping of his penis into the Nile symbolized its fertility, while his new phallus became an image to be worshipped by the masses. In fact, in his role as a symbol of fertility, the god is often depicted with a full erection. The ancient Egyptians filled their empire with phallic symbols of Osiris in the form of obelisks, monuments that would spread into the Middle East. The Tower of Babel can be interpreted as phallic in its design and imagery, with its purported builder, Nimrod, said to have experienced a dismemberment fate similar to Osiris.[8] This archetypal construction would be unknowingly carried on for thousands of years, with one of the best known modern examples being the Washington Monument, essentially a large phallus in the American capital.

The tale of Osiris was not the only example of mythological oral sex in Egypt. In the Heliopolitan creation myth, Atum, the original god, either masturbated or performed self-fellatio to begin creation. Upon ejaculating, he spit the semen from his mouth and thus created Shu and Tefnut, the wind and rain. These two gods produced Geb and Nut who represented the sky and the earth. Geb is often depicted in art as also performing self-fellatio, from which many additional gods were created. Occasionally, Geb and Nut are drawn in a 69 position, performing mutual oral sex and artistically depicting the connectedness of earth and sky. The frequency of myths concerning self-fellatio within Egyptian history is further represented by the culture's creation of the Ouroboros, an image of a snake eating its own tail. The symbol would be reused by different cultures throughout Western civilization well into the 20th century. Self-fellatio presents an interesting chapter in the larger study of the history of oral sex. In regard to the gods, the near physical impossibility of the action among mortals may have allowed the act to be viewed as more acceptable. Likewise, self-fertilization represented a purer accomplishment then relying on another for completion and compared well to the Roman and Greek view of fellatio which was largely negative based on the perceived passivity of the recipient.

The act is mentioned religiously in the famed Book of the Dead, also known as the Book of Coming Forth by Day. This series of funerary texts slowly developed over the course of a thousand years beginning with the advent of the New Kingdom and contained religious tales, magical spells, and funerary instructions. The texts were primarily designed to explain and guide the dead through the trials of the afterlife. In chapter 125, one of the more important vignettes of the entire work, the dead is brought before the gods to have his heart weighed and his sins judged. Among his pronouncements and negative confessions, the deceased would affirm, "I have never performed fellatio or copulated with a sodomite."[9] This appears to have been purely a prohibition against the homosexual variety of the act and is in fact the first recorded prohibition of any significant level against the act of oral sex. Again, this would seem to contradict the acceptance of the practice among the gods, including Osiris and Isis who were brother and sister.

Interestingly, though, despite a clear preponderance of oral sex tales in Egyptian mythology, the act itself is noticeably absent from the most of the nation's art. "Coitus is widely represented in hieroglyphics but all sources are discreet or uninformative about the variations of heterosexual activity such as cunnilingus and fellatio."[10] Surprisingly, it is even absent from one of the most famous of ancient sensual manuscripts. The Turin Papyrus, which was created around 1150 BC, contains 12 panels filled with sexually explicit scenes. Of all the different positions of intercourse contained in the text, there is not a single representation of oral sex. Was this simply an oversight or was the act so common as to make its inclusion pedantic to the ancient reader? Regardless, what is certain is that heterosexual sex in general and oral sex in particular did not bear any obvious social stigmas in ancient Egypt.

Across the Levant from Egypt was the other great ancient river valley civilization of the West, Mesopotamia. While its religious beliefs and institutions may have had less overt sexuality crafted into them, many examples still abound as to the extent of the practice in society. The Israel Museum has in its collection a clay tablet dated from around 2000 BC. Depicted on it is a Babylonian woman drinking beer from a straw while a man nearby drinks wine from a glass. Far from depicting actual practices, these were in fact thinly veiled, almost Freudian, allusions to oral sex.[11] The pun would have been well understood in the ancient world and clearly was drawn for that purpose. Another similar tablet depicts a woman being entered from behind by a man while she sucks beer from a straw. This again was most likely a thinly-veiled reference to a threesome, or at least showed a series of sex acts performed by the subject.

Whether Babylonian literature also depicted any acts of oral sex is debated. The vast majority of academics believe in either the complete absence of the topic or at least only a rare reference.[12] Arguably the only major references seem to come from religious tracts, much like in ancient Egypt. A particularly controversial work is Herbert Mason's translation of *Gilgamesh*. When the prostitute Shamhatu, which was originally her title, not her name, emerged from hiding to seduce the feral man Enkidu, she "bent down and moistened him with her lips then drew him / Slowly to the ground."[13] Other translations usually gloss over the act or simply refer to it as a sexual encounter. The larger implication within the tale is that sex drains a man of his wildness, civilizing him. Mason's translation, which portrays the harlot directly sucking the virility out of Enkidu, is perhaps the truest to the original moral message of the story. By employing fellatio, she becomes something of a succubus, perhaps serving as a cautionary to then-contemporary readers.

Alternatively, Shamhatu's use of oral sex could be seen as a way to attract and draw in her target, much as many animals use the act to garner interest from the opposite sex. Some historians have argued that lipstick originated with prostitutes of the Middle East who wore it for this particular reason. These women colored their lips to represent the female vulva or to advertise that they performed oral sex.[14] This ties in well with the second major reference to oral sex in

Mesopotamian literature within the myth of Inanna. Among the many *me*, or social mores, Inanna lays out for the people of Uruk was the gift of sexual intercourse, and among the practices she was taught by Enki and passed on was "the art of lovemaking, the kissing of the phallus."[15] Clearly anything presented as a divine gift to society would not have been officially frowned upon in daily life. In fact, both the myth of Gilgamesh and the tale of Inanna seem to portray sexual relations in general as having a civilizing effect on man. The understanding of the ancients is quite in keeping with more recent sociological studies which connect marriage and an active sex life with happiness and good health.

The worship of Baal that dominated much of the Levant coast embraced oral sex in its ritual practice. Here, young men performed or received fellatio as part of an initiation process. Some historians have speculated that the practice influenced later Jewish ritual and custom, specifically circumcision. Metzitza be'peh, or the ritualistic sucking of the recently circumcised penis in order to draw out blood, has been seen by some as a holdover of these ceremonies associated with Baal.[16] When one considers the normal taboos within the Jewish faith toward oral sex, homosexuality, and the impurity of blood, the act must have an earlier or foreign origin.

Cunnilingus has been noticeably lacking from ancient texts to this point. A thorough review of the literatures of the ancient Near East reveals only fleeting references to the act. A well-known one comes from a Sumerian poem: "Like her mouth her vulva is sweet, / Like her vulva her mouth is sweet."[17] Though the poem does not directly describe oral sex, the taste element of the chiastic line would clearly allude to nothing else. Another Babylonian poem compares the sweet taste of a woman's genitals to the taste of beer, again relying on an oral component.

The lack of reference to cunnilingus most likely represents shared cultural proscriptions against the practice, specifically ancient menstrual taboos. The ancient Greek phrase "to sleep in Phoenicia" was a reference to performing oral sex on a woman. It used the reddish purple dye famous from the region as an allusion to menstrual blood.[18] The fear of the transfer of disease is a possible reason for this taboo. All of this is not to suggest that the act wasn't practiced in the ancient Near East, simply that it was not the subject of art or literature as it was officially frowned upon or considered primitive. Concerns over the act being unclean paralleled primitive fears of it being a negative undertaking that would draw strength from men. The mouth-like shape of the vulva and darkened cave of the vagina implied to some a dark, draining element. The ancient Greek myth of Orpheus in which the hero must go down into Hades to rescue his wife can be seen as a metaphor for cunnilingus. Indeed, the basic tale is present in many ancient cultures including Japan, where Izanagi undertakes a similar quest for his deceased wife Izanami.

Many early societies expressed their fears of cunnilingus or sex in general with tales of vagina dentata. Though particulars of the story varied from culture to culture, the basic elements remained. The female protagonist was said to have teeth in her vagina which would injure or even kill the man or god who attempted to have sex with her. The association of death and an oral element was certainly intentional. A well-known Hopi tale involves two youth hurling bags of pebbles at Lowatamwuuti's vagina in order to break her teeth, thus enabling them to then "kill" her with arrows, clearly a phallic reference. Likewise, the Chiricahua Apache tell a tale of Coyote who uses a phallic rock to shatter the teeth of a woman's vagina. She subsequently thanks him, saying, "Hereafter I shall be worth a lot. I am worth horses and many things now."[19] The Kanamara Festival in Kawasaki, Japan, revolves around the celebration of a large penis. Local tradition holds that a sharp-toothed demon inhabited the vagina of a young woman, castrating those who attempted to marry her. A local blacksmith eventually constructed a steel phallus which was then used to break the demon's teeth and make the woman able to be married.

Judaism bore a similar negative view of menstruation in women. During *niddah*, the time when a woman was menstruating, contact with her husband was forbidden. "And to a woman in her state of *niddah* impurity you should not come close with intent to reveal her nudity."[20] Thus it was not surprising that the religion early on bore a similar negative attitude toward cunnilingus just as other ancient societies did. What was more, Judaism looked down on fellatio as well. Numerous cautionary tales appear in their sacred book and texts in an attempt to argue against the practice. In fact, the Bible remains one of the most complete texts on the opinion of oral sex in the ancient world.

One of the first occurrences of a discussion of the practice is the story of Lilith. Though she does not appear directly in the Talmud, her inclusion in a collection of medieval Jewish proverbs known as the *Alphabet of Ben Sirach* remains perhaps the most popular part of that work. Lilith is described as the first wife of Adam, created from either dirt like he was or from mud. As they were created at the same time and out of the same elements, equality penetrated their first sexual encounter. Lilith resented her husband's insistence that she take a submissive role and position, demanding instead to be the dominant sexual partner. "We are equal to each other inasmuch as we were both created from the earth."[21] Undoubtedly this extended into the realm of oral sex. When Adam refused to lie beneath his wife and presumably perform cunnilingus on her she flew up into the air and fled. The story of Lilith became a cautionary tale of pleasuring women in a way that was equal to men.

One of the possible geneses for Lilith may have been the demon Ardat-Lili. Originating in Sumerian mythology, the creature was portrayed in literature and art as a vampiric being who drained men of their seed which was then used by the Ardat-Lili to produce more monstrous offspring. Though exactly how the demon stole sperm from men was left out of Sumerian legends, the vampiric nature of the creature would seem to suggest an oral acquisition. This also helps to put in clearer perspective the ancient Mesopotamian view toward oral sex. While the practice in and of itself was not negative, it was the loss of sperm and/or virility from completing the act that was viewed as wrong. Like many other sexual activities, fellatio was to be undertaken as part of the greater act of conception, not as an end in itself.

Adam's next partner, Eve, was portrayed as a more submissive woman, yet Michelangelo painted her sexual side in one of his most famous scenes in the Sistine Chapel. In his *Temptation and Expulsion* panel, Michelangelo depicts the important scenes of Eve receiving the apple from the snake as well as being expelled with her husband from Paradise soon afterward, but a careful inspection of the layout of Adam and Eve in the temptation portion of the painting reveals a deeper allusion. Adam is pictured standing upright and nude, grasping firmly a branch of the Tree of Knowledge. Eve is on her side, her body in a position of submission before the genitals of Adam. While her head and arm are momentarily turned to receive the apple from Satan, her actions of only a moment before are clearly being hinted at. In fact, most Biblical scholars recognize that apples did not exist in the region, leading to speculation as to what fruit was meant. A favorite among commentators has been the fig, a fruit with traditional sexual overtones. Adam and Eve could actually have been expelled from Paradise for engaging in a wasteful and forbidden sexual act.[22] The Jewish play on words of Adam "knowing" his wife and their consumption of fruit from the Tree of Knowledge would seem to hint at this as well. Likewise, the very fact that the forbidden fruit was to be consumed orally implies that if the fruit was sexual satisfaction, then oral sex rather than reproductive intercourse was what was specifically forbidden by God. Finally, Eve's receiving the fruit from the snake is itself pregnant with allegorical references. Almost all ancient cultures alluded to snakes as a phallic symbol. One of the most notable myths features Persephone being impregnated by Zeus in the form of a snake. Therefore, the idea of Eve taking fruit from the snake may actually refer to her performing fellatio. "The woman said to the serpent, 'We may eat fruit from the trees in the garden,' but God did say, 'You must not eat fruit from the tree that is in the middle of the garden, and you must not touch it, or you will die.'"[23] "Dying" here may metaphorically refer to the dangers of over-utilizing sex and non-reproductive sex acts which would ultimately decrease human population. Regardless of the original intent of the story, religious and cultural concerns about oral sex have led to it being used as an allegory forbidding the act.

The next major instance of oral sex within the Bible is in the story of Noah. The mystical Jewish work *The Zohar* in fact attributes the entire episode of the flood to the sexual perversion of the people. "They were obliterated from the world in the very same manner as the sin they sinned."[24] That is, that the deluge of waters that obliterated man was an allusion to the deluge of semen and wasteful sexuality with which he concerned himself. Famed Talmudist Rav Chisda summarized the crime and punishment meted out by God: "With boiling passion they sinned, and with boiling water they were punished."[25]

Shortly after the flood, Noah settled down with his surviving family and began to farm. According the Genesis,

> Noah, a man of the soil, was the first to plant a vineyard. He drank some of the wine and became drunk, and he lay uncovered in his tent. And Ham, the father of Canaan, saw the nakedness of his father, and told his brothers outside. Then Shem and Japheth took a garment, laid it on both their shoulders, and walked backward and covered the nakedness of their father; their faces turned away, and they did not see their father's nakedness. When Noah awoke from his wine and knew what his youngest son had done to him, he said, "Cursed be Canaan; lowest of slaves shall he be to his brothers."[26]

Though later generations would make this story some sort of justification for slavery, the real controversy was actually explaining what the crime of Ham really was. Simply observing his father's nude figure seems to hardly justify eternal slavery for him and his descendants. From the nature of the story it seems to be more helpful to assume that Ham either had sex with Noah during his period of inebriation or performed fellatio on him.

This is not the only story of oral sex told about Noah. Once again the *Alphabet of Ben Sirach* has an expanded version of the episode. Noah is accused by a raven of seeking to have sex with a female raven.

> "The only reason you are sending me is so that I will be killed and you will be able to have intercourse with my wife. That is the only reason you made every animal come into the ark with its mate." Noah immediately responded by cursing the raven. "May you be cursed by that very thing which you slander me with. May you never copulate with your female except through your mouth."[27]

Thus, as a punishment for making such an accusation, the raven is forced to forever impregnate his mate by his beak. Once again cunnilingus was seen as a less than honorable method of sexual intercourse, saved only for those damned by either God or his prophets.

Though the Bible does not include an obvious provision against oral sex among its commandments, some commentators have taken chapter 18 of Leviticus to include a general prohibition of the practice.[28] "You must not do as they do in Egypt, where you used to live, and you must not do as they do in the land of Canaan, where I am bringing you. Do not follow their practices."[29] Interestingly, the Romans would later utilize Egypt as a setting in their own tales and paintings of wanton sexuality. Famed feminist and sexologist Shere Hite argued this traditional view in her groundbreaking *Hite Report on Men and Male Sexuality* in 1981. She pointed to a natural concern among early tribes and cultures for procreation that necessitated a ban on wasteful reproductive practices, thus making the act an abomination to the Jews. In fact, the difficult living conditions which confronted the Jews in the Near East drove many of their religious prohibitions. Included among these was the prohibition against consuming pork, as the maintenance of pigs was resource intensive compared to keeping cows or chickens.[30] Environmental necessity discouraged oral sex.

God's judgment of Sodom and Gomorrah is also sometimes taken to show a general prohibition of oral sex. Genesis chapter 19 recounts the story of Lot and the destruction of the cities of Sodom and Gomorrah as burning sulfur rains down on them. The crime of Sodom has been a matter of debate for thousands of years. The Bible itself seems to hint at sexual perversion as the sin of the inhabitants during a visit to the city by three angels. "Before they had gone to bed, all the men from every part of the city of Sodom—both young and old—surrounded the house. They called to Lot, 'Where are the men who came to you tonight? Bring them out to us so that we can have sex with them.' Lot went outside to meet them and shut the door behind him and said, 'No, my friends. Don't do this wicked thing.'"[31] Still other commentators have taken the entire episode to simply imply a lack of humbleness and hospitality on the part of the city. Finally, later Christian writers began to associate the sin of Sodom not merely with homosexuality but with all forms of what they deemed to be unnatural lovemaking, including anal sex and oral sex.

Still another warning against the degrading effects of cunnilingus in particular exists in the story of Samson. One of the last Judges to be visited upon ancient Israel, Samson was a model of physical strength and virility. After completing a number of near-mythical tasks in the manner of Heracles, Samson becomes enamored with a local woman named Delilah. After resisting her a number of times he finally succumbs and tells her the secret of his strength. According to Judges 19, "After putting him to sleep on her lap, she called for someone to shave off the seven braids of his hair, and so began to subdue him. And his strength left him." The association of Samson putting his head in her lap and subsequently losing his strength has been adopted by many commentators and authors, most notably John Milton, to stand as a metaphor for cunnilingus.

> Then swoll'n with pride into the snare I fell
> Of fair fallacious looks, venereal trains,
> Softn'd with pleasure and voluptuous life;
> At length to lay my head and hallow'd pledge
> Of all my strength in the lascivious lap [535]
> Of a deceitful Concubine who shore me
> Like a tame Weather, all my precious fleece,
> Then turn'd me out ridiculous, despoil'd,
> Shav'n, and disarm'd among my enemies.
>
> Chor. Desire of wine and all delicious drinks, [540]
> Which many a famous Warriour overturns,
> Thou could'st repress, nor did the dancing Rubie
> Sparkling, out-pow'red, the flavor, or the smell,
> Or taste that cheers the heart of Gods and men,
> Allure thee from the cool Crystalline stream. [545]
>
> Sam. Where ever fountain or fresh current flow'd
> Against the Eastern ray, translucent, pure,
> With touch ætherial of Heav'ns fiery rod
> I drank, from the clear milkie juice allaying
> Thirst, and refresht; nor envy'd them the grape [550]
> Whose heads that turbulent liquor fills with fumes.[32]

Milton's clear focus on the various smells and tastes that Samson enjoyed, in conjunction with the position of his head in Delilah's lap, would seem to allude to a particular sexual act rather than just general intercourse.

Overall, the religion has varying views on oral sex, with many texts and commentators coming out strongly against the practice. In the *Kallah Rabbah*, one of the minor tractates appended to the Babylonian Talmud, it is claimed that if a woman conceives after having received cunnilingus, her child will be born deformed. More specifically, the baby will have a closed mouth to visually represent the sin of the father.[33] As one of the disqualifications for *kohen*, or priests, in Judaism were visible blemishes, many undoubtedly sought to avoid the act. The *Orach Chaim* follows a similar path of thinking, arguing that one should not "look upon a place where others have embarrassment" without experiencing it themselves.[34] The author, Rabbi Jacob ben Asher, goes on to suggest that performing oral sex actually violated several of God's commandments. Notably the action would go against Micah 6:8 which commanded men to "walk humbly" and Leviticus 20:25 which advised, "thou shall not make your soul despicable." Rabbi Moses Isseries, though not outlawing the practice, recommends avoiding it, citing *Even Ha-Ezer*, "To make a fence, and not to engage in excessive marital relations."[35] Finally, many rabbis based their view on a misuse of the mouth. As man is the only creation granted by God the ability to speak, and thus can say His name and praise Him, performing such a lowly and filthy act debases that gift. A similar line of reasoning will also be used by the Greeks and Romans in relation to the mouth's ability to speak and debate as well as Christians who insist on the purity of the mouth to receive the body of Christ.

Not all segments of Judaism have historically looked down on oral sex, however. The Babylonian Talmud allows for the practice of oral sex, relating it to the right of cooking meat or fish in whatever way the purchaser desires. "A man may do whatever he pleases with his wife [at intercourse]: A parable; Meat which comes from the abattoir, may be eaten salted, roasted, cooked or seethed; so with fish from the fishmonger."[36] Perhaps the greatest expositor of the practice was the seminal scholar Maimonides. In his writings on the subject he took the stance that any act that was consensual between a husband and wife was perfectly fine. For him the larger danger was in excess or forced action. Sex of any kind "should be from mutual desire and happiness."[37]

The majority of Jewish scholars seemed to be concerned with the excessiveness of the practice and the misuse of sex for non-reproductive habits. This theme permeates the Bible, seen in the previously examined episodes of Adam and Eve, the flood, the Tower of

Babel, and the destruction of Sodom and Gomorrah. In all cases man's obsession with sex led to his punishment. Oral sex especially could become an idol, worshipped for its deliverance of only pleasure. Like most things in violation of the Second Commandment, these idols distracted man from loftier pursuits and purer pleasures.

Though little of early Jewish literature apart from the Bible exists, and thus a full appreciation of the sexual practices of the Jews is limited, some additional facts can be gleaned from the book *The Song of Songs*. Despite this work occasionally being taken to represent the allegorical love between God and man, it was originally much more poetical and sexual in nature. Several references to natural objects and actions in the book could in fact be references to specific oral acts. In chapter 2, verse 3, the woman says of her lover "his fruit is sweet to my mouth." Further on, in 7:6, the male refers to the female as "delectable," once again presenting an oral, taste-related adjective.

Overall, the ancient world of the Middle East had a mixed perception of oral sex. While the act was occasionally celebrated and even worshipped as a creative force in some societies, it was viewed quite harshly by others. As always a dichotomy existed between fellatio and cunnilingus, with one seen as positive and the other as negative, one catalyzing, the other enervating. Issues of religion, concerns over population growth, cleanliness and purity taboos, and gender inequality all played a role in these early views of oral sex.

2

The Greek
and Roman World

The sexuality of the classical Greeks has always been a subject of interest, to some for sheer shock value and to others for defending or moralizing their own behaviors. As with many attempts to use history as justification, though, the truth behind it often falls short of perceived reality. The image of the Greeks as liberal hedonists, as toga-clad philosophers engaged in orgies, as unrepentant homosexuals is a fantasy. The Bacchanalian feasts, Dionysian rites, and pederast couplings are often more fiction than fact. While writers, artists, and individuals centuries later would focus on these myths, the true history of sex, and particularly oral sex, in ancient Greece is nonetheless both scandalous and in itself instructive.

It is true that the Greeks were certainly not prudes when it came to the act and depiction of sex, yet many of the same taboos against oral sex that existed in the Middle East are found in ancient Athens and Sparta as well. In the land of democracy and individualism, oral sex was actually a rigidly restricted, class-based enterprise. Fellatio seems to have been regarded largely as the realm of prostitutes and homosexuals. Numerous pieces of Greek pottery depict female courtesans engaging in the act, but, interestingly, they often appear to be doing so under duress. The act was seen as in and of itself degrading for both people involved. For the man receiving fellatio, his inactivity during the act was viewed negatively by the Greeks, lovers of action and industry, and similar to Judaism, ejaculation was considered to be unclean, requiring ritual purification afterward. Thus any woman performing oral sex was polluting herself. Likewise, the classical physician Galen was quoted as stating, "We are more revolted by cunnilingus than by fellatio." Though the quote once again assumes the filthiness of the former act, it is also written in a way to cast derision on the latter. Perhaps this is why most of the women depicted in art and literature performing fellatio are forced or coerced into doing so.[1] Some examples of this include the Brygos Cup, the Attic Red Cup in Milan, the Florence Symposium Cup, and the Pedieus Cup, all of which depict women and boys performing oral sex while suffering different levels of forceful coercion.

The Florence Symposium Cup, which appears to have been crafted in 480s BC, shows a typical symposium scene in Athens at the time. In addition to drinking, singing, and general revelry, several sex scenes are portrayed. Two of these depict oral sex; in at least one the fellator has two individuals forcing her head down while the other has her being threatened by a man wielding a stick. The Pedieus Cup, while depicting a pleasant interaction between a young man and woman inside of the vessel, has a scene of violent sex painted on its exterior. A woman is shown having sex with two men, with several scenes suggesting forced fellatio. It is interesting that the raucous sex scenes on the outside would be those visible to guests while the interior of the cup would only be seen by the drinker.

A common motif on many such vases and vessels was a man brandishing a rod, threatening to beat a prostitute if she did not perform fellatio on him. Most Greek pottery that depicted sex did so with more accepted styles and positions. The portrayal of fellatio was extremely rare, and that of cunnilingus was virtually nonexistent. The famed orator Demosthenes once opined, "We have hetaerae for our pleasure, concubines for our daily needs and wives to give us legitimate children and look after the housekeeping." Oral sex was something to be avoided, in life and in art, unseemly for women of stature to perform, and degrading for men to receive.

Oral sex seems to have been left to mythology more than to real life. The myth of Io, as retold by Aeschylus in *The Suppliant Maidens*, portrays the impregnation of Io as more of an oral than a physical act.

> We (Danaus and the Danaides) flee with all speed over the waves of the sea and find a haven on Argos' shore. For from there descends our race, sprung from the caress and breath of Zeus on the gnat-tormented heifer [Io].[2]

Our champion from beyond the sea, the calf born of Zeus, the offspring of the flower-grazing cow [Io], our ancestress, the caress of Zeus' breath. The appointed period confirmed itself in a name suited to the event—Epaphos, to whom she gave birth.[3]

Father himself and lord, he planted us with his own hand; he is the mighty fashioner of our race, ancient in wisdom, who devises everything, whose breath makes all things prosper, Zeus himself.[4]

The myth of Zeus and Ganymede, built as it was around pederasty, would also seem to imply an at least partial oral relationship between the god and young boy. What stands out even more, however, is the central motif of Ganymede as the cup bearer of the gods. Upon his being carried to Mt. Olympus, the young captive replaced Hebe in carrying libations to Zeus. A number of metaphors emerge from Ganymede presenting his liquid-filled cup to the god to drink from, which blend into ancient Mesopotamian and Egyptian art which conflated oral sex with drinking.

The preeminent Stoic philosopher Chrysippus once beheld a famous erotic painting of Zeus and Hera. Housed in Argos, the artwork showed Hera fellating the king of the gods. Chrysippus explained the painting depicted the depositing of "reason" into the universe. In this, the myth was similar to Atum establishing creation with his semen, yet the prudishness of the majority of classical writers clearly stands out in Diogenes Laertius' discussion of the allegory. "He [the artist] interprets the story of Hera and Zeus coarsely; with details which no one would soil his lips by repeating. Indeed, his interpretation of the story is condemned as most indecent. He may be commending physical doctrine; but the language used is more appropriate to street-walkers than to deities; and it is moreover not even mentioned by bibliographers."[5] The idea of oral sex portrayed in art more than it was actually accepted in polite society seems to have its origins early in the Western experience.

Not surprisingly, the act seems to have been particularly favored and practiced by the most bestial of deities, satyrs. These horse-like companions of Dionysus were often depicted with enlarged phalluses and engaged in various wanton acts. Far from being a civilization of libertines, the Greeks viewed any form of excess, sexual or otherwise, as uncharacteristic of a civilized person. Therefore, as the non-reproductive nature of fellatio and cunnilingus would seem to lend themselves to little more than personal pleasure, both acts were viewed with a certain level of disgust. In ancient Greece, oral sex was often euphemistically referred to as "playing the flute," thus the musical depiction of these wanton creatures was more than a coincidence. The chief satyr himself, Silenus, was even renowned as a minor god of fertility. Perhaps the most famous story involving a satyr, however, was that of Marsyas who challenged Apollo to a musical contest. According to the legend, Athena invented the aulos, or double flute, but playing the instrument "impaired her facial beauty," a perhaps not-too-subtle reference to her abstention from performing fellatio. After she threw away the instrument, Marsyas the satyr picked it up and challenged Apollo. In the contest that followed the god of music was triumphant because he could sing and play at the same time, while Marsyas' mouth was occupied. The arrogant Marsyas was flayed and his skin hung as a trophy in Phrygia.

In keeping with their love of comedy, the Greeks produced satyr plays to commemorate festivals for Dionysius. They were far from a low class art form, and some of the greatest of the ancient playwrights tried their hand at them. Two of the more well known are Euripides' *Cyclops* and Sophocles' *Ichneutae*. The former even features a scene in which a drunken cyclops mistakes Silenus, the father of the satyrs, for Ganymede and carries him off into his cave. Much of the Dionysian cult itself revolved around specific sexual acts, including fellatio and cunnilingus. In fact, these practices have been argued to relate to the omophagy that was heavily present within the cult. Going back to the origin myths of Dionysius, eating raw flesh was practiced by the god and his devotees. Camille Paglia once opined, "there may be an element of omophagy in oral sex" as well.[6] It is not surprising then that Herodotus related the worship of the death and resurrection of Osiris through the oral actions of Isis to Dionysius. "For the Egyptians do not all worship the same gods, excepting Isis and Osiris, the latter of whom they say is the Grecian Bacchus."[7]

The myth of Orpheus, arguably the ancient world's most famous cunnilictor, ends with him being torn to shreds by a band of women he refused to share his gift with. After a snake killed Eurydice, his wife, Orpheus proceeded to go down into the Underworld to save his beloved. Apart from the phallic imagery of his wife's death, the descent of Orpheus into a dark cave was even more erotic in its own message. Upon his return to the land of the living, having failed to retrieve his wife, the skilled poet was sought by numerous women. According to Ovid's retelling of the myth,

> Three times the sun had ended the year, in watery Pisces, and Orpheus had abstained from the love of women, either because things ended badly for him, or because he had sworn to do so. Yet, many felt a desire to be joined with the poet, and many grieved at rejection. Indeed, he was the first of the Thracian people to transfer his love to young boys, and enjoy their brief springtime, and early flowering, this side of manhood.[8]

Outraged, a group of Thracian followers of Dionysius killed Orpheus, allegedly the Greek world's first pederast.

> "Behold, behold, this is the one who scorns us!" and hurled her spear at the face of Apollo's poet, as he was singing…. First, the innumerable birds, the snakes, and the procession of wild animals, still entranced by the voice of the singer, a mark of Orpheus's triumph, were torn apart by the Maenads. Then they set their bloody hands on Orpheus, and gathered, like birds that spy the owl, the bird of night, wandering in the daylight, or as in the amphitheater, on the morning of the staged events, on either side, a doomed stag, in the arena, is prey to the hounds…. Hoes, heavy mattocks, and long rakes lay scattered through the empty fields. After catching these up, and ripping apart the oxen, that threatened them with their horns, the fierce women rushed back to kill the poet. As he stretched out his hands, speaking ineffectually for the first time ever, not affecting them in any way with his voice, the impious ones murdered him: and the spirit, breathed out through that mouth to which stones listened, and which was understood by the senses of wild creatures—O, God!—vanished down the wind…. The poet's limbs were strewn in different places: the head and the lyre you, Hebrus, received, and floating in midstream, the lyre lamented mournfully; mournfully the lifeless tongue murmured; mournfully the banks echoed in reply.[9]

Orpheus' own oral predilictions and his cannibalistic execution by the scorned women of Dionyius were to become cornerstones of the god's cult as well as a possible cautionary tale to future men.

The third element of Greek culture associated with oral sex was homosexuals. Once again, though, the act was heavily inveighed against as was the receiving partner in any pederastic relationship. The practice itself is rarely depicted in art or mentioned in literature but can be surmised from several extant sources. The aforementioned Pedieus Cup depicts a symposium-type scene in which older men are having sex and receiving fellatio from young boys. As symposia were male-dominated events, same sex oral play by women is never depicted. Interestingly, though modern-day lesbianism can trace its name to the famed island home of Sappho, that location's appellation itself originated from the Greek word for fellatio.[10] This was confirmed by numerous ancient writers including Galen himself, who referred to the practice of oral sex as *lesbiari*. Likewise, the Greek comedic playwright Theopompus in his *Odyssesus*, of which only fragments survive, said, "Not to mention that well-known and ancient game devised, they say, by them of Lesbos' name."

Perhaps the most well-known symposium was that described by Plato in his work of the same name. As the party discusses the lofty concepts of love and beauty, a drunken Alcibiades stumbles in and begins to narrate his own sordid history with Socrates. Drawing upon both the metaphor of a flute player and the myth of Marsyas, Alcibiades proclaims to all present the skill of the great thinker at fellatio.

> And now, my boys, I shall praise Socrates in a figure which will appear to him to be a caricature, and yet I speak, not to make fun of him, but only for the truth's sake. I say, that he is exactly like the busts of Silenus, which are set up in the statuaries, shops, holding pipes and flutes in their mouths; and they are made to open in the middle, and have images of gods inside them. I say also that hit is like Marsyas the satyr. You yourself will not deny, Socrates, that your face is like that of a satyr. Aye, and there is a resemblance in other points too. For example, you are a bully, as I can prove by witnesses, if you will not confess. And are you not a flute-player? That you are, and a performer far more wonderful than Marsyas. He indeed with instruments used to charm the souls of men by the powers of his breath.[11]

The double entendre of Alcibiades, referring to both of Socrates' oral talents, was often glossed over by much-later puritanical translators and commentators who settled instead for a celebration of the great thinker's rhetorical skills. However, a sound understanding of Greek views of oral sex as well as their coded references to it combined with a thorough knowledge of the background and character of Alcibiades make the identification much more obvious. Alcibiades, having had his most recent advances scorned by Socrates in favor of a younger man, sought to lay his anger before all those present.

Oral sex did not escape the notice of other great thinkers of ancient Greece. To Pythagoras, "semen is a drop of the brain," thus implying that the vital fluid should not be wasted on frivolous sex acts.[12] Aristotle continued this line of thinking almost two centuries later. To him, too much oral sex could lead to sunken eyes and possible blindness, as man's sperm was generated from the liquid of his eyeballs.[13] This warning re-emerged as an urban legend in postwar America where young boys were chided that too much masturbation would make them go blind. The philosopher also argued that as the production of semen competes with the body for food and energy, wasteful sex acts are not beneficial to man. Plato, in his *Symposium*, differentiated between forms and acts of love. To him the basest forms of the concept, of which oral sex most certainly would have been included, were referred to as belonging to the goddess Aphrodite Panademos, or Aphrodite of the masses. Plato as always employs Socrates as the mouthpiece for his ideas. The latter claims in *The Symposium* to have learned this lesson from the philosopher Diotima. She apparently first introduced him to the concept that love created and drained and therefore needed to be reserved for necessary and productive encounters. Perhaps this female philosopher was basing her argument at least in part on a class-conscious disdain for performing oral sex. The Greeks were hardly unrestrained hedonists, but they always sought to maintain a level of modesty in balance in all of their acts, including sex.

Socrates was not the only famous Greek to be lambasted for his sexual exploits. The 4th-century AD poet Palladas cleverly recast some of Homer's own lines to paint him as a dedicated cunnilictor. In his epigram 9.395, the poet reworks Book IX, Lines 34–35 of the *Odyssey* into a series of erotic metaphors. "Homer said 'nothing is sweeter than a man's fatherland,' for in Circe's isle he never ate cheesecake. If he had seen even the smoke curling up from that, he would have sent ten Penelopes to the deuce." While in the original Homer has Odysseus say "nothing is sweeter than a man's own country," Palladas has Homer transfer his tastes to the cake of Circe. "Smoke curling up from that" was another ancient euphemism.[14] Palladas in fact made several references to the oral predilections of Homer, notably in epigrams IX, 218 and X, 50.

As always, the best source for information on the oral habits of the Greeks is their own literature. One of the first ancient poets to mention the topic was Archilochus of Paros, a jilted suitor who expressed his anger at his prospective bride and father-in-law in verse. Archilochus was to marry Neoboule, the daughter of Lycambes. When Lycambes suddenly terminated the arrangement, the scorned poet penned a series of works against father and daughter. At one point Neoboule likened to "a Thracian or Phrygian drinking beer through a tube she sucked; and she was hard at work astoop." This public reference to one of the Lycambids performing oral sex, when combined with dozens of other invectives hurled at the family, allegedly drove them all to commit suicide.[15]

Similarly, the satirical poet Hipponax, who lived in Ionia in the 6th century BC, used oral sex to lambast and attack his enemies. The perennial target of the poet was the sculptor Bupalus. Besides accusing Bupalus of committing incest with his own mother, Arete, Hipponax savages the poor woman as well by suggesting that she had the sexual habits of a common prostitute. In fragment 17 he describes Arete as "bending over for me towards the lamp," an allusion to her performing fellatio on the poet or her own son. In another line of poetry, he states, "She demands eight obols to give him a peck on his prick," a measly sum of money at the time.[16] During the Peloponnesian War, the Athenian comic Eupolis, who died during one of the war's many battles, once joked that the Lambda, or letter L, that proudly emblazoned the Spartan shields stood not for Lacadaemonia but for *leikhein*, to lick, in the sense of cunnilingus.

It is perhaps not surprising that of the great Greek playwrights, Aristophanes the comic poet was the one to most often mention oral sex in his plays. In *The Wasps*, the character Philocleon prides himself on having rescued a barmaid "from the solicitations of those fellators, who wanted you to make love to them in their own odd way."[17] Barely a breath later, though, he requests a similar act from the girl as his reward. Her identification as a "flute girl" reinforces her role as fellator. In *Ecclesiazusae*, the poet even has the women judge each other harshly for partaking in the act, with one proclaiming, "But you seem to be the Lambda of Lesbians." Here the Greek letter most likely stands for *leikhein*, "to lick," which Eupolis threw at the Spartans as an insult as well. Aristophanes also made several references to cunnilingus in his works, a rarity in ancient literature. In *Ecclesiazusae*, a satirical play about female empowerment, the author mentions Smoius, a supposed cunnilinctor. "The youngest girls are boiling pots of pea soup, and Smoius in his riding suit is among them, licking the women's bowls clean."[18] Another target of the playwright was Ariphrades, who Aristophanes claims invented the practice of cunnilingus. He appears in four different works, *Peace, Knights, Wasps*, and *Ecclesiazusae*. The leader of the chorus in *The Knights* calls him "Ariphrades the wicked. Actually, wicked is what he sets out to be, he gloats in vice, is not merely a dissolute man and utterly debauched—but he actually invented a new form of vice; for he pollutes his tongue with abominable pleasures, licking 'the abominable dew' in brothels, soiling his beard, disturbing women's sacred hearths."[19] Apart from the clear connotations of the filthiness of the act, the inclusion of Ariphrades highlights one of the psychological complaints against cunnilingus, that it was seen as a sexual tool of the old and impotent. A reliance on the tongue over the penis was a revealing and coded reference for the ancients. Sex for the young and virile was meant for reproduction, therefore sperm should not be wasted in frivolous pursuits and activities.

Writers were not the only ones to employ the idea of fellatio or cunnilingus to damage an enemy. Aeschines, one of the great Athenian orators of the 4th century BC, was accused of treason by his political enemies Demosthenes and Timarchus. The slandered official quite cleverly turned the tables on his accusers by claiming that Timarchus had lost his right to speak in front of the people due to his history of engaging in oral sex. In his *Against Timarchus*, Aeschines builds his case against his enemy by reminding the public that Athenian law forbade anyone who had prostituted himself from holding office in the state or even addressing it. He then proceeds to accuse Timarchus of precisely that crime. The charges are again taken up in his speech *On the Embassy*, in which Aeschines now moves on to attack the morality of Demosthenes. He accuses the latter of being a fellator of men for money, and blames this pastime for his famed speech impediment.[20] "I call him a lewd rascal, unclean of body, even to the place whence his voice issues forth."[21] These attacks helped to discredit

Demosthenes and his allies, harming the anti–Macedon party in Athens and thus abetting the rise of Philip and later Alexander the Great. In fact, the rhetoric of Aeschines was so effective and the actions of Timarchus so known, that the later Greek satirist Lucian used the persona of Timarchus to attack his own enemies. The Greeks and Romans bore a similar view of the mouth's purity as the ancient Jews. For them, oratory was the highest art of man, and thus anything that would take dignity away from the mouth cheapened not only it but also its possessor. Those who practiced oral sex lost the ability and right to address the public assembly, a pure body.

One of the more famous real-life Greeks to be involved with the act of oral sex was the previously mentioned great general Alcibiades. A towering figure from the Peloponnesian War, Alcibiades was also renowned for his youthful good looks and ambiguous sexuality. Yet the one lover he could not conquer appears to have been Socrates. Confronting the philosopher in *The Symposium*, Alcibiades states, "he is like Marsyas the satyr … are you not a flute player?"[22] The references to oral sex are blatant, with the youth praising Socrates' apparent skill at fellatio. Alcibiades would play a rather controversial role in the war between Athens and Sparta. His apogee in that conflict took place during the Sicilian Expedition in 415 BC. The night before the fleet was to embark, vandals mutilated the penises of the Herma statues that populated Athens. The blow to this symbol of luck and fertility weighed heavily upon the psyche of Athens and helped to speed the downfall of Alcibiades and eventually Athens as well. Generals were recalled, trials were held, and the unsupported expedition resulted in failure.

The fall of Athens and the rise of Rome initially saw little change in the overall tenor of sexuality in the ancient Mediterranean. Pederasty, prostitution, and a predilection for anal sex all existed in Italy just as much as they did in Greece, yet a certain air of prudishness existed among the Romans. Women were expected to uphold their sexual virtue, avoiding intercourse before marriage and not straying from their husbands. Lucretia, whose rape helped to bring about the rise of the Roman Republic, was utilized for centuries as the epitome of a Roman woman. As Livy himself wrote, "The prize in this contest of womanly virtues fell to Lucretia."[23] Even in Roman erotic art, women were still generally clothed even when participating in the most pornographic of acts.

Yet amidst all of this Puritan-like prudishness, a certain flair for sexuality, including oral sex, existed among the Romans. Prostitution existed in every corner of the empire, sex slavery was common and only grew larger following the Emperor Augustus' prohibition against adultery in the 1st century AD, and erotic graffiti and inscriptions adorned Pompeii and gravestones throughout the Mediterranean. Notably, one public piece of graffiti in Pompeii urged citizens to "vote Isidore for aedile, he's the best at licking cunt."[24]

The true litmus test for acceptable sexuality in ancient Rome was whether an act was active or passive in nature. The latter was the domain of women, and though acceptable for them, being a receiving partner and male was considered not only not virtuous but often even criminal. Thus, while the rapes suffered by the Sabine women or Lucretia were in and of themselves seen as horrible, they paled in comparison to the rape of Chrysippus, a male. Unsurprisingly, homosexual oral rape was seen as the most degrading form of sex to the ancient Romans.[25] The other aspect to consider was whether the act was excessive or unnecessary. The Stoic and Epicurean schools tended to view proper sex as being within the bonds of marriage and for the purpose of procreation, thus it was natural but largely unnecessary outside of reproduction. Obviously this was an ideal for behavior whose acceptance varied with era and social class. Suetonius' harsh judgment of the sexual depravities of the emperors in his famous history, though, can be understood as a moral verdict on these actions among the elites in general.

Once again, oral sex emerged as the basest form of sexuality, seen as unnecessary and unclean. The Romans referred to those who partook in it as *os impurum,* or those who suffered from an unclean mouth. The belief that the mark of a true citizen was his ability to employ speech over strength was the basis for much of the concern about oral purity, much as it was in classical Athens. Further evidence of this can be gleaned from records detailing prices charged by prostitutes for such acts. Invariably fellatio or cunnilingus cost more than any other sex act. The city of Pompeii contains some of the best evidence of daily life in the empire.

"Lahis fellat assibus duobus" or "Lahis gives head for two ases." Many Roman brothels accepted spintriae, tokens purchased for a set amount which were then exchanged for specific sex acts. Coins which depicted oral sex tended to be of higher value than those used for almost anything else.

Perhaps the more interesting aspect of oral sex among the Romans was its use as a form of punishment. Under Roman law, a person convicted of theft or adultery could be legally raped as recourse by the affected party. The great poet Catullus himself recorded just such an incident in which he "just found a young boy having sex with a girl: May it please Diana, I attacked him with my rigid thing, using it as a spear."[26] It appears that the exact method of rape was left up to the wronged party and could be carried out by either the person or his agent. Writers joked about obviously homo-sexual thieves who purposefully got caught in order to be raped. To counter this, the erotic set of poems known as the *Priapea* suggested, "I'm warning: a youth ill split open; a girl ill force to fuck. A bearded thief will get a third penalty."[27] This "third penalty" most likely referred to irrumation, or the practice of having active sex with a partner's mouth. This was seen as distinct from oral sex because of its perceived forcefulness, unwelcome nature, and failure to terminate in actual sex. Another poem in the same collection warns a potential thief that he would be anally raped for the first offense and irrumated for the second, again implying the second punishment to be worse than the first. The *Priapea* warns, "Walk in the vineyards, and if you steal any of the grapes, you shall have water, stranger, to take in another way."[28] The line employs metaphor to connect the drinking of liquid with the results of irrumation. The satirist Martial warns a would-be adulterer of this as well. "O Gallus, you who are smoother than Venus's shells, I warn you, flee the deceitful nets of the famous adulteress. Are you relying on your butt? The husband does not pen-etrate asses; there are two things that he does: he penetrates mouths or he fucks pussy."[29]

That is not to say that the practice of oral sex was eschewed by all Romans. Much like the Lesbians of the ancient Aegean, several inhabitants of Italy were recorded as being particularly fond of either giving or receiving fellatio. The 4th-century poet Ausonius identified the inhabitants of Campania as partaking frequently in the act.[30] Sextus Festus argued that the Osci, inhabitants of that region, because they gave and received oral sex, gave their name to the word "obscene." Horace referred in his *Satires* 1.5.62–64 to a disheveled, deformed man who was suffering the *Campanum morbus*, or Campanian disease. Though some have speculated that this may refer to a venereal disease, perhaps acquired from oral sex, it more likely simply references a taste for the act itself and the primitive look of those who partake in it. Undoubtedly, the region's association with early Greek colonization and Hellenic culture played a role in the view that they engaged in acts that were viewed as unclean and foreign.

It is therefore not surprising that numerous Roman-era writers and politicians used the idea of oral sex to attack and belittle their rivals, much as the Greeks had done before them. Lucian especially employed oral sex to assault the morals of his time. "In the name of the gods tell me what you are thinking of, when it is bruited about publically that you Lesbianize and even Phoenicianize?"[31] In his *Satires* Juvenal employs a failure to perform cunnilingus to show the moral superiority of two women over corresponding men. "Tedia never licks Cluvia … but Hispo yields to young men and gets sick both ways."[32]

The earliest Roman writers tended to eschew references to the act out of concerns of propriety, but several poets and playwrights did employ double entendres that would have been noticed by listeners. Plautus, who wrote at the end of the 3rd century BC, produced a number of comedies that reference irrumation. In his play *Amphitryon*, the author references the act in a verbal argument between Mercury and Sosia.

> **Mercury:** I'll check that tongue of yours today, you criminal.
> **Sosia:** You can't, I keep it nice and pure.[33]

The obvious reference to irrumation as a punishment and Sosia's concern for *os impurum* would still have been vague enough to confuse those more modest audience members as they certainly were for future generations of readers. Plautus uses a similar device in his play *Casina* where he suggests that a slave routinely fellates his libertine master.

Lysidamus: Be quiet, Chalinus.
Chalinus: Force hirn to be quiet.
Olympio: You'd do better to force hirn. He's used to that son of thing.[34]

The slightly-later playwright Terence also used several references to fellatio and irrumation in his plays. In his *Adelphoe,* Terence has the slave Syrus suggest that a young man be treated well. In reply, the character Sannio, a pimp, says, "How could I have been nicer today than by offering him my mouth?"[35] The combination of Sannio's profession and his reference to his mouth suggests little else than the performance of fellatio on the young man. A similar example occurs in *Hecyra* where a prostitute complains about a soldier forcing her to be quiet. The character Parmeno responds, "I think that the soldier put an end to your talking in a terrible way."[36] The suggestion of irrumation here is quite clear.

One of the most invective-filled works to accuse an enemy of being a lover of oral sex is Lucian's *Pseudologista,* or *The Mistaken Critic.* While the actual critic being skewered by Lucian remains a matter of conjecture and debate, the acts he is accused of are clearly from the realm of oral sex. Lucian's method of attack copied that of Aeschines, discrediting his adversary's mouth so as to negate his ability to use it as a weapon. The Critic, in the persona of Timarchus, is said to have been expelled from a wedding in Cyzicus for fellating other guests. "Why dost thou become furious, for the people all say thou art fellator and cunnilingus ... perhaps thou takest them for honorable titles.... All persons who have found thee in public places know thee very well, since they have seen thee kneeling on thy knees and doing that which thou knowest how to do so well."[37] Still later, Lucian claims that his enemy developed a sore throat while in Egypt after a painful encounter with a sailor. "You were called quinsy" refers to a popular herb that was used in cases of sore throats. Finally, he alludes to the story of the cyclops in the *Odyssey,* claiming that the Critic also had a sharpened stick plunged into him, and that he in turn "swallowed this noman whole."

One of the most notorious hedonists alive during the reign of Augustus was Hostius Quadra. Seneca said his "obscenity formed a model for everything that was lewd on the stage. He was rich and avaricious, a very slave to his millions. He was eventually murdered by his own slaves, but the late Emperor Augustus considered his murder undeserving of punishment, and as good as declared that he had been justly slain. This man's lust knew no distinction of sex."[38] Apart from engaging in homosexual relations and pederasty, Quadra was also said to have performed cunnilingus on a woman, once again showing the derision cast upon the act by the imperial Romans, one on par evidently with the other base forms of love he was accused of.

Perhaps the writer who most adroitly employed allusions to oral sex in his writings was the famed satirist Martial. Well known for his caustic verses aimed at enemies and everyday Romans, Martial often employed the imagery of fellatio and cunnilingus. In keeping with the mores of the time these references tended to be used negatively. For instance, "You sang badly, Aegle, in the days when you were fucked. Now you sing well—but you're not to be kissed"[39] refers to the polluting effect of Aegle performing oral sex. Thus despite the improvement in his singing career, he had become more debased through his actions.

> What is the female opening to you, Baeticus Gallus?
> This tongue is supposed to lick men.
> Why was your penis cut off with a Samian shard,
> if pussy was so satisfying to you, Baeticus?
> Your head should be castrated,
> for though you have the groin of a Gallus priest [castrated],
> nonetheless you betray the rites of Cybele, for in your
>   mouth you are male.[40]

The 81st epigram of Martial alludes to the priests of the cult of Cybele. As part of their initiation they were castrated, with many taking part in homosexual encounters afterward. Yet to Martial, the ignominy of Baeticus Gallus arose not from his frequent encounters with other men, but from his apparent enjoyment of performing cunnilingus. "They are twin brothers, but they lick different groins: Tell me, are they more unlike than like?"[41]

Epigram 88 continues the discussion of cunnilingus, this time questioning whether twin brothers are actually alike if one performs fellatio and the other cunnilingus. Though Martial does not directly pass judgment on either one, an underlying tone is evident from his frequenting lambasting of the latter act: "You lick my girl, but don't fuck her, while you chatter like an adulterer and pussy-fucker. If I catch you, Gargilus, you will shut up."[42]

Seven epigrams later, Martial combines a number of oral sex references in discussing his unfaithful lover. Yet the poet seems less concerned with the actual affair, than with the disconnect between Gargilus' claims about the relationship and his actions. While the latter is bragging in public about having sex, in reality he is only performing cunnilingus. Appalled by the act, which Martial feels is below a Roman gentleman, the poet then threatens to quiet Gargilus through irrumation, a fitting punishment, he feels, for a practitioner of oral sex. This negative view of cunnilingus, even for the receiving female, is also mentioned in epigram 6 of Book VI, "Paula loves a *muta persona*." The term "silent face," was often used to describe a cunnilictor, who out of necessity was unable to speak. Again, the ancient Greek and Roman view of oral debate and speaking skills as the hallmark of a truly refined citizen are viewed as impaired by the silent necessity of performing oral sex.

> Our Sotades is in danger of losing his head.
> Do you think Sotades is on trial?
> He isn't. Sotades has stopped being able to get an erection: he licks.[43]

Epigram 26 clearly lays out the aforementioned Greek view that cunnilingus was a practice reserved for old men who were unable to perform intercourse. Yet even in this case, the action was still viewed in a negative light. It seems that the same view was often held of women, with the contemporary Greek epigramist Nicarchus writing:

> A fine and largely built woman attracts me, Similus,
> Whether she be in her prime or elderly.
> If she be young she will clasp me,
> If she be old and wrinkled, δικάσεται.

The final Greek "δικάσεται" is a later insertion and correction which does not fit the rhyme scheme or meaning of the poem well. Lucia Floridi argues that the line was most likely referring to fellatio using a contemporary slang word.[44] This practice was perhaps associated with elderly women due to either a biological reason or their lower status and desirability.

Last night the soft charms of an exquisite whore fulfilled
    every whim of my mind.
Till with fucking grown weary, I begged something more.
One bliss that still lingered behind.
My prayer was accepted; the rose in the rear was opened
    to me in a minute.
One rose still remained, which I asked of my dear—
Twas her mouth and tongue that lay in it.
She promised at once, what I asked her to do.
Yet her lips were unsullied by me.
They'll not, my old friend, remain virgins for you,
Whose penchant exceeds even her fee.[45]

Finally, in his 67th epigram, Martial gives a clue of the opinion of oral sex among prostitutes. While the woman he hires has no reservations about vaginal or anal sex, "her fee" for performing fellatio far exceeds Martial's willingness to pay. Even among professionals, oral sex was somewhat taboo.

While one would expect a writer such as Martial to include references to oral sex in his work, one might be surprised to discover that more refined Roman poets did as well. The difference is in the subtle nature of the latter's approach. In his poems about his pining for Lesbia, Catullus occasionally referenced more erotic imagery. One of his more well-known poems expresses his desire to take the place of Lesbia's sparrow, "with whom she is accustomed to play, whom she is accustomed to hold in her lap, for whom, seeking greedily, she is accustomed to give her index finger and to provoke sharp bites."[46] Read literally, the poem simply suggests that Catullus wanted to replace his lover's pet. Yet if examined as erotic literature, the author is suggesting far more. Could Lesbia's pet sparrow represent another lover or her anatomy itself? Catullus could potentially be referring to Lesbia receiving cunnilingus from her lover or using her finger to pleasure herself.

At the same time, the great poet Horace was recommending his "ancient whore ... rouse it from a fastidious groin ... your mouth must labor hard."[47] Not unsurprisingly, Horace's renown as a refined Latin poet meant that this particular poem went largely untranslated for almost 2,000 years. The few translations that were made before the 1990s tended to either obscure the true message of the epode or cloak it in such poetic language that the reader was unsure of what Horace was referring to. Christopher Smart's translation in 1756 is a good example. "Or are their limbs less stout? But for you to raise an appetite, in a stomach that is nice, it is necessary that you exert every art of language." Here the mention of the phallus is removed and replaced with an ode to the poet's "limbs."

Finally, the erotic novel *Satyricon* dealt vividly with a variety of topics, including oral sex, in a way that continued to shock readers more than a millennium later. The typical jokes about, stereotypes of, and references to oral sex occur throughout the book. For example, in chapter 26 an older male lover is described as "the catamite, also at the soldier's order, began to beslaver me all over with the fetid kisses of his stinking mouth," once again belaboring the idea of the fellator as a filthy mouth.[48]

The *Satyricon* is also a treasure trove of classical Roman terms for different sex acts and classes of prostitutes. One of the most relevant for this topic is the *lupae*. This group of women received its name from the story of the she-wolf who nursed Romulus and Remus. The commentator Servius alludes to the wolf's licking of the two youths as a reference to the oral ability of this class of prostitute. Clearly the fact that a particular class of prostitutes existed just to deliver fellatio demonstrates a demand for that specific act among Roman men.

Roman art also contained numerous depictions of oral sex, especially pieces commissioned for the private residences of the upper class. In these paintings, dwarves especially were employed for different reasons to portray more risqué sexual acts. Several pieces of Nilotic art exist showing them engaged in fellatio with a female dwarf in a tergo position within a threesome.[49] Also common in Roman art were references to the exotic and the sexual promiscuity of Egypt. In fact, most of the more scandalous sex scenes portrayed in Roman art tended to be drawn as taking place in Egypt, but in true Roman fashion the subjects usually remained at least partially clothed. Not unsurprisingly, very few of the hundreds of erotic frescos in Pompeii depicted oral sex. One exception is the piece of wall art labeled scene VII in a dressing room of the Suburban Baths which depicts a woman being pleasured orally by another kneeling woman while she herself fellates a cinaedus, a homosexual male often working as a prostitute. The piece itself is particularly risqué for the assorted social taboos being broken by multiple characters.

As the Roman Empire expanded it absorbed not only lands and their people but also different cults and religions. Some of the more esoteric gods from the east brought with them erotic practices that were rather alien to the Romans. Take for example the Cult of Cybele which most likely originated in modern-day Turkey. Official Roman history recounts the arrival of the goddess during one of the darker phases of the Second Punic War as Hannibal camped outside the walls of the Eternal City itself. Regardless of the origins of the cult, its practices became quite well known and quite scandalous. The priests of Cybele, known as Galli, were eunuchs, men who castrated themselves as part of their initiation ritual. The practice was abhorred by the general Roman population and was in fact illegal for citizens. Writers and historians recorded that the castrated priests dressed as women and performed oral sex on each other or the gathered worshippers. Apuleius alludes to these priests, whom he calls "puellae," or "daughters," wishing to perform oral sex on a young shepherd boy.[50] "'Behold my daughters' … yet were these daughters a band of lewd and naughty fellows … they led me into the stable and tied me to the manger; and there was a certain stout young man with a mighty body, well skilled in playing on flutes." As seen earlier, the poet Martial used the practices of the Galli to berate one of his enemies: "though you have the groin of a Gallus priest, nonetheless you betray the rites of Cybele, for in your mouth you are male."[51]

As the Roman Republic under Julius Caesar expanded to the eastern edge of the Mediterranean, perhaps the most popular practice was the worship of the goddess Isis. Going back to the Osiris resurrection myth, priestesses performed certain sexual acts, including oral sex, in their worship. Various Roman emperors are alleged to have donned female garb to take part.

In fact, the sex lives and sexual perversions of the emperors have been better recorded than almost any other aspect of Roman society. Once again the impetus for this seems to have been an attempt by historians to normalize behavior. This was hardly just a post-imperial, Christian tone imposed on the records; it pervaded the writing of Roman historians and moralists as well. It is not surprising that one of the most notable targets of both was Cleopatra. Her non–Roman ethnicity, her status as a female ruler, and her well-known affairs with prominent generals made her an obvious target for contemporary authorities and later historians. She also became known as an ardent practitioner of oral sex. She allegedly fellated 100 Roman noblemen in one night, a feat that earned her the nickname *cheilon*, or thick-lipped, and helped to inspire a song by the band Adam and the Ants almost 2,000 years later. While many of the stories about Cleopatra were simple Roman propaganda, their existence tells us much about contemporary views of her, Egypt, and oral sex in general. The prevalence of the tales and the power of their message is evident in the views of the character Cleopatra over the next 2,000 years. None other than Shakespeare bawdily referred to her oral skills with double entendres in his play *Antony and Cleopatra*; for example, he wrote, "Quicken with kissing: had my lips that power, / Thus would I wear them out."[52] Yet her skills as a fellator are unable to save Antony whose sexual and physical death is referenced several lines later as his "pole is fall'n."

Her lover, Julius Caesar, was also often attacked for his own sexual exploits. Plutarch records that on the night before he crossed the Rubicon and began the civil war that brought down the Republic, "Caesar dreamt of having abominable sex with his mother."[53] While ancient and modern analysts take the mother in his dream to represent Rome, not all commentators and dream analysts agreed on the nature of the "abominable sex." Some have taken this to refer to oral sex, that Caesar irrumated the Republic, submitting it to himself in the most base of ways. Suetonius in *Twelve Caesars* states that upon seizing power, Julius Caesar, "transported with joy at this success, he could not keep from boasting a few days later before a crowded house, that having gained his heart's desire to the grief and lamentation of his opponents, he would therefore from that time mount on their heads."[54] Yet Caesar himself was still a product of his time. Seneca records that he once rejected a sum of money from Fabius Persicus because he was a well-known fellator. "What! Am I to accept the service of a man from whose cup I should decline to drink?"[55]

Roman writers utilized their often puritanical views toward oral sex in particular and hedonism in general to help explain disasters. After the disastrous Battle of Carrhae stories spread that among the other items recovered from the baggage train of Crassus' legions were copies of Milesiaca of Aristides. This "gave Surena occasion to heap much insulting ridicule upon the Romans, since they could not, even when going to war, let such subjects and writings alone."[56] The book was a famous eastern collection of erotic literature that included references to oral sex as well as other practices. To the moralists in the Senate, the soldiers' loss of virtue led to and justified their loss in battle.

The great Roman politician and moralist Cicero used allegations of oral sex to attack one of his greatest opponents, Publius Clodius Pulcher. A *populari* tribune, Clodius became known after his infiltration of the most sacred rite of the Vestal Virgins while dressed as a woman. Cicero helped to lead the prosecution of the former tribune, later on referring to Clodius as "that most impure of gluttons, the taster of your lusts, to that most needy and most impious man, Sextus Clodius, the companion of your family, who by his tongue alienated even your sister from you."[57] The great orator's attack impugned not only the honor of Clodius but also that of his sister Clodia. The pairing of cunnilingus and incest as crimes with equal weight is telling of the view of Republican Rome.

The idea that the fall of the Roman Republic was brought about by a similar collapse in Roman virtue was not lost on historians and moralists of the time. The first emperor himself was exposed as an effeminate letch; it was openly said that he once fellated a priest of Cybele. Lead sling bullets which have been unearthed from the time period of the civil war even bear references to Augustus performing fellatio on his adopted uncle and other males, naming him Octavia to emphasize this effeminizing practice.[58]

His successor Tiberius, though more renowned for his martial skill and rather lackluster reign, was also known to be perverted. He had numerous affairs and compelled many women to become his mistresses. "Even illustrious ones" were forced to perform oral sex on him, a particularly egregious act considering their rank.[59] One of these, allegedly, was a woman named Mallonia, who, after denouncing the emperor for his actions, kills herself in shame. Suetonius accused him of being a cunnilictor of women, a common charge against numerous ancients. His habits were so well known that they became the subject of an Atellan farce, a vulgar comedy show quite popular among the masses of Rome. Tiberius's lifestyle inspired a famous quip at one of these farces: "the old Billy goat is licking the sex of the does."[60] Again the conflation of age, impotence, and cunnilingus were brought forth as an insult against the majesty of the ruler. It is perhaps not surprising then that these performances soon became a target for the emperor; a number of them were banned and their performers seized. Yet worse than his predilection for cunnilingus were his abominable practices concerning children. It was rumored that he took unweaned infants and used them to fellate himself, an action seen as appalling even by modern standards.[61] Mention is also made in contemporary sources that in the imperial bedroom itself hung a painting by Parrhasius of Ephesus. This erotic work allegedly depicted Atalanta fellating or performing mutual oral sex with Meleager. Either way, it represented a work of art that the Roman public would have found unsuitable for the sleeping chamber of the emperor. Suetonius writes that Tiberius himself was offered a million sesterces, a princely sum, or the painting. His decision to accept the painting was used as yet another example of his moral failing.

The personal, political, and moral faults of Tiberius paled in comparison to those of Caligula and Nero. With all of the tales of incest, orgies, and violence associated with these rulers, it is not surprising to find references to degenerate oral sex practices as well. Seneca the Younger hinted at Caligula's predilection for engaging in cunnilingus, comparing him to the libertine Mamercus Scaurus.

> Why did it make Gaius Caesar the ruler of the world?—a man so greedy of human blood that he ordered it to be shed in his presence as freely as if he intended to catch the stream in his mouth! ... Why, when you yourself were supporting Mamercus Scaurus for the consulship, were you not aware that he would try to catch in his open mouth the menstrual discharge of his own maidservants? Did he himself make any mystery of it? Did he wish to appear to be decent?[62]

Rather than the act itself, Seneca focuses on the filth associated with it to emphasize the level of degredation to which the men had lowered themselves. Earlier in the work, Seneca even states that Scaurus not only engaged in cunnilingus with his wife and prostitutes but also with common household slave girls, a far greater insult.[63]

More shocking to Roman audiences, however, were the sexual exploits of Messalina, the wife of Claudius. According to contemporary histories she walked the streets of the capital at night working as a common prostitute. "Then she'd leave, exhausted by man, but not yet sated, a disgusting creature with filthy face, soiled by the lamp's black, taking her brothel-stench back to the Emperor's bed."[64] Pliny even recorded a contest she had with a legendary prostitute in which the empress managed to pleasure 25 men in 24 hours.[65] Numerous writers attacked her befouled mouth and, in a manner familiar by this point, impugned any advice or ideas that emerged from it. Tacitus records that in the year 47, Publius Suillius Rufus brought charges against the former consul Decimus Valerius Asiaticus on behalf of Messalina. Asiaticus had purchased the famous pleasure gardens of L. Licinius Lucullus, a property desired by Messalina. Suillius accused him of committing adultery with the empress's mother and of "unmanly vice."[66] "It was at this last that the accused broke silence, and burst out with the words, 'Question thy own sons, Suillius; they will own my manhood.'" The eventual conviction of Asiaticus bothered him less than the fact that it occurred "by the treachery of a woman and the shameless mouth of Vitellius."[67] That he was accused by two notorious practitioners of oral sex was the true insult to the fallen consul.

Likewise, the Emperor Domitian, a figure reviled by the Senate because of his dictatorial reign, was lambasted by the 1st-century female poet Sulpicia in her famous poem *The Complaint*. "And now the man who is ruling as king among the Romans, a degenerate not with his beam but with his back, and white in the throat."[68] She said he was the receiving partner in a sexual relationship and performed fellatio to completion. Quite ironically, Domitian renewed the *Lex Iulia de Adulteriis* of Augustus that banned adultery. Martial famously took the opportunity to attack the irony of the law and skewer one of his enemies. "The sacred censorship of the highest leader forbids adultery. Be happy, Zoilus; you do not fuck."[69] Thus, Zoilus' preference for performing fellatio on other men remains legal, a bizarre irony to Martial.[70] His penchant for sodomy is also utilized by Martial in another epigram which the poet uses to lambast the typical Roman punishment irrumation. "We are not able to get our revenge, he sucks cock."[71] To the Romans, it was not the act itself which was seen to be negative, but the passive nature of the person being irrumated. Zoilus' active practice of it therefore removes the associated stigma and punishment.

Roman imperial history is replete with stories and anecdotes of emperors and generals who were disgraced in the public eye because of their oral preferences. While the charges leveled against such men as Nero and Elagabalus are certainly true, those against many others were more likely simply personal attacks or meant to explain failure and downfall from a moral perspective. Regardless of whether the oral sex was practiced or simply implied we have a strong and continuing condemnation of fellatio and cunnilingus by the Romans. It is safe to assume that as their empire expanded across Europe and North Africa, these prejudices spread with them. Little information exists as to the sexual practices of pre–Roman groups such as the Celts, Germans, Numidians, and others. However, once Rome was firmly in control of these lands, prohibitions against oral sex became securely rooted in these now hybrid cultures.

3

The Middle Ages

The fall of Rome, though a politically shattering event for the classical world, did little to change the view or practice of oral sex around the Mediterranean. The Romans of the late empire continued to have the negative opinion of fellatio and cunnilingus that had dominated their moral view for almost a thousand years, and the new Germanic rulers who took power in the 5th and 6th centuries did not really change this. Late imperial literature and art continued to be the vehicle by which social opinions and mores were transmitted to both Romans and Germans. The concurrent rise of Christianity and its establishment as the new civilizing force in Europe with the decline of Roman imperial power also hardened pre-existing views of oral sex.

An example of this moralizing late Latin literature can be found in the writing of Artemidorus of Ephesus, who, during the 2nd century, mentioned the practice in his work on the meaning of dreams. "If one dreams of performing oral sex on someone else and that person is an acquaintance, whether man or woman, he will develop an enmity with that person, because it is no longer possible to share mouths. If it is an unknown person, the dream is bad for all except for those who earn their living by their mouths, I mean flutists, trumpet players, rhetors, sophists, and others like them."[1] Clearly, this is far from the view of most modern people who have a dream about oral sex. Though the view of individuals of the time on oral sex dreams is impossible to discern, Artemidorus does represent the conventional opinion of the previous millennium.

One of the last great poets of the empire, Decimus Magnus Ausonius, wrote a series of epigrams against his enemy Eunus during the late 4th century similar to Martial's. Much like his earlier poetic model, he focused the brunt of his attacks on the Eunus's penchant for cunnilingus. His epigram number 85 describes the act using Greek letters because it was still scandalous.

> Λαὶς, Ἔρως et Ἴτυς Χείρων, et Ἔρως Ἴτυς alter,
> Nomina si scribis, prima elementa adime,
> Ut facias verbum, quod facis, Eune magister.
> Dicere me Latium non decet opprobrium.

Lilly, Irene, Cassie and Karl; if you write out these names, and take the first letter of each, you can form the word which describes what you do, master Eunus! But I can't mention something so scandalous in Latin.

Ausonius' inclusion of Greek to describe the obscene acts of Eunus appears again in Epigram 87, where we find the latter pleasuring his mistress Phyllis.

> Eunus Syriscus, licker of groins,
> Master boor (or so he tells Phyllis),
> He sees the female member as a quadrilateral.
> He literally observes a three sided triangle Δ.
> On the other side of the valley in the wrinkles between the thighs,
> where there is a split slot,
> he says the path is a Ψ:
> with a three-pronged form.
> To whom he gives his tongue, he is a Λ.

Ausonius' description of Eunus as a Λ harkens back to the Athenian comic poet Eupolis who famously ascribed the presence of that letter on the Spartan shield to their predilection for cunnilingus.

An epigram later, Ausonius viciously attacks his opponent for providing oral sex to his pregnant wife, an even worse sin. "Eunus, when you're licking your pregnant wife's rotten vagina, you're hurrying to give your unborn children some tongue." As previously mentioned, Judaism had a similar proscription against performing cunnilingus on a pregnant woman, fearing that it would deform the child. Interestingly, recent medical research states that performing cunnilingus during pregnancy can result in death in very rare cases if enough air is blown into the vagina. In total, Ausonius composed eight epigrams against Eunus, utilizing deviant sexual practices in most as a way to discredit his rival. Finally, all of these were set in

Campania for the previously mentioned reason that the area was renowned for its oral proclivities.

The rise of Christianity largely only reinforced pre-existing Roman ideas toward sex and sexuality. Various Platonic, Neo-Platonic, and Stoic thinkers all argued for a limitation on sexual activity and recommended refraining from non-productive forms of pleasure. Lucretius, in his *De Rerum Natura*, spends much of Book IV discussing the fickleness of sex, especially non-reproductive sex such as fellatio and cunnilingus. "Poor fellow, kisses on the doors—Admitted at last, if haply but one whiff Got to him on approaching."[2] His philosophy became the cornerstone of Roman thought for the next several centuries. Thus, the teachings of the early Church concerning oral sex were not actually that revolutionary. The last great Roman philosopher, Boethius, whose thinking was an amalgamation of Christian and Neo-Platonic dogma, suggested that people should limit themselves to sex only once a month, and generally refrain from oral sex or other forms of sex which did not lead to reproduction. In his most famous work, *The Consolation of Philosophy*, one of the first acts by the visiting Lady Philosophy is to drive away the transitory forms of pleasure in his life, including sexual gratification. "Who let those whores from the theatre come to the bedside of this sick man?" she said. "They cannot offer medicine for his sorrows; they will nourish him only with their sweet poison. They kill the fruitful harvest of reason with the sterile thorns of the passions; they do not liberate the minds of men from disease, but merely accustom them to it."[3] Though Boethius himself was not necessarily an adherent of Christianity, his more contemporary Roman view on sex shows why the new religion was able to attract new adherents and become accepted: it did not significantly alter pre-existing social views.

Christianity tended to rely on pre-existing Jewish prohibitions against the practices of fellatio and cunnilingus as it did with most other social prohibitions. While no direct reference to the practice exists in the New Testament, many commentators have attempted to read a prohibition in Romans 1:24–27.

> Therefore God gave them over in the sinful desires of their hearts to sexual impurity for the degrading of their bodies with one another. They exchanged the truth about God for a lie, and worshiped and served created things rather than the Creator—who is forever praised. Amen.

> Because of this, God gave them over to shameful lusts. Even their women exchanged natural sexual relations for unnatural ones. In the same way the men also abandoned natural relations with women and were inflamed with lust for one another. Men committed shameful acts with other men, and received in themselves the due penalty for their error.

The Epistle of Barnabas, which Eusebius regarded as a spurious text, is perhaps the only work written in the century following the death of Jesus to address oral sex. The author incorporates the classical metaphors of various animals to condemn the practice.

> Again, neither shalt thou eat the hyena; thou shalt not, saith He, become an adulterer or a fornicator, neither shalt thou resemble such persons. Why so? Because this animal changeth its nature year by year, and becometh at one time male and at another female.
> Moreover He hath hated the weasel also and with good reason. Thou shalt not, saith He, become such as those men of whom we hear as working iniquity with their mouth for uncleanness, neither shalt thou cleave unto impure women who work iniquity with their mouth. For this animal conceiveth with its mouth.[4]

The medieval Church tended to group oral sex with other abhorred practices under the loose term sodomy. Therefore it is often difficult to identify specific acts committed by monarchs or commoners that are mentioned in literature and historical chronicles from the time. Both oral sex and homosexuality were judged deviant forms of love as they did not lead to conception and were practiced solely for pleasure. One of the first Church fathers to write on the subject was Tertullian. Around the beginning of the 3rd century, Tertullian, though married, took a vow of celibacy and wrote extensively on the morals of sex and marriage. In his *Apologeticum*, he defends the Church against different charges leveled by Roman pagans. Countering claims that Christians take part in secret atrocities, Tertullian adroitly points out the forms of human abuse and sacrifice practiced by the Romans. In doing so he also makes a veiled reference to a contemporary fondness for oral sex. "But do they do less who with beastly lust open their mouths to human bodies, because they devour what is alive? Are they the less consecrated to filth by human blood because they lick up only what is about to become blood? They eat not infants indeed, but rather adults."[5] Based on the position of his argument, Tertullian is actually equating fellatio and cunnilingus with cannibalism, a connection made by both the ancients and more modern researchers. Tertullian would have agreed with Camille Paglia's opinion that "there may be an element of omophagy in oral sex."[6]

St. Augustine continued this line of thinking several centuries later. In his work *Of the Good of Marriage,* he also comes out against sodomy, referring to it as "changing the natural use into that which is against nature, which is more damnable when it is done in the case of husband or wife."[7] Like the ancients, St. Augustine viewed oral sex as unnatural since it did not lead to conception, one of the three requirements of a good marriage. He himself had been something of a notorious letch earlier in life before converting to Manichaeism. A dualistic religion from Persia, it preached total abstinence from sexual activity for its followers. "The unrighteous law of the Manichaeans, in order to prevent their god, whom they bewail as confined in all seeds, from suffering still closer confinement in the womb, requires married people not on any account to have children, their great desire being to liberate their god."[8] At other points, Augustus suggests that these practices actually led the Manichaeans to practice oral sex instead. In many ways these two aspects of his youth helped to moderate and shape his later Christian view of sexuality. To Augustine, sex was quite natural and necessary, but like many other natural and necessary acts, it must be practiced to an end and not become an end in and of itself.

Not all followers of the Church agreed with these prohibitions against oral sex. Epiphanius of Salamis, a 4th-century bishop from Cyprus, discussed sects that either allowed or actually celebrated oral sex in his work on Gnosticism. "But others honor one Prunicus and like these, when they consummate their own passions with this kind of disgusting behavior, they say in mythological language of this interpretation of their disgusting behavior, 'We are gathering the power of Prunicus from our bodies, and through their emissions.' That is, they suppose they are gathering the power of semen and menses."[9] Origen further explains this particular sect in his work *Contra Celsus,* in which he explains that Prunicus was "a certain kind of wisdom, of which they would have the woman afflicted with the twelve years' issue of blood to be the symbol; so that Celsus, who confuses together all sorts of opinions—Greek, Barbarian, and Heretical—having heard of her, asserted that it was a power flowing forth from one Prunicos, a virgin."[10] The adherent's practice of cunnilingus was therefore religious in nature as it allowed him to gain power and strength, the opposite of the view of many in the ancient world who saw emission as a loss of strength.

Epiphanius also discussed another prominent group referred to as the Borborites, who considered sexual fluids sacramental. It seems that this Gnostic sect believed in a similar cosmology to the ancient Egyptians. They held that the creation of the universe was a sexual act between heavenly beings or by God himself, thus semen became the center of their worship rather than the teachings and crucifixion of Jesus. Epiphanius recounted that they "have also enslaved their bodies and souls to fornication and promiscuity. They foul their supposed assembly itself with the dirt of promiscuous fornication and eat and handle both human flesh and uncleanness."[11] General distaste for their practices caused them to be ostracized: "no one can eat with them. Food is served to them separately in their defilement, and no one can eat even bread with them because of the pollution."[12] Their ceremony seemed to involve ritual sex as well as the worship and consumption of seminal fluid afterward.

> For after having made love with the passion of fornication in addition, to lift their blasphemy up to heaven, the woman and man receive the man's emission on their own hands. And they stand with their eyes raised heavenward but the filth on their hands and pray, if you please—the ones they call Stratiotics and Gnostics—and offer that stuff on their hands to the true Father of all and say, "We offer thee this gift, the body of Christ." And then they eat it partaking of their own dirt, and say, "This is the body of Christ; and this is the Pascha, because of which our bodies suffer and are compelled to acknowledge the passion of Christ." And so with the woman's emission when she happens to be having her period—they likewise take the unclean menstrual blood they gather from her, and eat it in common. And "This," they say, "is the blood of Christ." But although they have sex with each other they renounce procreation. It is for enjoyment, not procreation, that they eagerly pursue seduction, since the devil is mocking people like these, and making fun of the creature fashioned by God. They come to climax but absorb the seeds of their dirt, not by implanting them for procreation, but by eating the dirty stuff themselves.[13]

This practice of ritualized oral sex and the consumption of its products only made more detestable to the early Church fathers the Borborites' practice of aborting and cannibalizing fetuses as well.[14]

As the Greeks and Romans had waged a moral war against a culture of sodomy, the Church spent much of its time fighting against systemic oral sex in various cults. It was always connected in early Christian literature to both excess and more extreme practices such as cannibalism, murder, and blasphemy. Oral sex was a gateway sin, a seemingly harmless practice which actually conditioned the practitioner for more extreme, personally-focused sins. In this light it was seen by Christians, as by Jews, to be in direct violation of the 2nd Commandment.

Early Christian penitentials, or texts on sins and their punishments, remain one of the best sources for studying the views of Western Europeans toward the practices of fellatio and cunnilingus. In the *Penitential of Theodore*, compiled by the archbishop of Canterbury in the 7th century, fellatio is punishable by seven or more years of penance and fasting. "Whoever ejaculates seed into the mouth, that is the worst evil."[15] If practitioners were habitual in their sinning, then "they repent this up to the end of their lives."[16] This is all the more extraordinary when one considers that Theodore only recommended four years of penance for adultery and one year for "murder without reason."[17]

This negative view of oral sex and harsh penalties can be seen in penitentials over the next few centuries. Saint Columbanus in the 6th century referred to fellators as "those who befouled their lips." A century later, the *Penitential of Cummean* recommended four years of penance for "those who satisfy their desires with their lips…. If it has become a habit, seven years." As late as the 10th century, these books still highlighted the sin of oral sodomy, though the great *Liber Gomorrhianus* of St. Peter Damian omits the crime entirely.

The Church has always feared that its spread to other cultures would result in the retention or re-emergence of ancient, tribal practices, many of which involved folk remedies and popular practices for ensuring love. From several medieval references, it appears that semen was used by women as an aphrodisiac at several places across Europe. Burchard, the bishop of Worms during the 10th century, warned, "Have you swallowed your husband's semen in the hope that because of your diabolical deed he might burn all the more with love and desire for you? If you have done this, you should do penance for seven years on legitimate holy days." Theodore of Canterbury in his penitential likewise addresses women baking semen into bread to attract the attention of their husbands or lovers. While the former may have been more practical on the woman's part for attracting and keeping a lover, the latter was firmly rooted in pre–Christian religious magic. Interestingly, magical food was never really eliminated from Continental society despite the best efforts of Church authorities. As late as the 1690s, a resident of Salem named Mary Sibley had a slave bake a witch's cake containing urine to prove whether several girls in the town were practicing black magic.

Much of the opposition to oral sex was likely the result of two beliefs. In keeping with the thought of the ancients, sex which did not lead to conception was viewed as excessive. Saint Thomas Aquinas summed up the Church's view:

> I answer that, as stated above wherever there occurs a special kind of deformity whereby the venereal act is rendered unbecoming, there is a determinate species of lust. This may occur in two ways: First, through being contrary to right reason, and this is common to all lustful vices; secondly, because, in addition, it is contrary to the natural order of the venereal act as becoming to the human race: and this is called "the unnatural vice." This may happen in several ways. First, by procuring pollution, without any copulation, for the sake of venereal pleasure: this pertains to the sin of "uncleanness" which some call "effeminacy." Secondly, by copulation with a thing of undue species, and this is called "bestiality." Thirdly, by copulation with an undue sex, male with male, or female with female, as the Apostle states (Romans 1:27): and this is called the "vice of sodomy." Fourthly, by not observing the natural manner of copulation, either as to undue means, or as to other monstrous and bestial manners of copulation.[18]

Unnatural sex acts and the pursuit of pure lust confined one to more earthly pursuits and not the heavenly pursuits of Christian theology.

The second reason for Church opposition to oral sex may be attributed to the Eucharist. As with Timarchus in classical Athens, where pollution of the mouth prohibited his right to speak in the assembly, so could it now restrict a parishioner's access to Holy Communion. Transubstantiation, the belief that the bread physically became the body of Christ, made the bread an enviable object, one that could not be placed into an unclean mouth. This may also explain the harsher penalties assigned to oral sex versus other methods of fornication. Rather than a new concept, the idea clearly has antecedents in the Jewish view of the mouth as a clean object used to praise God and the Roman view of oratory as the highest function of man.

The veneration of the Eucharist was joined in the medieval Church by the adoration of any object that could be connected to the life of Jesus or the lives of the saints. One of the more interesting holy relics of the time was the foreskin of the infant Jesus. According to some traditions, Mary saved it after his circumcision to unite him with it in heaven. It was claimed that the foreskin was in the possession of the popes until the invasion of Rome in 1527 by imperial troops under Charles V. Agnes Blannbekin, a 14th-century Austrian beguine, left a series of confessions regarding her ecstatic visions of the foreskin of Jesus. The oral fetishism present in her stories were deemed pornographic and condemned by the Church.

> Crying and with compassion, she began to think about the foreskin of Christ, where it may be located [after the Resurrection]. And behold, soon she felt with the greatest sweetness on her tongue a little piece of skin alike the skin in an egg, which she swallowed. After she had swallowed it, she again felt the little skin on her tongue with sweetness as before, and again she swallowed it. And this happened to her about a hundred times. And when she felt it so frequently, she was tempted to touch it with her finger. And when she wanted to do so, that little skin went down her throat on its own. And it was told to her that the foreskin was resurrected with the Lord on the day of resurrection. And so great was the sweetness of tasting that little skin that she felt in all [her] limbs and parts of the limbs a sweet transformation.[19]

Her orgiastic response to swallowing the foreskin of Jesus in a manner resembling fellatio gave additional fuel to the later arguments of Luther, Calvin, and others of the Freudian oral fixation of medieval Catholics with the Eucharist.

Interestingly, illustrations from the time which portrayed Christ's wounds often did so in ways that resembled vulvas.

The Catholic Church was not alone in its condemnation of oral sex. The equally Christian and equally Greco-Roman Byzantine Empire saw fellatio and cunnilingus in a similar light to western Europeans. The holy fathers and commentators in the Eastern Church largely assigned the same prohibitions against these acts as their counterparts in Rome. Theodore Balsamon, the patriarch of Antioch during the 12th century, interpreted St. Basil's 70th Canon, which discussed priests and deacons who defiled their lips, to refer to cunnilingus. He chastised those who "inflamed with a sexual fire use the female privy parts as a cup, and by it drink the abominable drink and defile their lips."[20] Meanwhile, Russian Orthodox sources, which rarely listed the crimes of oral sex being committed, did mandate a penance of two to three years of fasting for the sin. Like the *Penitential of Theodore*, this was on par with the punishments for adultery and incest.[21]

The most prominent individuals associated with oral sex in the Byzantine Empire were perhaps the most notable pair to ever rule the nation, Justinian and Theodora. In fact, the woman who inspired her husband to remarkable ends and saved Byzantium from the Nikka Riots came to power primarily through cunnilingus and bestiality. Beginning as an entertainer, Theodora found herself working as an actress and a prostitute. Historically this was not an uncommon joining of professions and is one of the reasons why the Church and later sects of Christianity frowned upon or outright banned theatrical employment. Regardless, apart from sexually servicing customers, Theodora allegedly made a name for herself by recreating the story of Leda and the Swan on stage. The myth centered on Zeus' mating with Leda, taking the guise of a swan to hide from his perennially suffering wife. According to Procopius,

> Often, even in the theater, in the sight of all the people, she removed her costume and stood nude in their midst, except for a girdle about the groin: not that she was abashed at revealing that, too, to the audience, but because there was a law against appearing altogether naked on the stage, without at least this much of a fig-leaf. Covered thus with a ribbon, she would sink down to the stage floor and recline on her back. Slaves to whom the duty was entrusted would then scatter grains of barley from above into the calyx of this passion flower, whence geese, trained for the purpose, would next pick the grains one by one with their bills and eat. When she rose, it was not with a blush, but she seemed rather to glory in the performance.[22]

This act of bestial cunnilingus attracted the attention of generals, nobles, and suitors, and after Theodora's return to Byzantium several years later, the Emperor Justinian. Once she became empress, rumors spread that she continued her sordid lifestyle. The author Procopius recounted numerous tales of her perverted behavior.

Perhaps ironically, Justinian passed a law forbidding sodomy in the Byzantine Empire. Following a series of earthquakes, harsh weather events, and the outbreak of plague, the emperor set about rectifying the moral failings of the nation much as Augustus did 500 years before. The term "sodomy" was allegedly created to encompass these perceived unnatural and sinful acts, and those convicted of engaging in homosexual unions or aberrant sex could be castrated or put to death. To date these were the harshest penalties applied for oral or anal intercourse as well as a host of other sexual transgressions.

Due to a combination of the increasingly harsh view of oral sex in both the Church and the Byzantine Empire and a decline in the arts during the Dark Ages, art and literature of the next several centuries rarely touched upon the subject. Among the rare pieces that depict the practice is the Veroli Casket, a 10th-century storage box. It is covered in various classical motifs, including the story of Europa, and the back depicts a small child or cupid fellating a horse. The use of a cupid here would allow the artist to condemn pre–Christian beliefs while still portraying the practice. This parallels the Roman use of dwarfs and Egyptian motifs in Nilotic art.

Medieval Western art was a little more risqué than that of the East. Surprisingly, what few depictions of oral sex did exist were mostly in religious art and architecture. The Saint-Omer Book of Hours housed at the Morgan Library in New York City, besides containing prayers and Bible passages, displays on page 16 a drawing of a man performing cunnilingus on a reclining woman. Ironically, the page is a copy of Psalm 87: "Indeed, of Zion it will be said, this one and that one were born *in her*, and the Most High himself will establish her." The placement of this image within a holy book drawn by hand for a wealthy woman is surprising. The addition of a large beaked bird which appears to be sodomizing the man from behind may add a certain element of divine punishment to the act, though, turning a seemingly erotic addition into a statement on morals.

The decorated capitals that graced church columns were another common location for depictions of strange creatures and bizarre acts.

These included gargoyles, dragons, demons, and the erotic Sheela na gig, an Anglo-Irish figure who is often shown with an open or exaggerated vagina. More prominent examples include churches at Colegiata de Santillana and Conzac Charente, which has a capital on a column depicting two people fellating tendrils that emerge from each other. These and other erotic and grotesque capitals and corbels seem to be morality pieces or, according to some historians, meant to depict pagan and Muslim practices. This would especially be true in churches built along the religious borders of Europe. As the single largest producer and sponsor of art and literature during the era were religious groups, it is not surprising to see an almost total lack of discussion of oral sex. The few exceptions resulted from attempts to portray the sinful nature of the act or were jokingly produced in attempts to circumvent the censors.

Medieval literature also discussed oral sex on a much smaller scale than the writings of the classical world. Perhaps this was because of a combination of royal and religious restrictions on the publication of such material with the fact that the literate class was mostly composed of religious figures. Oswald von Wolkenstein, a German writer and diplomat of the early 15th century, included among his poems a line that some have taken as a veiled reference to oral sex. "The young women skillfully allowed him to enter her mouth passing by the white battlement of her teeth in memory of St. Jonah."[23] Fellow German writer Heinrich Wittenwiler penned a satirical poem at the beginning of the 15th century which featured a scene where a young woman named Matzli gave in to a doctor's request for fellatio: "then she ate the root."[24] Some have read cunnilingus into an episode of *The Miller's Tale* by Geoffrey Chaucer. Toward the end of this ribald story, Alison projects her naked butt out of a window and spreads her legs, tricking Absalon into kissing her "hole." "Ful savoury, er he were war of this. Abak he stirte, and thoughte it was amys, For wel he wiste a womman hath no berd. He felte a thyng al rough and long yherd, And seyde, 'Fy! allas! what have I do?'"[25] Even the erotic French fabliaux of the 12th–15th centuries bear no reference to any acts of oral sex despite the inclusion of other sexual situations within the 100 or more extent stories.[26]

Some of the most blatant allusions to oral sex, perhaps not unsurprisingly, occurred in medieval literature that was modeled after the legends of pre–Roman people. One of the best examples of this is the Welsh legend of Ceridwen. An enchantress, she set about to create a potion to give her hideous offspring wisdom. The mixture spilled on the thumb of Gwion, who sucked it and gained the wisdom instead. The idea of auto-fellatio as a creative or enlightening process has existed since at least the time of the ancient Egyptians with the myths of Atum and Geb. Infuriated, Ceridwen chased the boy who kept shape shifting to escape her. The enchantress assumed dominant forms each time, a greyhound to his hare, an otter to his fish, until finally she became a chicken when he became a seed of grain. Swallowing his seed, she then became pregnant and eventually gave birth to the Welsh bard Taliesin. The concept of oral impregnation has also been seen in earlier myths and served as a caution against performing fellatio.

The Icelandic Sagas were another early example of what could be considered pre–Christian literature. In the *Ljosavandsfolkenes Saga*, a character is accused of not only performing oral sex, but of performing it on an animal. The joining of cunnilingus and bestiality is yet another attempt to portray the act as primitive. "You would be better occupied with picking out of your own teeth the bits of mare's ass which you ate before you came here; your shepherd saw you do it and was amazed at such disgusting behavior."[27]

The few other references to oral sex during this thousand-year period usually occurred in folklore. Some of the more erotic tales involve the demonic succubae, evil spirits who visited unsuspecting men at night and had sex with them. In some versions the succubus pleasured the man until his vitality was sucked dry; in others, the succubus forced the man to perform cunnilingus on her unclean vagina.[28] A succubus often worked in partnership with an incubus, draining sperm from her male victim with her mouth, which the incubus then used to impregnate another human female. Once again these acts of oral sex were seen as lowly and filthy. In fact, medieval legends claimed that engaging in the practice produced children with leprosy.

In keeping with the association of oral sex with the demonic, the illuminated painting *Mouth of Hell* by Meester van Katharina van Kleef seemingly portrays an entrance to the Underworld, yet in a classic example of double entendre, the animalistic entrance represents a rather convincing portrayal of a woman's vagina. Combining elements of the succubus, vagina dentata, sin, and the enervating element of the practice, the painting represents a clear warning against cunnilingus.

It should not come as a surprise then that the most well-known folk tale of the Middle Ages, the legend of King Arthur, also contained allusions to oral sex. Different versions of the tale are rife with metaphors and sexual innuendo. The most famous one, Chretien de Troyes' *Perceval, the Story of the Grail,* can be read as a reference to cunnilingus. The search by the knights for the Holy Grail bears many of the hallmarks of earlier and later allusions to oral sex. The shape of the vessel, much like the Greek cornucopia, lends itself to phallic imagery, as does the act of putting it to one's mouth.

Lust in the form of either oral sex or promiscuity was to be avoided by knights. The idea of chivalry, based on medieval religious and classical philosophical themes, stood staunchly opposed to fellatio or cunnilingus. Though written much later, Edmund Spenser's *The Faerie Queen* contains a scene of seduction between the witch Acrasia and the knight Verdant. In Book II, Canto XII, the hero Guyon makes his way into the Bower of Bliss and finds the naked Acrasia sucking life from the unconscious Verdant in a way reminiscent of a succubus.

> And all that while, right ouer him she hong,
> With her false eyes fast fixed in his sight,
> As seeking medicine, whence she was stong,
> Or greedily depasturing delight:
> And oft inclining downe with kisses light,
> For feare of waking him, his lips bedewd,
> And through his humid eyes did sucke his spright,
> Quite molten into lust and pleasure lewd;
> Wherewith she sighed soft, as if his case she rewd.
> The whiles some one did chaunt this louely lay;
> Ah see, who so faire thing doest faine to see,
> In springing flowre the image of thy day;
> Ah see the Virgin Rose, how sweetly shee
> Doth first peepe forth with bashfull modestee,
> That fairer seemes, the lesse ye see her may;

Lo see soone after, how more bold and free
Her bared bosome she doth broad display;
Loe see soone after, how she fades, and falles away.

That she "did sucke his spright" through his eyes can be seen as a warning against the act in particular and unrepentant sexuality in general. Her withdrawal of his spirit, "through his humid eyes," is also interesting as it parallels Aristotle's view of the eyeballs as the source of seminal fluid in the body. The passage was not only clearly representative of the medieval views toward the act, but was also written as a morality play for readers of the Elizabethan era.

In regard to actual historical figures, written records are again scarce as to oral sex practices. Much of what can be gleaned comes from accounts of confessions by monarchs to the sin of sodomy. Medieval tales recall how Charlemagne once committed an act so sinful and unspeakable that he had to seek forgiveness directly from God. Opinions of whether this was incest, necrophilia, or oral sex have been passed around for years without a resolution. Richard the Lionheart of England made two public confessions in 1191 and 1195 and has been rumored for years to have partaken in either anal or oral sex with any number of male soldiers and monarchs in Europe and the Middle East.

Soldiers returning from the Levant brought back tales of Muslims forcing Christian prisoners of war to perform oral sex and other acts. Regardless of whether these initial stories were true, the rumor was soon spread as a way to portray the Arabs as immoral. Long after the conflict was over, accusations of fellatio and sodomy were also leveled against the Knights Templar as part of the effort to discredit and destroy the organization.[29]

Frederick Barbarossa is the subject of numerous stories and legends during this time. Perhaps none is more scandalous than his treatment of the Milanese following their revolt in 1162. References to his actions appear in a number of sources, most notably in chapter 45 of the book *Gargantua and Pantagruel*. The citizens of the northern Italian city rose up against their German king, expelling his wife from the town on a donkey. To further insult her they mounted her on the animal backwards, "with her bottom turned towards the mule's head, and her face to its rump." The sexual implications here were meant to embarrass her and infuriate the emperor. Upon re-conquering the town, Frederick offered the leading citizens the option of being hanged or using their mouths to remove a fig from either the anus or vagina of the same mule used to expel the empress. According to legend, so many Milanese were offended at the prospect of performing cunnilingus or analingus on an animal that they chose to be hanged. This is most likely the origin of the Italian gesture of "making the fig," as the Italian word for fig, *fico*, is only one letter different than the word for vagina, *fica*.

As Frederick Barbarossa was allegedly forcing cunnilingus on the citizens of Milan, Pope Gregory IX was actively fighting against it in other parts of Europe. Following a startling report written by Konrad of Marburg detailing the frequency and depravity of rites being practiced by witches across Germany, Gregory issued a papal bull entitled *Vox in Rama* in the 1230s. According to Konrad, those wishing to become witches would "kiss the rear of a cat," possibly a sanitized reference to oral bestiality. After this the new witches, both male and female, engaged in an orgy of sodomy. The pope's bull ordered German authorities to tamp down these practices, and even led to accusations that Henry II, the count of Sayn, engaged in witches' orgies for opposing Konrad's investigations. Interestingly, the witch hunts that followed led to the decimation of black cats in Western Europe.

Though the term "Dark Ages" has fallen out of favor for describing society during the medieval period, it still is an apt descriptor for the practice of oral sex during the time. Greco-Roman morality and Church restrictions combined to further bury the practice. Associating it with witchcraft, foreign religions, heresy, and archaic rites, medieval society pushed oral sex deeper into the private sphere, essentially removing it from the public sphere for a thousand years, yet continued concerns about it show it was alive and well.

4

From Asia
to the Americas

The Western world, inspired by the traditional ideas of the classical Near Eastern civilizations, maintained a prevailing view of oral sex for more than 2,000 years fed by various philosophical trends and new religions. In fact, the success of these different schools of thought was due to their embracing what was seen as a norm for the time. Not surprisingly, though, as the practices of fellatio and cunnilingus also occurred in every other civilization and corner of the globe, a variety of views and opinions evolved. In fact, oral sex was viewed in many of these cultures much differently than it was in the West. The reasons for these divergent attitudes most likely have to do with religion, philosophy, sanitation, social hierarchies, and demographics.

As could be predicted, the Islamic world viewed oral sex in relatively the same light as Jews and Christians did. The Quran itself does not directly mention the practice and thus opinion on it has historically been divided among commentators. Some authorities have relied on surah 7:157 to discern a view on oral sex. "Those who follow the Messenger, the unlettered prophet, whom they find written in what they have of the Torah and the Gospel, who enjoins upon them what is right and forbids them what is wrong and makes lawful for them the good things and prohibits for them the evil/impure." The question then usually becomes one of whether semen is considered clean, like spit or breast milk, or unclean, like blood or menses. Regardless, most scholars tend to prohibit the ejaculation of sperm into the mouth for similar reasons as Judaism and Christianity.[1] As for cunnilingus, the presence of discharge so frequently in the area of the vagina was one of several factors leading to a less than favorable view of the practice. Because of this, and perhaps a number of other reasons, there are no reported references to oral sex anywhere in medieval Islamic literature.[2] In fact, European works that mentioned oral sex, such as Artemidorus' book on dream interpretation, were repeatedly censored upon their translation into Arabic. Perhaps the most renowned commentator on the topic of Islamic jurisprudence after the death of the prophet Muhammad, al-Ghazali, recommended severe limitation of nudity during sex and oral sex, much in keeping with the views of contemporary Scholastic philosophers in Europe.[3]

Not surprisingly, Europeans at the time had a far different view of the sexual practices of Muslims much as the Romans did of the Egyptians. The Saracens were often accused of the most obscene practices, including oral sex, which they committed against each other and the invading Crusader armies. These accusations even found their way into Dante's famed work in which he relates the punishment of Muhammad to the sodomy and oral sex practices that he permitted among his followers.

> A cask, split down the middle or the end,
> Gapes not so wide as one I witnessed there,
> Ripped from the chin to where the haunches bend.
> Between his legs the entrails hung; meanwhile
> The midriff, and the paunch were seen confest—
> Receptacle of what is foul and vile.
> While, all intent, on him my sight I bend,
> He eyed me, opening with his hand his breast,
> And said, "Behold how I my bosom rend!
> Behold how Mahomet is rent in twain!
> Before me, cloven upward from the chin
> E'en to the brow, walks Ali."[4]

The splitting in half of Muhammad served as a double entendre, representing not only his splitting of religion, but also the sodomy that he and his followers were accused of.[5] In the end, though, major religions and societies actually held similar views regarding oral sex.

This general prohibition against oral sex that dominated in both Europe and the Middle East rapidly changes as one crosses the Indus River. Over the past 3,000 years, India has generally not held the same negative views toward oral sex as most other civilizations and cultures. This is not surprising considering the rather prevalent and frank depiction of sex in general in Indian art and literature. In contrast to Western churches, some temples in India have an abundance of sexual iconography. Referred to as maithuna, these portrayals of tantric sexual unions serve a number of purposes in Hindu theology. They represent the joined nature of all components of creation and are a celebration of all natural and life-producing activities, while at the same time, in keeping with the Second Commandment, are warnings to avoid earthly pursuits to achieve higher forms of enlightenment.

The Markandeshwar Temple is a 12th-century shrine to Shiva located in Puri in eastern India. According to local tradition it was constructed in only one night by the Danavas, the sons of the primordial goddess Danu. Among the numerous carvings on its exterior is a scene of fellatio between a man and woman. Not far from the Markandeshwar Temple is the Sun Temple of Konarak, one of the greatest architectural accomplishments of the Hindu religion and dedicated to the sun god Surya. Its walls are covered with maithuna, including many depicting oral sex and several portraying rare instances of mutual oral sex. The slightly earlier Bhoramdeo Temple was built in the late 11th century and is also dedicated to the god Shiva. On its exterior walls are numerous maithuna showing oral sex and other practices. Further to the west, Hindu and Jain temples of Osian are also replete with sexual carvings. Finally, the 10th-century Lakshmana Temple dedicated to Vishnu, as well as the other temples in the vicinity of Khajuraho, feature hundreds of erotic sculptures. Many of these show not only oral sex but also bestiality and homosexual encounters.

In regard to Indian literature, one would expect the *Kama Sutra* to contain frequent references to and instructions on the practice. In what would be a shocking inclusion in the West, the book contains an entire chapter on fellatio as performed by male eunuchs on other men. "The acts that are done on the Jaghana, or middle parts of women, are also done in the mouths of their eunuchs and is called Auparishtaka. These eunuchs derive their imaginable pleasure and their livelihood from this kind of congress."[6] The author then goes on to describe eight different techniques of fellatio, all equally suited to men or women.

1) When holding the man's lingam in his hands and placing it between his lips, the eunuch moves about his mouth, it is called the "nominal congress."

2) When, covering the end of the lingam with his fingers collected together like the bud of a plant or flower, the eunuch presses the sides of it with his lips, using his teeth also, it is called "biting the sides."

3) When, being desired to proceed, the eunuch presses the end of the lingam with his lips closed together, and kisses it as if he were drawing it out, it is called the "outside pressing."

4) When, being asked to go on, he puts the lingam further into his mouth, and presses it with his lips and then takes it out, it is called the "inside pressing."

5) When, holding the lingam in his hand the eunuch kisses it as if he were kissing the lower lip, it is called the "kissing."

6) When, after kissing it, he touched it with his tongue everywhere, and passes his tongue over the end of it, it is called the "rubbing."

7) When, in the same way, he puts the half of it into his mouth, and forcibly kisses and sucks it, this is called, "sucking the mango fruit."

8) And lastly, when, with the consent of the man, the eunuch puts the whole lingam into his mouth, and presses it to the very end, as if he were going to swallow it up, it is called "swallowing it up."

Yet following the description of the methods by which a eunuch could please a man, the author advises, "the Auparishtaka is practiced only by unchaste and wanton women, female attendants, and serving maids ... never by Brahman." The *Kama Sutra* is actually quite shockingly in line with ancient Western views of oral sex, arguing that "this Auparishtaka is the work of a dog and not of a man, because it is a low practice, and opposed to the orders of the Holy Writ, and because the man himself suffers by bringing his lingam into contact with the mouths of eunuchs and women." At the end of the chapter, the author does acknowledge that despite prohibitions, many people do engage in the act, including harem girls on each other. The book also vividly describes mutual oral sex between two partners, which it calls "the congress of the crow." In a similar way, the classic Mahabharata, in the chapter describing the destruction of the world by a great flood, lists oral sex as one of the evils that caused the gods to destroy the planet.[7]

Indian religion and mythology, with its focus on the sacred penises of its gods, also contains a number of stories and allusions to the practice of oral sex. The god of beauty and war himself, Kartikeya, or Skanda, is said to have been born after Agni collected the semen of Shiva in his mouth and impregnated the Ganges River with it.

Even the trunk of the elephant god Ganesha can be seen to represent a phallus. The god himself is often portrayed in a number of erotic encounters. For instance, in Tibetan iconography of the god he is pictured being fellated by a goddess with a cat's head. Interestingly, the fellating goddess is often pictured with blood pouring from her own genitalia, representing the flow of power and fluids through the partners. Other paintings and bronzes from the Himalayan region feature scenes of Ganesh engaging in oral sex with either cat- or monkey-headed goddesses. These representations are rare in general in Buddhist art in the region. Gudrun Buhnemann suggests that Ganesh's tantric association with seeking world pleasure or perhaps his earlier origins as a vinayaka, or wild demon, may explain his portrayal in this manner.[8]

Shiva especially became associated with sex due to his role as the god of creation and its creative power. The god is often pictured with his consort Parvati engaged in ritual sex as part of the creative process. South Asia is replete with carved stone yoni and linga made to represent their respective genitals. This association between Shiva and sex may help to explain the presence of erotic maithuna on the exterior walls of temples dedicated to his worship.

The beginnings of tantric practices and worship involved the extraction, worship, and consumption of bodily fluids. While made more philosophical and perhaps ultimately trite by medieval commentators and modern New Age practitioners, the original theology of the movement closely resembled that of the Borborites in early Christianity. Early adherents focused on the acquisition of power and the pleasing of female deities through the extraction and offering of seminal fluid. Oral sex almost certainly played a role here in ritualistic or non-ritualistic habits.[9] Tantric sex, if it ever did exist, was concerned with pleasing powerful female gods, not the sexual satisfaction of its followers.

Indian folklore has a creature that resembles the succubae of European legends. Known as chuiaels, these demons were formerly women who died in childbirth. Appearing as a beautiful temptress, the chuiael lures a man into bed and performs fellatio on him until his life has been sucked out. Perhaps because of the cultural and religious influence of Indian traders, many of these religious concepts and cultural tales regarding oral sex made their way to the East Indies. The town of Pontianak, the capital of its own sultanate in Indonesia in the 18th–20th centuries, was allegedly built on the site of a nest of female succubae. These pontianaks tracked down and seduced men, devouring their genitals afterward. The founder of the city, Syarif Abdurrahman Alkadrie, is said to have destroyed the nest and driven out the demons before building the town.

India's traditional acceptance and even encouragement of oral sex is difficult to explain. As has been discussed, the root of prohibitions against it may be in the Middle East and the diffusion of its views to Greece and the rest of Europe through cultural exchange and the spread of religion. As ancient India was relatively isolated from these interactions, it maintained a more primitive, or at least less formally restricted, outlook on oral sex. Alternatively, the citizens of Mohenjo-Daro may have been more concerned with hygiene than those to the west, eliminating one of the prime reasons for the aversion to fellatio and cunnilingus. The discovery of the Great Bath at Mohenjo-Daro and rather sophisticated plumbing and bathing facilities at other sites have led archaeologists to describe the Indus River civilization as one of the most modern in terms of cleanliness. The Hindu philosophical obsession with birth and rebirth may play into a more general acceptance of these practices as they are connected to procreation. Compared to this, the Middle Eastern and Western philosophical concern with death led to a greater emphasis on moral and spiritual purity rather than physical happiness. Finally, the abundant food and increasing population of India would have meant sex wasn't for reproduction only. Tribes to the west struggling to survive in the deserts and competing with each other for power demanded constant population growth.

India's oral promiscuity was not to last. Outside religious and cultural influences altered its perceptions of sexual practices over the previous 700 years. While Buddhism initially bore no general prohibition against oral sex, it did speak out against sexual misconduct. The Pali Canon, the earliest collection of Buddhist scriptures, includes in its categorization of genders the term *pandaka*. Covering a wide range of definitions, it is generally taken to mean those who perform homosexual fellatio and other sexually deviant acts.[10] Over the next millennium, as Buddhism spread and was interpreted by various cultures, the definition of sexual deviance evolved. In some cases, constraints on sexuality that were originally prescribed for clergy became adopted by followers. "If the contact involves the three organs [oral sex with the male or female mouth, and anal sex], the offense of sexual misconduct is committed."[11] Perhaps due more to cultural than originally religious mores, Tibetan Buddhists particularly take a harsher stance toward oral sex. The 12th-century master Gampopa in his work *Jewel Ornament of Liberation* includes fellatio as a forbidden act, one that would lead to the base desires that Buddhism sought to avoid. This opinion holds today, with the current Dali Lama recommending in his book *Beyond Dogma*, "Even with your own wife, using one's mouth or the other hole is sexual misconduct." Overall, the Buddhist view again fits in well with Jewish and Christian views, seeing oral sex as a destructive act that could become compulsive and take the place of traditional sex. As one of the prime tenets of Buddhism was an effort to rid oneself of desire, oral sex could be seen as a purely desire-oriented activity.

The arrival of Islamic invaders, beginning in the 8th century and progressively increasing thereafter, introduced that religion's proscriptions against oral sex to India. Though the vast majority of Indians did not convert to the new faith present in their country, the rulers of the Ghurid Dynasty and Delhi Sultanate, among others, tried to instill their morality in the subcontinent and certainly impacted art and literature. Likewise, the arrival of the British several centuries later brought that nation's views on oral sex to India. Two centuries of English rule and reform would help to strip any remaining vestiges of the practice from Indian society and produce many of the same taboos and laws that existed in London. By the 19th century oral sex was dismissed as a Bengali practice, emphasizing the more primitive nature of that group, much as the ancient Romans saw it as an act confined to Campanians and Egyptians.[12]

Moving further eastward from India to China, the general attitude toward oral sex softened even more. Once again, it seems that the further a culture was from the Middle East, the more it lacked any general prohibition against these practices. Fellatio seems to have been considered a perfectly normal act for the Chinese, being mentioned frequently in both history and literature. The only prohibition placed on the act involved the release of semen, as this would weaken the man. The Chinese believed that ejaculation reduced a man's "yang" and enervated him. The disorders and diseases that could result from this were generally referred to as *shenkui* and were moralizing warnings against sexual over-indulgence. Men were often encouraged under Daoist doctrine to practice retrograde ejaculation, returning the semen to the brain so its power could be reabsorbed. Cunnilingus, on the other hand, was wholeheartedly approved of as it allowed the man to acquire "yin," a force which women were believed to have an endless supply of.[13]

This concern about the loss of yang in men also stands at the center of the Chinese version of the classic succubus tale. Later Ming and Qing literature dealt with the character of the fox, a sexualized creature that could assume human form to seduce unsuspecting people. In at least one case the parasitic nature of the fox is shown through its performance of fellatio on a man, thus draining his life from him.[14]

Chinese literature has many examples of couples engaging in oral sex acts, often described in the most poetic of ways. Popular stories refer to women servicing "jade stalks," "red stalk," "swollen mushrooms," and "heavenly dragon pillars," while men knelt before "open peony blossoms," "golden lotuses," and the "cinnabar gates." Classic novels like *Gold Plum Vase* contained detailed scenes of oral sex including one in which the character Golden Lotus is described as quite adept at "playing the flute." In another Ximen Qing is fellated by a wet nurse. Chinese literature also features sexual handbooks including *The Handbook of the Plain Girl* and *The Art of the Bedchamber*. The former was allegedly written for the Yellow Emperor in early antiquity and was a commentary on the careful use of sexual energy to prolong life and youth to the point of immortality. According to the book, for most of a girl's life her body must balance itself between "Jade Gate secretions" of yin and "absorption of yang forces." By the age of 35, as her fertility declines and the chances for birth defects increase, a woman "needs more frequent releases of secretions, but less invasion of her Jade Gate in order to maintain youthfulness." Clearly cunnilingus would be the best method to achieve this. It seems that fellatio is largely recommended for older women as "when she reaches the age of forty-nine ... in order to prevent old age from permanently settling in she needs frequent stimulation of her Jade Gate secretions, increased production of saliva, and frequent absorptions of yang essences."[15] The 12th-century Daoist master Zhang Sanfeng recommended "blowing the flute," or fellatio, as a way to open up the passage and allow for energy to flow more directly between the man and woman. Not only was sex in general and oral sex in particular necessary for a full life, if done properly they could prolong life.

The Mawangdui tombs of the early Han Dynasty, discovered in 1973, contained a treasure trove of texts written on silk. Among the philosophical writings, historical works, and military canons were a series of writings on health and medicine. One of these directly referenced sexual activity and oral sex, recommending that a woman "give breath to the penis; give food and drink to the penis. Feed it as if nourishing a child." This near-worship of the male sex organ finds parallels in the Hindu worship of the lingam of Shiva, though as always, oral sex was mainly seen as merely a component of the larger sexual practice.

The overall acceptance of oral sex, bordering on a fixation with the practice, has long been of psychological interest to Western researchers. Beginning in the 1950s many have attempted to apply Freudian concepts of sexual development toward the Chinese acceptance of oral sex, suggesting that it is a by-product of the strong mother-son relationship in the culture as well as prolonged breast feeding.[16]

Competing with Daoism's acceptance of oral sex was the Confucianism's moral rigidity which adopted the familiar Middle Eastern view of sex as serving only a procreative purpose. This is perhaps not surprising when one considers the larger emphasis placed by Confucius on the importance of continuing the family line and obtaining personal perfectibility and dominance over lesser desires. As recorded in the *Book of Rites*,

> The things which men greatly desire are comprehended in meat and drink and sexual pleasure; those which they greatly dislike are comprehended in death, exile, poverty, and suffering. Thus liking and disliking are the great elements in men's minds. But men keep them hidden in their minds, where they cannot be fathomed or measured. The good and the bad of them being in their minds, and no outward manifestation of them being visible, if it be wished to determine these qualities in one uniform way, how can it be done without the use of the rules of propriety (implied in the ceremonial usages)?[17]

The inherent patriarchal view of the philosophy was also not above employing the idea of cunnilingus to denigrate a man or demonize a woman. The most well-known examples were the stories and rumors about Wu Zetian. A powerful woman, Wu plotted her way upward from consort to become the first female empress of China at the end of the 7th century. Not surprisingly, her adversaries sought to sexualize her reign to discredit her. It was widely rumored that she forced visiting dignitaries and her own officials to perform cunnilingus on her, "licking the lotus stamen" as a sign of respect.[18] Similarly, a thousand years later, rumors that eunuchs were having "vegetarian affairs" with women in their harems, performing cunnilingus on them, led the Yongle emperor to order the execution of more than 2,000. Finally, the powerful Empress Dowager Cixi is rumored to have used British sinologist Sir Edmund Trelawny Backhouse as her own personal paramour. The openly homosexual Backhouse had fled England for China in the 1890s and soon began to provide a number of sexual services, including cunnilingus, for the 69-year-old woman. Backhouse later wrote of his encounters in a much debated autobiography entitled *Decadence Mandchoue* in the 1940s.

On the whole, Chinese views regarding oral sex seemed to have waxed and waned with the power struggle between Daoism and Confucianism. Where and when the former philosophy was strong, oral sex enjoyed a certain level of acceptance and near-worship, but in elite circles and within the Confucian bureaucracy, it held many of the social stigmas that it did in the West. This switch in thinking mainly occurred after the fall of the Tang Dynasty. By the advent of the Song, Confucianism had been wedded to the imperial government and had gained traction in society. Neo-Confucianism attempted to provide a more secular belief system, supplanting much of the esoteric mysticism of Daoism.

The geographic trend of greater acceptance of oral sex as one moves to the east continues onward to the Japanese islands. Like Orpheus of ancient Greek mythology, the Japanese god Izanagi journeyed to the land of the dead to save his wife, Izanami, who had died in childbirth. The metaphor presented by Izanagi, "going down," stands out strongly here due to the sexual nature of his wife's death. In the end, after going down, the god mistakenly looks at his wife, an action that is also rife with symbolism. As he flees to the surface from his now-hideous deceased spouse, he is chased by Shikome, an ugly hag. He manages to make it to safety and throws peaches at Shikome to momentarily distract her, then rolls a boulder in front of the entrance to Hades, sealing it off. It should be noted that the peach also is pregnant with sexual connotation in traditional Japanese and modern Asian society.[19]

Japan's history of moral relativism meant that only the arrival of outside philosophies led to the casting of dispersion upon the practices of fellatio or cunnilingus. In fact, the founding of the Tachikawa-ryu school of esoteric Buddhism by the monk Ninkan in the 12th century sought to create a purely Japanese school of tantric sex to balance the moral and sexual restrictions of foreign philosophy. For believers in this sect the sharing of sexual fluids was part of the initiation process and oral sex was seen as not only normal but as a desirable way to reach enlightenment. Ultimately, the immoral elements of the new sect led to its dissolution and the destruction of its texts in the 16th century during the Muromachi Period.

As Buddhism and Confucianism gained more ground in Japan, the practices of fellatio and cunnilingus once again faced challenges. A Buddhist text published in 1661 has the Buddha himself referring to those who practice oral sex as "beasts in men's flesh."[20] These foreign religious influences led to fewer references to homosexual fellatio in the literature of the nation to only several from the Middle Ages to the 19th century. One of the few still in existence is a scene from the erotic Chigo no sōshi scroll in which a young man fellates a priest, describing him as "a bit salty."

Despite these restrictions, the generally progressive view of oral sex continued well into the modern era and is reflected by its recent portrayal in the *shunga* erotic art of the 18th and 19th centuries. Numerous watercolors and prints depict both men and women performing oral sex among numerous other acts of intercourse and bestiality.

One famous print shows that not only were fluids clean, but also desirable enough to collect as shown by the vase or cup positioned underneath the woman. This particular notion was mostly likely Daoist in origin reflecting the concepts of yin and yang and the power inherent in the female. These pictures often depict elites as well as monks and commoners engaging in the process. To the Japanese oral sex was a universal and uniting practice. Interestingly, fellatio is less often depicted than cunnilingus. Gary Leupp argues that this may have simply been due to the artistic limitations of *shunga* which tended to portray exaggerated penises and very small mouths.[21] Conversely, this may once again be due to the yin and yang philosophy brought over from China a thousand years before.

Perhaps the greatest example of orally-focused *shunga* is the uniquely Japanese story "The Dream of the Fisherman's Wife." In this tale and its associated artwork from the early 1800s, a Japanese pearl diver is seized by an octopus which then proceeds to perform cunnilingus on her. The story inspired numerous pieces of artwork and literature and was a precursor to the well-known tentacle porn of modern Japan.

All of these pieces were part of the larger ukiyo-e art, "pictures of the floating world," movement. Its pictures and prints dominated the artistic world in Japan after the 17th century. In keeping with the idea that art reflects the general zeitgeist of society, life in post–Sengoku Japan tended toward exaggerated hedonism. This would be similar to the Lost Generation of the Roaring Twenties or the escapism that dominated Chinese life and philosophy in the Northern and Southern dynasties.

Sexual practices and attitudes toward oral sex remain liberal as we move across the Pacific Ocean and the islands of Melanesia and Polynesia. In fact, the remoteness of these cultures provide a unique area of study for modern-day anthropologists seeking to understand the sexual proclivities of early man. Early European explorers and traders for their part would have focused on the primitiveness of these people to reinforce their own 18th- and 19th-century views of oral sex.

One of the more well-known groups was the Sambia people who inhabited the highlands of Papua New Guinea. Like many primitive tribes, the Sambia practiced initiation rites for young men. These involved the ritualistic fellating of older warriors during which semen was ingested so as to pass on strength and virility. Often these actions would continue until the men were married. The basis of this ritual centered on the tribe's worship of "secret bamboo flutes of great and mysterious power."[22] To the Sambia, masculinity must be induced in young boys through the ingestion of semen which then allows for the production of sperm in the body. The boys were taken from their mothers and over the course of several days were exposed to beatings, spiritual lessons, and mock fellatio. "You kwulai'u—open your mouths for the flute, they will place it inside."[23] The initiation bonded the male warriors in the tribe, as similar rites among Amerindian and African tribes did.

Interestingly, the Sambia, along with most other tribes of New Guinea, refused to practice cunnilingus. Concerns over menstrual blood pollution as well as the fact that power resided in male spiritual cults caused the practice to be viewed with outward disdain. Gilbert Herdt recorded that Sambian men would involuntarily spit if the subject was broached by outside anthropologists.[24] The one apparent exception appears to have been the Ilahita Arapesh people of northeastern New Guinea. Donald Tuzin reported in his seminal work, *The Cassowary's Revenge*, that men of the tribe regularly performed cunnilingus on their wives and that the practice was considered ancient.[25] Yet it should be mentioned that the culture was more known for its concurrent destruction of its ancient male-dominated cults. This may bear some relevance to its localized acceptance of the practice of cunnilingus.

During his exploration of Tahiti, Captain William Bligh witnessed a chief perform fellatio on one of his attendants.[26] "It is strange that in so prolific a country as this, men should be led into such beastly acts of gratification, but no other place are they so common or so extraordinary as in this island," he wrote.[27] Clearly this role reversal was not viewed negatively by the Tahitians themselves. English explorers chronicled the *mahu* of Tahiti, homosexual males who fellated other members of the tribe. As the captain of the missionary ship *Duff* recounted in 1799, "we are obliged here to draw a veil over other practices too horrible to mention."[28] The Hawaiian Islands had a similar tradition which Captain Cook observed during his third voyage there in the late 1770s. *Aikane* were same-sex relations based on societal levels rather than sexual attraction. These young men who participated seem to have played an important role in Hawaiian society and were far more than simple courtesans.[29]

Oral sex was not simply consigned to initiation or same sex relationships in the Pacific. Visitors to Pohnpei in Micronesia noted the regular occurrence of oral sex on the island, especially cunnilingus. Hermann Heinrich Ploss, a German anthropologist who visited in the late 19th century, recorded that Melanesian men placed a fish in a woman's vagina and then proceed to dine on both delicacies. Young boys and girls of the Cook Islands were actually instructed in oral sex techniques by older members of the tribe.[30]

Otto Finsch, a German explorer who visited in the 1880s, recorded other oral peculiarities of Pohnpei. Girls were thought to be exceedingly unwelcoming of sex, so older men of the village worked as cunnilictors, seeking to induce the young women to desire sex. It was reported that they also sometimes used biting ants to excite the clitorises of the girls. Even after the women began to partake in sex with the men of the island, "the men, at the desire of the women, must use not only their tongues but their teeth to produce a local stimulation of the female genitals."[31]

Other tribes and primitive civilizations stretching around the globe practiced different and unique forms of oral sex. The Manchu of northeastern China practiced a custom in which mothers would fellate their young sons as a greeting. James Webb recorded similar scenes in his 2001 book *Lost Soldiers*, set in Thailand during his time in the Vietnam War. A multitude of other groups from the Telegu of India to various rural people in Cambodia also partake in this seemingly harmless play.

Pieces of Incan and Moche art that have been unearthed and depict graphic representations of oral sex would seem to suggest that the practice was also generally well received in more civilized parts of the New World. The Moche inhabited the coastal area of northern Peru during the first millennium of the modern era. In addition to their construction of pyramids and their irrigation systems, the people were famous for their erotic pottery. At least 500 sex-themed ceramics produced at that time have been found and catalogued. In a sharp departure from European and Asian erotic art, the vast majority of sex acts in this art involve anal sex or fellatio. In fact, vaginal sex is almost non-existent among the pots found so far. Interestingly, like those of ancient Greece and Rome, the Moche sculptures tend to depict the man being fellated dressed in a superior fashion to the fellator.[32] Though the reasons behind the Moche's choice of subject material remains unknown, the sheer volume of the pots stands in sharp contrast to the limited portrayal of the act in other cultures.

Notable among the Northern American Amerindians were the Crow who possessed classes of effeminate men known as "messengers" whose purpose was to fellate other male members of the tribe in addition to their normal sexual intercourse with women.[33] In fact, one of the few Amerindian groups that frowned upon both fellatio and cunnilingus were the Inuit who viewed most sexual acts undertaken with the mouth to be taboo. Another was the Yurok Indians who lived along the Klamath River in Oregon. This tribe held a similar view, preferring not to mix different fluids. Cunnilingus was seen as mixing fluids, the consequence of which would harm the annual salmon run on the river.[34]

The attitude of most of the rest of the world toward oral sex was markedly different from those cultures impacted religiously or philosophically by the Middle East. Prohibitions against fellatio and cunnilingus due to sanitary concerns, fear of losing virility, the need to procreate and expand the tribe or concerns about personal control and over-indulgence were either non-existent or else countered in argument. Formerly, anthropologists and historians speculated that civilizations developing in warmer climes tended to have more liberal sexual practices. While the sterner morality of the Europeans and the Inuit may seem to support this notion, the equally puritanical bent of Judaism and the Greeks does not. Our lack of knowledge regarding the sexual practices of Europeans before the rise of Rome and Christianity makes this unable to be proven. Racial origin also seems to play no part in either a penchant for or prohibition against oral sex as Indians and Europeans, despite a common origin, had divergent views on the subject.

5

15th to 17th Century Europe

For a number of reasons, the Renaissance marked a change in Europe's long-held attitude toward oral sex. Almost 2,000 years of moral and societal opposition to the practice began to deteriorate. While this change would not be sudden and would take another 500 years to reach its climax, it was in many ways inevitable. Institutions in the West and Middle East, such as religion and state morality, were fighting a losing battle against human nature. The evolution of art, science, religion, and economics as the Middle Ages receded, pushed fellatio and cunnilingus from the shadows of immorality to a certain level of acceptance and normalcy.

Some have speculated that the shift from feudalism to independent family units may have contributed to a softening of the prohibitions against oral sex in marriage.[1] The increased individualism that accompanied the transition from the medieval to early modern period led to greater concerns for privacy in both the household and the bedroom, yet other factors may have played an even greater role. Advances in art and literature, when combined with the advent of the Protestant Reformation, began the acceptance of oral sex in the public sphere. The rise to prominence of the family structure may have localized the practice, but it would take great changes in both art and religion to bring it to national attention.

The Black Death plays a certain minor role in this reappearance of oral sex through its effects on politics and society. Foremost, the destruction wrought by the plague helped to break down many of the feudal bonds that had dominated on the Continent. Likewise, the power of the Church began to wane due to its inability to cope with the pestilence, thus weakening its power over social customs and leading invariably to the rise of Protestantism. Finally, the art and literary movements that developed in response to the arrival of the plague, including the Danse Macabre, tended to focus on a more hedonistic lifestyle.

Perhaps nowhere is this more represented than in Giovanni Boccaccio's *Decameron*. This epic collection of 100 tales as told by a group of young people seeking to avoid the effects of the plague on Florence contain some of the first references in literature to oral sex in nearly 1,000 years. During the first day of storytelling, in the middle of the last tale, Alberto proceeds to deliver an anecdote meant to imply that women make poor choices in life, especially in the selection of mates. Yet the metaphor he uses is itself a commentary on the general aversion of most of them to oral sex.

> I have often taken a light meal with women and I have seen them eating lupini beans and leeks. Although there is nothing good at all about the leek, its head is the less disagreeable part. But you women, seduced and deceived by your desire, hold the head in your hand and you eat the stalk, which not only is worthless but tastes really nasty. So who am I to say, madam, that you don't do the same as you choose your lovers?[2]

The great Italian Renaissance satirist Pietro Aretino wrote frequently about what he saw as the Church's unnatural obsession with limiting human sexuality. "What harm is there in seeing a man mount a woman? Should beasts, then, be freer than we?"[3] In fact, by the 16th century, holy feast days had adopted much of the often erotic carnival atmosphere that they would become known for. This included the consumption of phallic-shaped or -inspired meats and treats in a manner which seemed to allude to oral sex. Aretino was not the only Italian writer to attack the often hypocritical beliefs of the Church. Bishop Blosio Palladio was lampooned in poetry in the 16th century for "dining alone on a huge pheasant," a satirical reference to his penchant for performing oral sex on other men.[4]

Among these Renaissance works which attempted to revive the classical pattern of using metaphors and double entendres to discuss oral sex were the poems of Johannes Secundus. The Dutch poet compiled a collection of epigrams dedicated to his love, Neaera, which he entitled *Liber Basiorum*, or Book of Kisses. Another poem of dubious authorship is often attached to the collection. Entitled "A Fragment: To Lydia," it is far more risqué in content than the preceding love sonnets.

> Soft! You suck my breath away,
> Drink the life drops of my heart,
> Draw my soul from every part;
> Scarce my senses can sustain
> So much pleasure, so much pain!

The influence of both Marital and Catullus comes through strongly in the writing of Secundus, showing a clear return to the classical form.

Artists have always pushed the boundaries of what was acceptable in culture, presenting through art what was often taboo to discuss in public. The new techniques that began to surface in the Renaissance, when combined with the resurrection of classical themes and tales and sponsorship by private individuals, allowed artists to portray subject matters that would have been unthinkable during the Middle Ages. The woodcut "Sacrifice to Priapus" in Francesco Colonna's *Hypernerotomachia Poliphili* of 1499 bears witness to this. It portrays a group of mostly female Dionysian worshippers, many playing flutes or holding phallic symbols, gathered in front of the god Priapus. He is at the center, behind a lectern mounted on a podium on the front of which is secured a phallus. The sexualized imagery of the book was deemed acceptable due to its classical nature, a loophole that other artists exploited.

Fruit and vegetables were frequently used as metaphors for sex in Renaissance and Baroque art. A certain level of wishful naiveté on the part of the clergy and general population allowed artists to hide these objects in paintings much as Michelangelo did in the Sistine Chapel ceiling. And this wasn't simply bawdy humor. In 1588 Italian writer Giambattista della Porta published *Phytognomica*, a book which sought to not only study and categorize various plant species but also compared them to human organs in an attempt to prove the existence of God's hand in creation.

Raphael's paintings of Cupid and Psyche at the Villa Farnesina in Rome is framed by a border of plants and fruits drawn by his student Giovanni da Udine. Giovanni took the opportunity to draw numerous phallic-shaped fruits and vegetables, some within grasp of the outstretched hands of the painted characters and some oriented toward their mouths. Niccolo Frangipane's *The Madrigal Singers* portrays a similar scene, a collection of men, all open-mouthed, seated around a table filled with sausages and peaches. Complementing the obvious erotic nature of the painting are the figure of a man to the right lifting a pitcher to his mouth and a classic satyr to the left.

As was discussed in Chapter 1, Michelangelo's *Temptation and Expulsion* panel on the ceiling of the Sistine Chapel represents a rather blatant depiction of oral sex between the first two people created by God. It is bordered by eight triangular spandrels which Michelangelo filled with pictures of the ancestors of Jesus. Atop each spandrel is an elegant ram's head which has long seemed out of place amidst the Biblical narratives. Recently, several historians and art critics have claimed that the artist included these images as a coded reference to the female anatomy, representing the vagina, uterus, and fallopian tubes.[5] If true, then one image in particular would seem to show two female figures performing oral sex on the ram's head. Given the sheer number of lay and sexual jokes and innuendo throughout the rest of the piece, this would not be surprising.

A century before Michelangelo, Taddeo di Bartolo painted a fresco in the lower level of the Collegiate Church of Santa Maria Assunta in San Gimignano. Depicting the Last Judgement, the artwork illustrates the punishments to be meted out for those who commit any of the seven deadly sins. Two of the sufferers drawn by di Bartolo are being punished for having committed sodomy during their lifetimes. One of the unfortunate sinners, who can be assumed to have been the penetrator in the act, is himself penetrated by a devil holding a long metal rod. The other sinner, the passive partner, receives the same rod into his mouth in the manner of fellatio. All the while numerous others in the piece are being tormented and tortured by demons.

South of the town of San Gimignano is the small village of Massa Marittima where in 2000 a 13th-century fresco was discovered in a public fountain. Once restored it was revealed to depict a scene of women gathered beneath a tree bearing penises as fruit. These erotic horticulturalists are shown harvesting these fruits while a flock of birds circles the tree. While some have suggested that the scene represents simple eroticism or even witchcraft, others argue for a thinly-veiled reference to oral sex, as fruit grown on trees is consumed by the mouth.[6] Finally, it could be an advertisement for marriage, suggesting to men that there is an ample supply of suitors available for women and that they risk the devouring of their virility the longer they stay unpicked. The concept of penis-bearing trees was not a new or unique creation. Drawings of them had appeared in illuminated manuscripts since the Middle Ages, with a number of theories existing as to their meaning.

Thus, though oral sex was beginning to make itself seen in art, it was often only as a warning against the act. The famous German Chiaroscuro artist Hans Baldung Grien created a series of woodcuts on the theme of the witches' sabbath. In keeping with the thought of the day, one of Baldung's creations shows a witch receiving a dragon's tongue from behind. The action is then magnified to the right, where the beast's tail resembles a stylized vulva, penetrated by two objects. Witches, to whom every other abominable act was prescribed, were considered well-known practitioners of oral sex. Surprisingly, one of the most well-known manuals on the subject, the *Malleus Maleficarum*, does not broach oral sex, though it does detail the other sexual exploits of these women. In fact, the book is quick to point out that there are certain sexual activities that even demons would not take part in.

> Also it must be carefully noted that, though the Scripture speaks of Incubi and Succubi lusting after women, yet nowhere do we read that Incubi and Succubi fell into vices against nature. We do not speak only of sodomy, but of any other sin whereby the act is wrongfully performed outside the rightful channel. And the very great enormity of such as sin in this way is shown by the fact that all devils equally, of whatsoever order, abominate and think shame to commit such actions. And it seems that the gloss on *Ezekiel* XIX means this, where it says: I will give thee into the hands of the dwellers in Palestine, that is devils, who shall blush at your iniquities, meaning vices against nature.[7]

Records from witch trials held at this time in England bear several references to oral sex as part of the witching process. Margaret Flower, one of the notorious Witches of Belvoir who were accused of poisoning and murdering the Earl of Rutland's children, confessed in 1618 "she hath two familiar spirits sucking on her, the one white, the other black spotted. The white sucked under her left breast, and the black spotted within the inward parts of her secrets."[8] Though demons were rumored to suck the blood of witches, especially from their breasts, the actions of the second demon in Flower's testimony seems to imply cunnilingus. A similar confession was made by Elizabeth Sawyer three years later in 1621. "Whether did you pull up your coats or no when the Devil came to suck you? No, I did not, but the Devil would put his head under my coats, and I did willingly suffer him to do what he would."[9] Not only therefore was it seen as sinful to perform cunnilingus, it would be equally abominable to request and enjoy it.

The issues of oral sex and heresy began to be seen as one and the same by both secular and ecclesiastical leaders. In 1524 Pope Clement VII granted the Inquisition in Aragon power over investigation of sodomy in addition to overseeing the trials of heretics. In fact, the court was not required to present a connection between the sodomite and any belief in heresy, as the former practice was considered spiritually damning in its own right.[10] Less than a decade later, Emperor Charles V extended these punishments for oral sex to lesbians. Anyone caught committing any of these acts could be sentenced to death by burning.

This renewed concern about proselytizing against the practice of oral sex and other forms of sodomy emerged partly due to the onslaught of the Bubonic Plague. The vast population reduction experienced by almost all parts of the Western world, with some as high as 50–60 percent, became a serious issue for European nations and city-states. Feudalism, as an economic model, depended on a large population of peasants. Likewise, in an era of warfare, intercity competition, and continued Mongol and Muslim expansion, an increasing population was also a security concern. Oral sex and other non-reproductive practices which were formerly considered as perhaps only damaging to spiritual health were now seen by many to also be a threat to the health of the kingdom. As one preacher, Bernardino of Siena, lectured in the 15th century, "if you wish to exterminate your city and motherland, I tell you, keep on being sodomites."[11] Thus, though the hedonism that was associated with the onslaught of the Black Death led to an explosion of formerly banned sexual activity, local political authorities were forced to confront it for more practical purposes.

As has been seen, the perceived savagery of those who practiced sodomy in all of its forms led to accusations of it being leveled against various non–European groups. With the discovery of the New World, these views were extended to the natives there. Michele da Cuneo, who accompanied Columbus on his second voyage in 1495, recorded not only many instances of cannibalism among the inhabitants of the Caribbean, but also sodomy. Keeping with the omophagic nature of the latter, the two crimes were given equal weight by the Spanish explorer. In fact, these crimes were used as justification for the enslavement of natives in subsequent years.[12]

Literature followed the lead of art, beginning to more actively engage in discussions and tales of oral sex. Pietro Aretino, previously mentioned for his humanistic writings against the Church, is also regarded as one of the first modern pornographic writers. In a series of erotic poems entitled the *Sonetti lussoriosi*, Aretino detailed a number of sexual adventures including an episode of cunnilingus. "I lifted her up to devour her chamber of love which I could not otherwise reach, wishing to put her in a position to devour her in turn the weapon which wounded her to death without taking her life."

Aretino was only matched in his erotic writing by Francois Rabelais, a man renowned for his overall bawdiness. The Frenchman's writings contain numerous oblique references to oral sex. In chapter 15 of *Gargantua and Pantagruel*, during the discourse of the drinkers, one character asks, "If there came such liquor from my ballock, would you not willingly thereafter suck the udder whence it issued?" Earlier in the book as Pantagruel and Panurge discussed marital love, the latter went on at length about oral sex.

The words of the third article are: She will suck me at my best end. Why not? That pleaseth me right well. You know the thing; I need not tell you that it is my intercrural pudding with one end. I swear and promise that, in what I can, I will preserve it sappy, full of juice, and as well victualled for her use as may be. She shall not suck me, I believe, in vain, nor be destitute of her allowance; there shall her justum both in peck and lippy be furnished to the full eternally. You expound this passage allegorically, and interpret it to theft and larceny. I love the exposition, and the allegory pleaseth me; but not according to the sense whereto you stretch it. It may be that the sincerity of the affection which you bear me moveth you to harbour in your breast those refractory thoughts concerning me, with a suspicion of my adversity to come. We have this saying from the learned, That a marvellously fearful thing is love, and that true love is never without fear. But, sir, according to my judgment, you do understand both of and by yourself that here stealth signifieth nothing else, no more than in a thousand other places of Greek and Latin, old and modern writings, but the sweet fruits of amorous dalliance, which Venus liketh best when reaped in secret, and culled by fervent lovers filchingly. Why so, I prithee tell? Because, when the feat of the loose-coat skirmish happeneth to be done underhand and privily, between two well-disposed, athwart the steps of a pair of stairs lurkingly, and in covert behind a suit of hangings, or close hid and trussed upon an unbound faggot, it is more pleasing to the Cyprian goddess, and to me also—I speak this without prejudice to any better or more sound opinion—than to perform that culbusting art after the Cynic manner, in the view of the clear sunshine, or in a rich tent, under a precious stately canopy, within a glorious and sublime pavilion, or yet on a soft couch betwixt rich curtains of cloth of gold, without affrightment, at long intermediate respites, enjoying of pleasures and delights a bellyfull, at all great ease, with a huge fly-flap fan of crimson satin and a bunch of feathers of some East-Indian ostrich serving to give chase unto the flies all round about; whilst, in the interim, the female picks her teeth with a stiff straw picked even then from out of the bottom of the bed she lies on. If you be not content with this my exposition, are you of the mind that my wife will suck and sup me up as people use to gulp and swallow oysters out of the shell? or as the Cilician women, according to the testimony of Dioscorides, were wont to do the grain of alkermes? Assuredly that is an error. Who seizeth on it, doth neither gulch up nor swill down, but takes away what hath been packed up, catcheth, snatcheth, and plies the play of hey-pass, repass.

A fellow Frenchman, Nicolas Chorier, published an equally licentious book in the late 17th century. Falsely attributed to the Spanish poetess Luisa Sigea de Velasco, *The School of Women* contained numerous references to oral sex.

The day before yesterday, Crisogono came to see my mother in the afternoon. All was quiet and silent. He had scarcely begun to wanton a little with her, when he became very importunate. "Yesterday morning," he said, "I learned a new kind of pleasure. One of our grand personages, who had certainly tasted it, says there is nothing so disgusting and repulsive as those parts of his wife which stamp her as a woman,—and he has a very pretty wife, mind! In that sink everything is foul, while in this (kissing my mother on the mouth), dwells the true Venus. He therefore abominates that ill favoured cavern, and adores the pure mouth, that charming head. He looks to nothing else, his member rises for nothing else. His wife is as spirited as she is beautiful, and even more obliging ... so she lends him the service of her mouth. What would you do Sempronia, if I asked you? If you were to refuse I should say that you have forgotten all your promises and your pledged faith. You know that Socrates said, the beautiful body of a pretty woman is nothing but a living treasure chamber of voluptuousness, the storehouse whereto men resort to finding their pleasures, whereto they direct the burning floods of their lubricity. What matter whether you fulfill your duty through that pure canal (kissing her mouth), or through that other (touching below), which is infect?"

After such a deft philosophical argument for fellatio, the woman dropped to her knees and replied,

"Oh, what an air you want me to play, and upon what a flute, in our concert!" taking in her hand his member, which began to rise. She seized the point of his dart between her lips and turning her tongue around it, caused novel transports of delight to the member that slid into its new receptacle. But feeling that the fountains of the brine of Venus were on the point of bursting forth, she recoiled with horror. "You would not degrade me so far," said my mother, "as to drink a man in a liquid form?" She had scarcely spoken when an abundant shower fell upon her robe. He showed some anger, "How could you be so foolish," he cried, "as to spoil such good work!" She replied: "Forgive me, the next time you will find me more obedient." She kept her word, and actually drank men in a liquid state—a spicy thing.[13]

Slightly later in the work, another character is also easily persuaded into a once forbidden act.

"Your catapult, my Alfonso," said I, "is not made for breaching this door, you are mad, and want to make me the same." "No! I would fain have you mad, not myself; for that you love me, I owe to your madness, not to any merits of my own. If I get delirious, I may forget the respect that I owe you, and I would rather die than to cease to live for you alone." These words softened my heart, and decided me to assist him in that game. I seized his inflamed dart with a good heart between my lips.[14]

The Whore's Rhetoric, written by Ferrante Pallavicino in 1683, contained numerous references to both fellatio and cunnilingus, but once again, the fact that oral sex was being discussed by prostitutes was meant to denigrate the practice rather than encourage it.[15]

Cracks in the once-monolithic edifice of the Church also helped bring erotic matters to the forefront of Western thought. Much as art slowly broached the subject of oral sex, so did the Roman Catholic Church. Theologians of the late Middle Ages, most notably Nicole Oresme and Martin Le Maistre, argued for the expansion of sexual practices in marriage beyond simply that needed for reproduction. "Nature granted carnal pleasures to the animals only for the purpose of reproduction; but it accorded the human species this pleasure not only for reproduction of its kind but also to enhance and maintain friendship between man and woman. This is implied in Pliny's statement that no female, after she has become pregnant, seeks sexual union, except woman only (*Nat. Hist.* VII, 5). And this greater unity is a cause of greater friendship."[16] While Church thinkers like Oresme were hardly arguing for free love, they did see the value to marriage from engaging in sex for non-reproductive ends or by non-reproductive means.

With the advent of the Reformation much of Europe departed from not only the theological but also the sexual teachings of the Church. Luther's questioning of total Catholic dogma encouraged others to tear down other edifices of tradition and faith. As has been seen, this was no doubt helped by a trend of liberalism that had been emerging within the Church itself for several centuries. Luther questioned and then flaunted Church teachings on the celibacy of the clergy, advocating marriage and with it sex as a gift from God. Sexual desire and sexual pleasure needed no justification as long as they were kept within the ordered bonds of matrimony. Though the state and Calvin still targeted unnatural sexual activities such as bestiality or homosexuality, oral sex between husband and wife could be seen as consistent with the will of God especially when it helped to preserve monogamous marriage, a far loftier goal.

This is all the more interesting when one considers that Luther and later Protestant apologists highlighted the flaunting of rules of celibacy by some monks and nuns as signs of corruption and decadence within the Catholic Church. Luther himself frequently invoked the term sodomy when discussing the papacy, monks, and nuns. His contemporary, Erasmus, in one of his dialogues sought to dissuade a young lady from entering a convent because of the frequency of cunnilingus between the nuns.

> **Eubulus:** What's more, not everything's virginal among those virgins in other respects, either.
> **Catharine:** No? Why not, if you please?
> **Eusubus:** Because there are more who copy Sappho's behavior than share her talent.

Catharine: I don't quite understand what you mean.

Eusubus: And I say these things in order that the time may not come when you do understand, my dear Catharine.

Later English Puritan poet Andrew Marvell combined cunnilingus and religious deception by nuns in his poem "Upon Appleton House," remarking, "the Nuns smooth Tongue has suckt her in." While many of the stories of this kind of trickery were certainly lies and exaggerations, a number of incidents and sex scandals have occurred within the Church over the past 2,000 years. One involved the Sant'Ambrogio Convent. It was eventually disbanded by the pope in 1861 due to reports of sexual activity among the nuns, especially cunnilingus. Numerous other stories published in the 19th century claiming to expose the dark sexual secrets of nunneries, such as Maria Monk's *Awful Disclosures* in 1836, were little more than tabloid fare. This Black Legend continues today, with historian Karma Lochrie suggesting that the veneration and kissing of Christ's wounds by medieval nuns amounted to a metaphor for their practice of lesbian oral sex.[17]

This new drive toward reinterpreting both theology and morality was due to Luther's rejection of Aristotelianism and Protestantism's subsequent trend of individual interpretation and relativism. Later philosopher Alasdair MacIntyre's statement that man must either follow Aristotle or Nietzsche hits at this point. A community's newfound freedom to interpret the Bible would seem to imply that oral sex was also open to debate. While the Reformation did not usher in an era of pure libertine living, it laid the groundwork for the acceptance of a philosophical worldview that would.

Calvin and his followers sought even stricter control over the lives of their followers than the Church did. In 1557 a case came before the Consistory in Geneva regarding alleged incest between Andre Duplot and his aunt, Jeanne Court, from Avignon. Though Court testified that "a man" attempted to have oral sex with her, she declined to name him. The Calvinists eventually fined and imprisoned both of them, ordering them to cease sexual activity with each other.[18] Interestingly, Calvin, in his commentary on the Book of Genesis, preferred to argue that the sin of the citizens of Sodom was not sexual but a lack of proper hospitality.

The Jesuits, known among conservative Catholics and Protestants of the time for their more pragmatic justification of certain acts, as lampooned by Blaise Pascal in his Fifth Provincial Letter, even began to question the Church's rigid stance on oral sex. While the order attempted to justify other forms of foreplay as important for social bonding in marriage or conception, oral sex was still seen as a sin. Tomas Sanchez, a 16th-century Jesuit, wrote a work discussing these issues in a Catholic marriage. In his 17th Disputation, Sanchez argued that while foreplay and oral sex were useful in some ways, they should still be treated as venial sins by the priest during confession.

The theological competition between Catholicism and Protestantism soon turned to force of arms for resolution, culminating in the disastrous Thirty Years' War. Writer and mercenary Hans Grimmelshausen mentions the use of forced oral sodomy as a form of punishment in his magnum opus on the conflict. "They had cut off his nose and ears, yet before that had forced him to render to five of them the filthiest service in the world."[19] Described by the author as "ihnen den Hintern zu lecken," the act was apparently so degrading to the prisoner that he begged for death afterward. The act bears parallels to Frederick Barbarossa's treatment of Milan during its rebellion several centuries before. Interestingly, the earliest references to the latter were written slightly after the time of the Thirty Years' War. To a Catholic audience, the actions of these Protestants would also harken back to the punishments inflicted by the Muslims on captured Crusaders.

Thus the 16th and 17th centuries saw a move toward a more open attitude regarding oral sex. Much as with previous periods, this can best be examined through the art and literature of the time. Though Erasmus denied the very existence of the practice, "the term remains of course, but I think the practice [of oral sex] has been eliminated," the works of Shakespeare tell a different story.[20] In fact, it appears that the immortal bard took an early liking to erotic tales and humor. In 1593, at the very start of his career, Shakespeare wrote his own erotic version of the classic story of Venus and Adonis. In it, Venus propositions Adonis for cunnilingus

I'll be a park, and thou shalt be my deer;
Feed where thou wilt, on mountain or in dale:
Graze on my lips; and if those hills be dry,
Stray lower, where the pleasant fountains lie.[21]

As was observed in the introduction, the play *Hamlet* also contained witty reference to cunnilingus, with Hamlet asking to put his head in Ophelia's lap to discuss "country" matters, certainly a crowd pleaser at the turn of the 17th century, but these were not isolated references. In fact, a thorough analysis of a number of plays by Shakespeare reveal either veiled or obvious references to oral sex.

What, with my tongue in your tail? nay, come again,
Good Kate; I am a gentleman
[Antonio in *The Taming of the Shrew*, Act II, Scene I].

That man that hath a tongue, I say, is no man, if with his
   tongue he cannot win a woman
[Valentine in *Two Gentlemen of Verona*, Act III, Scene I].

Well, the best is, she has no teeth to bite
[Launce in *Two Gentlemen of Verona*, Act III, Scene I].

Come, I'll drink no proofs nor no bullets: I'll
drink no more than will do me good, for no man's
pleasure, I
[Mistress Quickly in *Henry IV, Part II*, Act II, Scene IV].

This compell'd fortune!—have your mouth fill'd up
Before you open it.... How tastes it? is it bitter? forty pence, no.
There was a lady once, 'tis an old story,
That would not be a queen, that would she not,
For all the mud in Egypt: have you heard it?
[Old Lady in *Henry VIII*, Act II, Scene III].

Shakespeare also kept with the negative connotations of the act. In Part 1 of *Henry VI*, an argument between Plantagenet and Suffolk ends with the latter threatening to irrumate Richard of York. "I'll turn my part thereof into thy throat."[22] Apart from the threat of violence, the line harkens back to the punishment handed out to robbers and adulterers in the Roman republic. Likewise, in Part 2, Suffolk again references fellatio, this time implying that the captain of the ship isn't even worthy to fellate him. In this he compares himself to

Zeus, often represented in mythology by the eagle, and pictures the captain as Ganymede.

> O that I were a god, to shoot forth thunder
> Upon these paltry, servile, abject drudges!
> Small things make base men proud: this villain here,
> Being captain of a pinnace, threatens more
> Than Bargulus the strong Illyrian pirate.
> Drones suck not eagles' blood but rob beehives:
> It is impossible that I should die
> By such a lowly vassal as thyself.[23]

Other Englishmen openly discussed the subject. Thomas Carew, in the poem "A Rapture," describes an oral tour of his body and those of his lovers.

> Swell my bag with honey, drawn forth by the power
> Of fervent kisses from each spicy flower.
> I'll seize the rose-buds in their perfumed bed,
> The violet knots, like curious mazes spread
> O'er all the garden, taste the ripen'd cherry,
> The warm firm apple, tipp'd with coral berry :
> Then will I visit with a wand'ring kiss
> The vale of lilies and the bower of bliss ;
> And where the beauteous region both divide
> Into two milky ways, my lips shall slide
> Down those smooth alleys, wearing as they go
> A tract for lovers on the printed snow ;
> Thence climbing o'er the swelling Apennine,
> Retire into thy grove of eglantine,
> Where I will all those ravish'd sweets distil
> Through Love's alembic, and with chemic skill
> From the mix'd mass one sovereign balm derive,
> Then bring that great elixir to thy hive.[24]

Likewise, John Donne in his Elegy XVIII, "Love's Progress," traces his erotic, oral voyage of discovery from his lover's head to her vagina.

> The hair a forest is of ambushes,
> Of springs, snares, fetters and manacles;
> The brow becalms us when 'tis smooth and plain,
> And when 'tis wrinkled shipwrecks us again—
> Smooth, 'tis a paradise where we would have

Immortal stay, and wrinkled 'tis our grave.
The nose (like to the first meridian) runs
Not 'twixt an East and West, but 'twixt two suns;
It leaves a cheek, a rosy hemisphere,
On either side, and then directs us where
Upon the Islands Fortunate we fall,
(Not faint Canaries, but Ambrosial)
Her swelling lips; to which when we are come,
We anchor there, and think ourselves at home,
For they seem all: there Sirens' songs, and there
Wise Delphic oracles do fill the ear;
There in a creek where chosen pearls do swell,
The remora, her cleaving tongue doth dwell.
These, and the glorious promontory, her chin,
O'erpassed, and the straight Hellespont between
The Sestos and Abydos of her breasts,
(Not of two lovers, but two loves the nests)
Succeeds a boundless sea, but yet thine eye
Some island moles may scattered there descry;
And sailing towards her India, in that way
Shall at her fair Atlantic navel stay;
Though thence the current be thy pilot made,
Yet ere thou be where thou wouldst be embayed
Thou shalt upon another forest set,
Where many shipwreck and no further get.
When thou art there, consider what this chase
Misspent by thy beginning at the face.
Rather set out below; practise my art.[25]

At the beginning of the poem, though, Donne warns against relying solely on oral sex to please a woman. "Love is a bear-whelp born: if we o'erlick our love, and force it new strange shapes to take, we err, and of a lump a monster make." This is a reference to the folk belief that bear cubs were born as a lump of fur which the mother then licked into a shape.

Some of this new praise of oral sex can certainly be attributed to the arrival of the Reformation in England during the reign of Henry VIII. Yet sexual license for that famously amorous king did not imply a state of hedonism for the people. In 1533, as part of the process of codifying state law, Parliament passed the Buggery Act which outlawed sodomy, including oral sex. With the termination of ecclesiastical courts in England, many actions formerly conceived of as sins became crimes instead. Though the rise to power of Mary in 1553 saw a reversal of the law, Queen Elizabeth would reinstate it in 1563. Interestingly, the law was championed in Parliament by Thomas Cromwell, a distant ancestor of the future Puritan dictator Oliver Cromwell.

One of the English writers most influenced by the works of the ancients was Ben Johnson. He frequently attempted to model his writings on the Roman poets and playwrights, and nowhere was this more evident than in his own marginal notes in a copy of Martial. Despite his own bitingly satirical poems and lines, Johnson refrained from making any reference, comedic or otherwise, in his works to oral sex. Indeed, his notes consisted of an almost ashamed indexing of sexual practices. To Martial's epigram 1.94 he simply wrote *"fellatrix"* while next to 6.6 he scribbled *"cuneling."* Though a man as well read in the classics as Johnson certainly understood the negative Roman view towards the practices, he could not bring himself to copy Martial's use of fellatio and cunnilingus in attacks upon his enemies.

Shortly after the time of Ben Johnson, John Milton wrote his monumental work *Paradise Lost*. Covering as it did both Biblical accounts of original sin and fantastical accounts of demonology, the book is rife with allusions intended and perhaps unintended to oral sex. Several commentators have pointed out clear differences in Milton's language concerning pre- and post-lapsarian sex between Adam and Eve.[26] The clearest evidence for this emerges in Book IX in which Milton portrays the event which led to the Fall.

> So said he, and forbore not glance or toy
> Of amorous intent, well understood
> Of *Eve*, whose Eye darted contagious Fire.
> Her hand he seis'd, and to a shadie bank,
> Thick overhead with verdant roof imbowr'd
> He led her nothing loath; Flours were the Couch,
> Pansies, and Violets, and Asphodel,
> And Hyacinth, Earths freshest softest lap.
> There they thir fill of Love and Loves disport
> Took largely, of thir mutual guilt the Seale,
> The solace of thir sin, till dewie sleep

Oppress'd them, wearied with thir amorous play.
Soon as the force of that fallacious Fruit,

That with exhilerating vapour bland
About thir spirits had plaid, and inmost powers
Made erre, was now exhal'd, and grosser sleep
Bred of unkindly fumes, with conscious dreams
Encumberd, now had left them, up they rose
As from unrest, and each the other viewing,
Soon found thir Eyes how op'nd, and thir minds
How dark'nd; innocence, that as a veile
Had shadow'd them from knowing ill, was gon,
Just confidence, and native righteousness
And honour from about them, naked left
To guiltie shame hee cover'd, but his Robe
Uncover'd more, so rose the *Danite* strong
Herculean Samson from the Harlot-lap
Of *Philistean Dalilah*, and wak'd
Shorn of his strength.

The inclusion of "fallacious Fruit" is a clear reference to classical Latin fellatio. Milton builds on the version of the Fall which blames the discovery of non-productive sex by Adam and Eve. Alternatively, by consuming the Fruit of Knowledge, Adam and Eve performed oral sex as their first act of rebellion against God. Milton's inclusion of the allegory of Samson is also interesting. The classical idea of the once-powerful prophet losing his strength is recast as another scene of perverted love. In lines 1059–1062 Milton writes that Samson "rose … from the Harlot-lap … shorn of his strength." Performing cunnilingus on Delilah led to the fall of Samson as much as oral sex led to the original fall of man. Milton would reiterate this version in his poem *Samson Agonistes*.

Softn'd with pleasure and voluptuous life;
At length to lay my head and hallow'd pledge
Of all my strength in the lascivious lap
Of a deceitful Concubine…[27]

Robert Herrick was another English poet of the 17th century who pushed the boundaries of what was considered decent. Famous for his poem "To the Virgins, to Make Much of Time," he wrote a number of other poems that took *carpe diem* to a much more sexual level. In "Kisses Loathsome," the author discusses his thoughts on the various types of kisses he prefers, but ends with his love for kissing lower lips. "What should poking sticks make there, when the ruff is set elsewhere?" This could either reference his own desire to perform cunnilingus or serve as a rebuff to her wish to fellate him, preferring sex instead. Another poem by Herrick entitled "The Shoe Tying" more directly references cunnilinugs.

> Anthea bade me tie her shoe;
> I did; and kissed the instep too:
> And would have kissed unto her knee,
> Had not her blush rebuked me.

Another erotic poet and author of 17th-century England was John Wilmot, the 2nd Earl of Rochester, who had a stay in the Tower and died at the age of 33 from venereal disease. His poems were far more vulgar than those of Shakespeare or Herrick, leaving little to the imagination and requiring almost no deeper reading.

> Naked she lay, clasped in my longing arms...
> She clips me to her breast, and sucks me to her face.
> Her nimble tongue, Love's lesser lightening, played
> Within my mouth, and to my thoughts conveyed
> Swift orders that I should prepare to throw
> The all-dissolving thunderbolt below.
> My fluttering soul, sprung with the painted kiss,
> Hangs hovering o'er her balmy brinks of bliss.
> But whilst her busy hand would guide that part
> Which should convey my soul up to her heart,
> In liquid raptures I dissolve all o'er,
> Melt into sperm and, and spend at every pore.
> A touch from any part of her had done't:
> Her hand, her foot, her very look's a cunt.[28]

His poems reference all manner of sex and forms of debauchery, frequently mentioning oral sex.

Other poets who wrote on the topic in England were Sir Charles Sedley, Charles Sackville, George Etherege, and Robert Gould. Gould wrote a play entitled *Love Given O'er*, which is filled with graphic references to the sex lives of English women in the 17th century.

> And now, if so much to the World's reveal'd,
> Reflect on the vast store that lies conceal'd.
> How, oft, into their Closets they retire,
> Where flaming Dildos does inflame desire,
> And gentle Lap dogs feed the am'rous fire.[29]

Here, Gould hints at a bestial use of lap dogs by English women for cunnilingus. Lap dogs were popular among the elite of the day and featured both literally and figuratively in 17th-century paintings.

London had a notorious red light district during the Restoration with not only girls but whole brothels specializing in various acts of depravity. Thus it is not surprising to find that one focused solely on fellatio. Known as the "Prick Office" or the "Last and Lyon," the business located at Smithfield only hired girls who were skilled at oral sex. Due to the rarity of the act, the owner Hammond allegedly made quite a profit.[30] Ultimately, the outbreak of the Black Plague in 1665 and the Great Fire in 1666 helped to devastate much of London and pushed the city's prostitution business further upriver.

The art of the Baroque period largely copied that of the Renaissance with its hidden or metaphorical references to the practice of oral sex. Cecco del Caravaggio's *Cupid at the Fountain* depicts an adolescent Cupid who has stripped off his clothing and weapons to satiate himself at a water fountain. The position of Cupid on his knees and the phallic shape of the fountain makes the painting a powerful metaphor for oral sex, and the painted curtain on the right seems to suggest a voyeuristic angle to the scene, as if the viewer just caught the god in his forbidden act.

Sculptor Benevenuto Cellini likewise made a number of works based on classical mythology which hinted at oral sex. A marble statue of Ganymede standing next to Zeus in the form of an eagle invokes images of fellatio based on the pose of the boy as well as the location of the bird's head. Another piece, *Apollo and Hyacinth*, shows the proudly nude god with his hand resting on the head of a kneeling Hyacinth.

Baroque architecture continued the hidden and jocular references to oral sex in both public and private spaces. They were even in the imperial palace of the Habsburg monarchs in Prague. Rudolf II, who ruled the Holy Roman Empire from 1576 until 1612, was a well-known patron of the arts and of the occult. On a side door of the Old Royal Palace, Rudolf had installed an elaborate doorknocker which, when closed, showed a woman performing fellatio on a man.[31]

At best, the 15th–17th centuries saw a minor re-emergence of oral sex in Western Europe. The practice, though depicted slightly more in art and literature, had yet to approach the even tacit acceptance it enjoyed by some in ancient history. In fact, with the codification of laws under various monarchs at this time, the crime of sodomy became officially condemned and had attached to it some of the harshest punishments.

6

18th and 19th Centuries

Whereas the advent of the Renaissance and the Reformation began to slowly introduce a modicum of acceptance or at least recognition of the practice of oral sex in Western Europe, the growth of the Enlightenment and the rise of Nationalism only hastened the process. The concept of natural law and natural rights and the rise of the autonomy of the individual meant that a practice such as oral sex would gain more acceptance over the next few centuries. For many Catholic countries, the Enlightenment helped to counterbalance their lack of a reformation in terms of changing social mores. Likewise, the move toward more secular nations meant that laws were to be decided by the populations through their elected governments, and therefore, unlike in theocracies, views and, in effect, truth could change. Finally, the more oral sex became popularized in both art and literature the more the general public would begin to accept an act that the vast majority was probably privately partaking in anyway.

Nowhere was the growing acceptance of oral sex more evident than in late Renaissance France. In fact, the increasing popularity of the act led to the adoption of the term "Frenching" as a euphemism for oral sex in many parts of Europe. Though King Henry IV is perhaps better known to history for his rise to power following the Wars of Religion in France and his subsequent assassination, he was also rumored to be quite a philanderer. One of his nicknames, "the Green Gallant," arose from this, with green being the color of sex during that era. Henry IV was also alleged to be a voracious cunnilictor of women. Perhaps it is not surprising to find that the king was born and raised a Protestant, only later converting to Catholicism after issuing the famous opinion "Paris is well worth a mass."

France quickly gained a reputation as a land of oral sex, a widespread belief that continues in popular culture even today. Literature from the Eldest Daughter of the Church began to feature numerous tales of fellatio and cunnilingus, yet all of these paled in comparison to the eroticism of the Marquis de Sade. Along with references to incest, orgies, and murder, de Sade's novels are awash in instances of oral sex. Even his first novel, *Justine: Or the Misfortunes of Virtue*, while tame when compared to his later works, still contains numerous depictions of fellatio and cunnilingus. "The idea of being together with a veritable executioner aroused the greatest passions in Juliette. She had herself flagellated and Delcour practiced cunnilingus."[1] Another character in the novella, Dorval, the master thief of Paris, was said to have enjoyed "cunnilingus post coitum," robbing even sperm from women.[2]

The Marquis de Sade's epic work, *The 120 Days of Sodom*, contained even more references to oral sex.

> A young abbot called for my sister a short time afterward … knelt down between her thighs … conveyed his mouth to my sister's cunt. He tickled its clitoris with his tongue, and managed so cunningly, so harmoniously, to synchronize the two activities, that within the space of three minutes he had plunged her into a delirium. I saw her head toss about, her eyes begin to roll, and heard the rascal cry. "Ah my dear Reverend Father, you're slaying me with pleasure!" The abbot's custom was simply to swallow the liquid his libertine dexterity made flow.[3]

Later, de Sade describes another encounter between Duclos and another oral lover.

> Another libertine, much older and in a different way disgusting, succeeded the one I mentioned a moment ago, and came to give me a second representation of the same mania; he had me stretch out naked upon a bed, stretched out himself, his head to my toe, popped his prick in my mouth, his tongue in my cunt, and having adopted this attitude, bade me return for the voluptuous titillations he declared his tongue was very certainly going to procure for me. I sucked as best I could, he had my pucelage, he licked, bubbled, splashed about, and without a doubt in all these maneuvers, labored infinitely more in his own behalf than in mine.[4]

Duclos then finished by "wringing the juice from his prick with my lips, by swishing it about in my mouth."[5]

Sade's third major work, *Philosophy in the Bedroom*, written in 1795, is at the same time a pornographic novel and an alleged satirical attack on the French Revolution. Much of the erotic corruption of its main character, Eugenie, involves vivid acts of oral sex. While Madame de Saint-Ange performs cunnilingus on the young virgin heroine, Dolmance advises her to "make your voluptuous tongues penetrate her womb, 'tis the surest way to hasten the ejaculation."[6] Sade's work can be seen as a philosophical argument for complete freedom and the rights of the individual, ideas and ideals at the heart of the French Revolution. The orgy of violence that accompanied the revolt is nicely mirrored by the orgy of base sodomy among his characters. Not surprisingly, Sade himself, once elected to the National Convention, came to represent the far left. His views on ultimate democracy, universal suffrage, and anarchic freedoms soon put him in as much trouble as his scandalous writings. After seizing power, Napoleon ordered his arrest and Sade spent the rest of his life in a mental asylum.

Giacomo Casanova was undoubtedly the greatest Italian libertine of the century. Among tales of his various conquests, the Venetian relates his having received oral sex from a 12-year-old girl while separated by a partition. Casanova had been regaling the girl with accounts of his other conquests when "she was moved to eat me, and she may have hoped to swallow me; but the too great pleasure she aroused in my soul liquefied my heart. She did not leave me until she was convinced of my exhaustion. I sat down, and in gratitude pressed my lips to the sweet mouth which had sucked the quintessence of my soul and my heart."[7] His memoirs are filled with numerous episodes of oral sex, most in plain and vivid detail. "When they were doing the Straight Tree, to my mind the most lascivious of them all, Leah behaved like a true Lesbian; for while the young man excited her amorous fury she got hold of his instrument and took it between her lips till the work was complete. I could not doubt that she had swallowed the vital fluid of my fortunate rival."[8] In the 1740s, Casanova traveled to the Ottoman Empire, where among various other sexual exploits he and his host participated in mutual fellatio while watching three harem girls bathe.

French literature of the time gave us the term "sixty-nine" when used with a sexual connotation. The earliest acknowledged occurrence of "*soixante-neuf*" can be found in *The Whore's Catechism*, a manual for revolutionary protests that has been attributed to Theroigne de Mericourt.[9] Though clearly the act had been known since the rise of man, this allegedly was the first recorded assignment of the most familiar name to the position.

The spread of the Enlightenment to all corners of Europe naturally brought an increased prevalence of oral sex stories. One of the most notorious banned books in England, *Fanny Hill* by John Cleland, contained, among tales of flagellation and mutual masturbation, an episode of cunnilingus between Mr. Barville and Fanny.

> He rush'd, as it were, on that part whose lips, and round-about, had felt this cruelty, and by way of reparation, glews his own to them; then he opened, shut, squeez'd them, pluck'd softly the overgrowing moss, and all this in a style of wild passionate rapture and enthusiasm, that express'd excess of pleasure; till betaking himself to the rod again, encourag'd by my passiveness, and infuriated with this strange taste of delight, he made my poor posteriours pay for the ungovernableness of it; for now shewing them no quarter the traitor cut me so, that I wanted but little of fainting away, when he gave over. And yet I did not utter one groan, or angry expostulation; but in heart I resolv'd nothing so seriously, as never to expose myself again to the like serverities.[10]

This scene was repeated in an edition of *The Ladies' Miscellany* published in 1718 which contained a poem about cunnilingus.

> Then sticking closely to the text,
> He fairy tipt the Velvet next;
> And straight the warm saliva Juice,
> Did wondrous Effects produce
> Her Pulse beats High, her Blood's inflamed,
> Symptoms so plain her Love proclaim'd.

Englishman Richard Payne Knight wrote perhaps the most sexually controversial book to date in the country, *The Worship of Priapus*. Published in 1786, the work focused on the ancient worship of reproductive organs, arguing that the appreciation for the generative power of the phallus and vagina actually continued well into the present. Numerous plates were included showing ancient depictions of phalluses as well as the worship of them. Some of these even depicted fellatio and cunnilingus among numerous other acts.

Meanwhile, Francisco Goya was painting Enlightenment themes in Spain. The care of the poor, prisoners, and mentally ill was a hallmark of Enlightenment thinking and discussion and showed up in both art and literature. Goya used his artistic abilities to depict the darker side of this topic, most famously in his painting *The Madhouse*. Composed shortly after the fall of Napoleon, the work shows a crowded dungeon filled with half naked primitive, maniacal figures. To emphasize the savagery of the situation, Goya's painting contains a scene of two men engaged in fellatio. Nestled in the shadows in a dark alcove to the right, the image is hard to see, but it is apparent. Even at the start of the 19th century and the end of the Enlightenment, oral sex was still portrayed as a degrading practice.

At the other end of Europe, Russia had gone through a process of Westernization since at least the time of Peter the Great. Besides copying the military, legal, artistic, and scientific advancements of the rest of Europe, the Russians apparently also adopted the West's growing acceptance of and fascination with oral sex. The ruler most associated with this was the late 18th-century czarina Catherine the Great. In addition to her advancement of Russia's geographical boundaries as well as its economy and society, Catherine was also something of a libertine. Rumors of her numerous male lovers were only overshadowed by the stories that she was a nymphomaniac. Sources point to cabinets of sexual toys as well as stables of horses with whom she allegedly copulated. Far from mere falsehoods, some of these rumors can be corroborated from the rather bizarre sexual furniture that remains from her reign now housed in museums. One piece is a well-appointed chair covered with depictions of nude figures in various graphic poses. Carved at the top of the chair's frame is the head of a young woman with an erect penis resting on her lips. Though the chair would be quite at home in Sade's chateau, its presence in the palace of Catherine the Great tells us much about the tastes of the eastern European elite. While rumors of her untimely demise underneath a horse are more hilarious than accurate, her appreciation of oral sex is reasonably apparent.

Perhaps the ultimate product of the Enlightenment was Napoleon Bonaparte. Though some have seen him as a perverter of the promises of the philosophy, he certainly reflected many of its ideas and traits. Most interesting of all seems to be his recorded appreciation of oral sex. By all accounts, the young general fawned over his new bride Josephine after the two were married in 1796. Numerous letters exist to attest to this affection, with some delving into rather pornographic details. One written in April of 1796 promised his new bride "a kiss on your heart, and one much lower down, much lower!" Despite Josephine's subsequent philandering, Napoleon remained passionately in love. A letter written while he was in Italy, shortly before his victory at Rivoli in January of 1797, reminded his wife, "You know, I never forget the little visits, you know, the little black forest.... I kiss it a thousand times and wait impatiently for the moment I will be in it."[11]

The Neoclassical artistic movement that characterized the latter half of the 18th century, with its focus on ancient themes and characters applied to modern philosophy, should be expected to portray a number of sexual themes. Jean-Antoine Watteau presents the ideals of the time, frivolous pursuits of passion by the middle and upper class, which undoubtedly also included sexual ones. His contemporary Jean-Auguste-Doninique Ingres' painting of Jupiter and Thetis expressed many of these. In the composition, a dominant, shirtless Jupiter sits on a throne holding a phallic staff in his right hand as a half-nude Thetis kneels before him, her hand on his lap and her head arching forward and up. Her pleas for the life of her son Achilles take on an assuredly sexual nature. Likewise, the Neoclassical poem *The Fable of Polyphemus and Galatea* by Luis de Gongora takes an ancient myth from Ovid and transforms it using not only Enlightenment ideals but also oral sex. In stanzas 40–42, Acis performs cunnilingus on Galatea, consummating the love that is only hinted at in the earlier version.

The advent of the 19th century saw the rise of various divergent forces around the world. The onset of the Industrial Revolution continued the slow road to modernity that had begun in the Renaissance. Populations shifted toward urban areas, mass migration brought different religious, cultural, and sexual norms to many nations, and basic hygiene improved for millions. As a result the practice of oral sex became more standard and more accepted. Yet as is often the case, the fast-paced change was resisted by different conservative movements. Despite these hindrances, the gradually-increasing acceptance of oral sex continued relatively unabated throughout the century.

Art continued to include acts of fellatio and cunnilingus as prominent themes, though occasionally, due to fears of censorship, artists were forced to still utilize only subtle references. Nicolai Abildgaard's *The Nightmare*, painted in 1800, is a prime example. The subject matter was modeled on Henry Fuseli's similar piece of a generation prior, but Abildgaard added a "tongue-wagging demon, bluntly suggesting cunnilingus," especially based on the creature's position on the sleeping woman's body.[12] While an artistic depiction of what amounted to an incubus was not revolutionary in and of itself, its appearance in popular art was. Even a century later, Abildgaard's piece is one of the main exhibits at the Sorø Kuntsmuseum in Denmark.

Characteristically, French art of the 19th century was early to unabashedly depict oral sex. A prominent example from mid-century is the work of Achille Devéria. His normal interest was portraiture, but Devéria also made a number of erotic pieces for libertine publications, many of which focused on cunnilingus. One famous work depicts cunnilingus in France and another shows it in the Ottoman Empire; a clear distinction can be drawn between how the act is viewed by these societies. The European woman stands and is pleasured in a rushed fashion behind a curtain. She looks nervously over her shoulder, expecting at any minute that the people in the next room will discover her engaging in this sinful act. Finally, the whiteness of both her outfit and skin, usually denoting innocence and purity, stands in sharp contrast to both the dark shadows around her and the typical negative opinion of the act. The Ottoman woman in the other painting reclines, seeming to enjoy every second of her intimate encounter. It is perhaps also interesting to note that her partner is an nude girl, showing a biased view of the depraved nature of either Eastern society or the act itself. Finally, the female couple makes no attempt to hide their lovemaking, leaving a nearby window uncovered, affording a view to a passing noble who appears to be more interested and aroused than judgmental.

Devéria assisted in illustrating Alfred de Musset's erotic lesbian novel *Gamiani*, published in 1833. While the book continued Voltaire's and Sade's attack on traditional society and morals, Devéria's lithograph is important for representing two lovers engaged in mutual oral sex for perhaps the first time in modern Western art. The sense of sexual equality expressed by the act of *soixante-neuf*, feared by some authorities since the time of Lilith, fit in well with the ideals of both the French Revolution and the 19th century.

De Musset's book was quite scandalous, featuring, among other scenes, an act of bestiality in which a large dog performed cunnilingus on a young girl. "At this cry a huge dog comes out of a cache, rushes on the countess and begins to lick a clitoris whose tip came out red and inflamed."[13]

Mihaly Zichy, a Hungarian artist who eventually became a court painter in St. Petersburg under Czar Alexander II, also tried his hand at erotica around the middle of the century. He produced numerous drawings which depicted all varieties of sexual gratification. A fair number of these involved cunnilingus rather than fellatio, continuing the popular trend that seems to have been developing at the time.

Despite its name, Romantic art contained very little sexual imagery, and perhaps no direct or indirect references to oral sex. In many ways the movement was a reaction to the more sensual aspects of the art of the previous century. Therefore, it returned to scenes and concepts from much earlier eras. While many paintings contained nude figures, these were intended to show human perfection and the role of nature rather than sexuality. One of the few exceptions was artist Francesco Hayez. Active throughout the 19th century, Hayez painted many notable pieces, the most famous of which was *The Kiss*, which became popular during the drive to Italian unification. Hayez also made a number of sketches of men performing cunnilingus on women.

Romantic literature proved much more risqué, undoubtedly encouraged by the expanding popular market for more realistic works of fiction. Men such as Lord Byron carried on the erotic traditions of the writers of the previous century both in their own lives and in their literary works. In his poem *Don Juan*, the narrator hinted at his love of cunnilingus. "My wish ... that womankind had but one rosy mouth, to kiss them all at once from North to South."[14] As a testament to the staying power of his escapades, Byron's predilections for various sexual practices remained a topic of conversation for a century. The movie *Gothic*, released in 1986, depicted the poet as a bisexual rake who performed cunnilingus on an unconscious woman before sucking her blood. Interestingly, the scene takes place in a bedroom in which hangs a version of Abildgaard's *The Nightmare*.

A close companion to Byron though less famous for libertine pursuits, Percy Bysshe Shelley was nonetheless responsible for several erotic poems and passages. The following piece represents a love poem, or epithalamium, between two French assassins, Francois Ravaillac and Charlotte Corday.

> Soft, my dearest angel, stay,
> Oh! you suck my soul away;
> Suck on, suck on, I glow, I glow!
> Tides of maddening passion roll,
> And streams of rapture drown my soul.
> Now give me one more billing kiss,
> Let your lips now repeat the bliss,
> Endless kisses steal my breath,
> No life can equal such a death.[15]

Shelley is clearly referring to fellatio, ending with an orgasm which he refers to as "death." Interestingly, since at least the 16th century it was common in both France and England to use expressions such as "la petite mort" or "fainting fit" to describe sexual release. The scandalous nature of this piece by Shelley led to its being ignored, glossed over in reprints, misquoted, or incorrectly analyzed for more than a century. In fact, that it actually referred to fellatio was not recognized by critics until 1974.[16]

William Blake, known for his unique sexual views, included oral sex in his epic poem *Milton*. In it, he becomes one with his predecessor in an act strongly suggesting fellatio. "Milton will utterly consume us & thee our beloved Father."[17] Though perhaps vague, the associated illustrated plate, drawn by Blake himself, leaves little to the imagination. Blake is shown kneeling before the god Los becoming impregnated by the spirit of Milton.

In 1866, Algernon Charles Swinburne published his poem "Anactoria," named for a woman mentioned by Sappho as one of her lovers. The work is narrated by the ancient Greek poetess and describes in detail a sexual encounter with Anactoria that features both tribadism and cunnilingus. Swinburn waxes poetic several times on Sappho's desires to use her mouth to "taste the faint flakes from thy bosom to the waist!"

As part of the Transcendental and Utopian movements active in antebellum America, Walt Whitman wrote frequently, though not always clearly, about sex and sexuality. His seminal work *Leaves of Grass* faced censorship both in America and in England due to its references to prostitutes, oral sex, erotica, and homosexuality. Frank allusions to fellatio also abound, though some are subtle enough to lead to endless debate. Sexuality and acts of oral sex can be read into Whitman's "Song of Myself," recognized by some as one of the most erotic poems ever written, and other poems depending upon one's own whims. In "I Heard You Solemn-Sweet Pipes of the Organ," Whitman could be harmlessly discussing the sounds of church music on a Sunday morning or referring to an episode of oral sex.

> I heard you solemn-sweet pipes of the organ as last Sunday
> morn I pass'd the church,
> Winds of autumn, as I walk'd the woods at dusk I hear your
> long-stretched sighs up above so mournful,
> I heard the perfect Italian tenor singing at the opera, I heard
> the soprano in the midst of the quartet singing;
> Heart of my love! You too I heard murmuring low through
> one of the wrists around my head,
> Heard the pulse of you when all was still ringing little bells
> last night under my ear.

In "Song of Myself," Whitman writes lines that seem to reference closed-off throats. "Loose the stop from your throat … the hum of your valved voice." He then proceeds to a connected and much more erotic scene.

> I mind how once we lay such a transparent summer morning,
> How you settled your head athwart my hips and gently turn'd
> over upon me,
> And parted the shirt from my bosom-bone, and plunged your
> tongue to my bare-stript heart,
> And reach'd till you felt my beard, and reach'd till you held my feet.

In another stanza from the same poem, he writes,

> The young men float on their backs, their white bellies
> bulge to the sun, they do not ask who seizes fast to them,

They do not know who puffs and declines with pendant
   and bending arch,
They do not think whom they souse with spray.

The scandalous nature of Whitman's poetry was recognized by his contemporaries. In fact, in 1865, his book cost him his job at the Department of the Interior. James Harlan, Secretary of the Interior and a devout Christian, found Whitman editing a copy of his book. So appalled was he by the sexual tone and content of the work that Harlan fired him immediately. Whitman's relationship with the government did not end in 1865, however. One hundred and thirty years later, President Bill Clinton gave a copy of *Leaves of Grass* to Monica Lewinsky as a Valentine's gift during their White House affair. It is doubtful that the sexual connotations of the poems or possibly even the historical connection were lost on Clinton.

Increased censorship led to the adoption of new terms for fellatio and cunnilingus. Some of these involved the resurrection of previously used terms from the classical world such as "irrumation" while others were entirely new creations like "gamahuching," used in such works as *The Quintessence of Birch Discipline* and the anonymous *Romance of Lust*. The latter mentioned the act more than 100 times, containing vivid scenes and descriptions: "gamahuching me most rapturously as he swallowed every drop as eagerly as a bee sucking honey" and "so I began again to gamahuche her; this time it took a longer effort to produce the ultimate result; but apparently with still greater effect, and a more copious discharge. Her little cunt being now relaxed, and well moistened with her own discharge and my saliva." Richard Burton's English translation of *The Book of the Thousand Nights and a Night* also became known at the time for its addition of sexual content to the originally non-erotic Arab tales.

For those Englishmen who were solely interested in obscene material, the periodical *The Pearl* served as their main source of entertainment. Published from 1879 to 1880, when it was shut down by the government, *The Pearl* contained hundreds of erotic stories which relied largely on a combination of esoteric terms and new ones in an effort to avoid the censors. Its selections ranged from limericks to short stories that covered every possible sex act, including oral sex.

There was a young lady of Troy,
Who invented a new kind of joy:
She sugared her thing
Both outside and in,
And then had it sucked by a boy.[18]

A poem that appeared in December of 1880 utilized the term gamahuching to refer to cunnilingus in its celebration of "a woman's cunt."

It likes to be fondled with tongue and with lip,
And shuns not the touch of your hand.
You may frig and gamahuche and try every plan,
But fair fucking's the pride of an Englishman.

A famed English writer of erotic fiction at the time was Edward Sellon. He lived a scandalous and libertine lifestyle, and he authored a number of books in the 1860s. One of these, *The New Epicurean*, was published in 1865 and contained the following reference to gamahuching as another term for fellatio. "'Quick, quick, Blanche!' cried Cerise, 'come and gamahuche the gentleman.'"

A generation later, the first piece of erotic literature featuring homosexual love was published in England. Claiming to be the memoir of Jack Saul, a male prostitute at the center of the Cleveland Street Scandal, *The Sins of the Cities of the Plains* includes numerous stories of same-sex sexual encounters. One involves the famous 19th-century London transvestite Thomas Ernest Boulton, called "Laura" in the book. Boulton seduces a female milliner, convincing her that his penis is actually an enlarged clitoris. The two then engage in a bout of mutual oral sex.

Not surprisingly, Victorians and religious conservatives fought tooth and nail against many of the literary and artistic portrayals of oral sex. Numerous pieces of literature, including Radclyffe Hall's *The Well of Loneliness*, became the subjects of drawn-out censorship campaigns and legal battles. Interestingly, Hall's novel, like many others at the time, contained no actual description of oral sex, only general ideas of love deemed unnatural. Perhaps the most well-known sexual witch-hunter of the time in America was Anthony Comstock. As both a private citizen and postal inspector, Comstock devoted his life to attacking what he saw as vice. Due to the limitations of federal authority, he directed his efforts toward eliminating the use of the mail to spread sexual material. Many persons were jailed and many works of literature and art were either burned or banned because of the famed Comstock Law. Notable among the victims of this "Oral Sex Scare" was Ida Craddock, aforementioned founder of the sexualized Church of Yoga, who committed suicide rather than face a five-year prison sentence for distribution of her book *The Wedding Night*. In her suicide note left for her mother, the 45-year-old Craddock described Comstock: "The man is a sex pervert; he is what physicians term a Sadist—namely a person in whom the impulses of cruelty arise concurrently with the stirring of sex emotion…. I believe that Mr. Comstock takes pleasure in lugging in on all occasions a word picture (especially to a large audience) of the shocking possibilities of the corruption of the morals of innocent youth."

Another active campaigner against what was seen as the increasingly lax sexual morals of society was the Reverend Charles H. Parkhurst. Perhaps more famous for his efforts to bring down Tammany Hall, Parkhurst also used his influential pulpit to tackle the rise of French circuses in the Madison Square area of New York City. These were little more than extravagant peep shows in which girls performed oral sex on each other and occasionally audience members. French circuses had long been popular in New York, stretching back to before the Civil War. A famous one was Busy Fleas, a trio of women who would perform cunnilingus on each other for paying audiences. In May of 1892, Parkhurst personally witnessed just such a performance as part of a personal undercover operation and helped to convict and imprison two of the women. The owner, Hattie Adams, was sentenced to nine months on Blackwell's Island while one of her performers received a one-year sentence and a fine of $1,000. Parkhurst's hands-on style impressed Teddy Roosevelt, the new crusading police commissioner, and led to the creation of the Lexow Committee. It was aimed at cleaning up the noted corruption of the police department that often allowed people like Hattie Adams to escape justice.

By the Gilded Age, almost all major cities in America had a red light district, most of which had houses specializing in oral sex. The word French, when amended to any action, exhibit, show, or person, usually referred to fellatio or cunnilingus. The best known house in New Orleans was owned and operated by Norma and Diana. The property was narrow and well suited to acts that could be done standing up. Down the street, Emma Johnson offered free oral sex to any man who could last for more than a minute.

Ironically, the increased interest in erotic statuary and aping of the vulgar literature of the classical world led to an apocryphal story of the 19th century. The cautionary tale centers on John Ruskin, one of the most gifted art critics and minds of the Victorian era. At the age of 29, the already accomplished Ruskin married Euphemia Gray, a 19-year-old socialite known for her many admirers. Six years later, in 1854, the Ruskins' marriage was annulled on the grounds of non-consummation. To explain this odd ending, John Ruskin wrote his lawyer, "It may be thought strange that I could abstain from a woman who to most people was so attractive. But though her face was beautiful, her person was not formed to excite passion. On the contrary, there were certain circumstances in her person which completely checked it." As could be expected, these "circumstances" led to wild speculation over the next two centuries. Apart from the obvious rumors concerning Ruskin's sexuality, a much more popular theory involved a rather unfortunate attempt by the new husband at cunnilingus. It was said that John, accustomed as he was to the classical female figure of art, was shocked and appalled by the hair, sight, or blood of his new bride's vagina. The world's most unsuccessful cunnilictor then proved unable or unwilling to consummate the marriage for the next six years. While more recent theories argue that the financial situation or moral character of Euphemia was the problem, the rather Victorian cautionary tale of one man's attempt at oral sex is still the most well known and most influential of the time.[19]

About this time, the permissive Regency period was eliding into the more prudish Victorian era. The reign of King George IV, both as regent for his mentally unfit father and as king himself, lasted from 1811 to 1830 and oversaw a series of social, economic, and political changes in Britain. The horrors of the Napoleonic Wars, a subsequent baby boom, and more permissive sexual attitudes accompanied the literature, ideas, and art of Western Europe. While oral sex remained the realm of mistresses, extra-marital practices had at least become more commonly accepted. Yet the onset of the Victorian era, in many ways an upper-class reaction to the slipping morality of lower-class, industrialized England, once again saw many sexual practices become taboo. According to a sexual handbook for Victorian brides from 1894, "If he lifts her gown and attempts to kiss her anyplace else she should quickly pull the gown back in place, spring from the bed, and announce that nature calls her to the toilet. This will generally dampen his desire to kiss in the forbidden territory."[20]

Various monarchs and personages living on the Continent continued to practice oral sex, which the new scandal-filled periodicals were quick to bring to the public's attention. King Ludwig I of Bavaria, who ruled from 1825 until the outbreak of revolution in 1848, was known for a number of sex scandals. Despite having an enormous birthmark on his head, which his court painters managed to ignore in his official portraits, Ludwig charmed a number of women and carried on a lively correspondence with them. His letters to Lola Montez frequently mention his penchant for sucking on her feet and her skill at fellatio, probably necessary due to her repeated bouts with illness (including the syphilis of which she eventually died) and the danger of pregnancy.[21] Ludwig became so enthralled with both her feet and mouth that she quickly became a trusted advisor to the monarch. His subsequent decline in popularity and the eventual outbreak of the revolution of 1848 in Munich which led to his downfall can be traced in part to Lola.

The renewed campaign against oral sex was hardly just a European trend. Nearly all of the original 13 colonies had sodomy laws being enforced at the time America declared its independence from England. The one exception was Georgia, which, due to a number of factors, had neglected to adopt such a provision. The geographic spread of the opposition demonstrated that it couldn't be a matter of Puritan repression. Before the Revolution, though, there appears to have been only a handful of arrests for oral sex, specifically three separate women charged with performing cunnilingus in Plymouth and the Massachusetts Bay Colony in the 1600s. These crimes were prosecuted more for the lesbianism they involved rather than going against the general ban on oral sex. The first woman, Elizabeth Johnson, was charged in December of 1642 for "unseemly practices betwixt her and another maid" and subsequently fined and whipped. In 1650, Mary Hammond and Sarah Norman were arrested on similar charges. The former was released with a warning because she was young but the latter was forced to publicly apologize for her actions.

> Whereas the wife of Hugh Norman, of Yarmouth, hath stood presented [in] divers Courts for misdemeanor and lewd behavior with Mary Hammon upon a bed ... the said Court have therefore sentenced her, the said wife of Hugh Norman, for her wild behavior in the aforesaid particulars, to make a public acknowledgment, so far as conveniently may be, of her unchaste behavior, and have also warned her to take heed of such carriages for the future, lest her former carriage come in remembrance against her to make her punishment the greater.[22]

It is important to note the light punishment received by the three women in comparison to that received by men.

Georgia finally joined the rest of the states in 1817 and made sodomy a crime under state statute. Sixteen years later the state legislature adopted an even stricter law which would remain in force for almost a century and a half. Yet it was not the law itself that was to be a source of trouble for the state, as it was quite in keeping with general American and European law at the time, but the unique way in which it was written. "Carnal knowledge and connection against the order of nature by man with man, or in the same unnatural manner with woman." Though it was written mainly to combat anal sex, since sodomy by nature also included oral copulation, the law actually legalized cunnilingus between women by omission. The 1833 statute would go on to have a rather interesting and controversial history in later years as will be seen in another chapter.

Pennsylvania became the first state to specifically include oral sex in its legal definition of sodomy in 1879. "The terms sodomy and buggery ... shall be taken to cover and include ... penetrating the mouth." Massachusetts followed Pennsylvania in 1887 and was quickly joined by New York, Ohio, Wyoming, Louisiana, Wisconsin, Iowa, Indiana, Washington, Missouri, Oregon, Nebraska, North Dakota, Virginia, Georgia, South Dakota, North Carolina, Alabama, Nevada, Delaware, Kansas, Montana, Idaho, Oklahoma, Hawaii, Minnesota, Arkansas, and Maine. Though it would be 1938 before the last of these states amended its laws, a clear pattern of opposition to oral sex was evident. As with most progressive laws and programs, these pieces of legislation usually followed sex scandals involving oral sex which could not be charged under current law. Some states even employed clever euphemisms to satisfy their need for legalese. For example, California adopted the term "oral copulation" while Oklahoma and Oregon both referred to the crime as "osculatory relations."

An expansion of Georgia's anti-sodomy law came about in 1904 thanks to the *Herring* case. In keeping with both the sexual conservatism of the state as well as the popularity of progressive legislation at the time, the state's court argued that if the

> baser form of the abominable and disgusting crime against nature—i.e., by the mouth—had prevailed in the days of the early common law, the courts of England could well have held that that form of the offense was included in the current definition of the crime of sodomy. And no satisfactory reason occurs to us why the lesser form of this crime against nature should be covered by our statute, and the greater excluded, when both are committed in a like unnatural manner, and when either might well be spoken of and understood as being "the abominable crime not fit to be named among Christians."

Without adopting a new statute, Georgia had effectively criminalized fellatio.

Later cases further defined the moral law of the state. The 1921 *Comer* case ruled that cunnilingus performed by a man upon a woman was to be treated the same as fellatio. Yet in 1939, the court ruled in *Thompson* that two women performing cunnilingus did not fall within the purview of the law. Oklahoma would actually be the first state to hand down a conviction against two women for engaging in cunnilingus, but this would not happen until 1935. Several other states followed suit, extending sodomy laws to cover the actions of women.

Likewise, despite the fact that the Victorians were repulsed by the immorality of oral sex, England had no official law forbidding the practice. The vagaries of the acts of Henry VIII and Elizabeth had not yet been brought into the modern era. Following the salacious Eliza Armstrong affair, in which an undercover muckraking author was able to purchase a 13-year-old virgin for only £5, Parliament finally passed a comprehensive morality law for England. Known as the Criminal Law Amendment Act of 1885, this legislation targeted various aspects of what was then known as white slavery, or the forced prostitution of women and young girls. Prior to its passage,

Henry Labouchere submitted an amendment for consideration that eventually bore his name. Concerned with what he saw as rampant homosexuality in London society, especially the recent Cleveland Street Scandal which was rumored to have involved Prince Albert Victor, Labouchere proposed a section to the act focusing on other unspeakable sex acts. "Any male person who, in public or private, commits, or is a party to the commission of, or procures, or attempts to procure the commission by any male person of, any act of gross indecency with another male person, shall be guilty of a misdemeanour, and being convicted thereof, shall be liable at the discretion of the Court to be imprisoned for any term not exceeding two years, with or without hard labour." The law could and was applied as much to oral sex as it was to more traditional forms of sodomy.

The goal of Labouchere and others was to cover some of the gaps in the law exposed by a number of cases, most notably the trial of the two most famous transvestites of Victorian England, Ernest "Stella" Boulton and Fredrick "Fanny" Park. The two had been arrested, along with Lord Arthur Clinton, in 1870 and charged with conspiracy to commit sodomy. Unfortunately for the Crown's efforts at prosecution, the existing statutes required an excessive physical burden of proof that penetration had actually occurred. Lord Clifford conveniently died, allegedly of scarlet fever, shortly before the case, and therefore without enough evidence to convict, both men were freed. Likewise, the case of Rex versus Jacobs which was argued in 1817 ultimately ruled that penetration of the mouth did not constitute sodomy.

Probably the most well-known individual to be prosecuted under this law was famed playwright and hedonist Oscar Wilde. In 1891, Wilde began a five-year love affair with the much younger Lord Alfred Douglas. Despite being married with two children, the playwright became attached to the young and attractive college student. Their relationship was carried out in the truest imitation of the ancient Greek world, resembling the pederasty that was so common in earlier times between older and younger men of status. On the night of their first sexual encounter, Wilde fellated "Bosie," as Douglas was known, later writing to a friend, "he lies like a hyacinth on the sofa, and I worship him."[23] Wilde was a notorious fellator of other men, from delivery boys to minor celebrities, frequently remarking that "love is a sacrament that should be taken kneeling." When rumors began to circulate about the pederasty that was taking place between the young Douglas and Wilde, the boy's father, the famous John Douglas, 9th Marquess of Queensberry, quickly took action.

Queensberry began to publicly attack Wilde and a lawsuit was soon brought. The playwright was eventually forced to abandon his claims of libel against the Marquess as more and more evidence of the truth began to mount. Though advised by many to flee the country, Wilde remained and was shortly afterwards arrested and tried under Section 11 of the above mentioned Criminal Law Amendment Act of 1885. During the proceedings, Wilde was pressed to define his oral relationship with Douglas.

> **Gill:** What is the "Love that dare not speak its name"?
>
> **Wilde:** "The Love that dare not speak its name" in this century is such a great affection of an elder for a younger man as there was between David and Jonathan, such as Plato made the very basis of his philosophy, and such as you find in the sonnets of Michelangelo and Shakespeare. It is that deep, spiritual affection that is as pure as it is perfect. It dictates and pervades great works of art like those of Shakespeare and Michelangelo, and those two letters of mine, such as they are. It is in this century misunderstood, so much misunderstood that it may be described as the "Love that dare not speak its name," and on account of it I am placed where I am now. It is beautiful, it is fine, it is the noblest form of affection. There is nothing unnatural about it. It is intellectual, and it repeatedly exists between an elder and a younger man, when the elder man has intellect, and the younger man has all the joy, hope and glamour of life before him. That it should be so the world does not understand. The world mocks at it and sometimes puts one in the pillory for it. [Loud applause, mingled with some hisses.][24]

Not surprisingly, Wilde was soon found guilty and sentenced to hard labor. Though he was released after two years, his time in prison had broken him both physically and mentally. Three years later, while in exile in France, Oscar Wilde died, most likely from meningitis.

Wilde was not alone in his writings and predilections. As a writer he is usually included with the authors known as the Uranian Movement. Active between 1858 and the 1920s, the group devoted much of their poetry to classical Greek ideas, specifically pederasty, which they cloaked in metaphors and allegories. The Reverend Gerard Manley Hopkins is usually classed with this group due to the homoerotic nature of many of his poems. One of these, "The Bugler's First Communion," seems to convert the experience of receiving the Host to one of fellatio.

> Here he knelt then in regimental red.
> Forth Christ from cupboard fetched, how fain I of feet
> To his youngster take his treat!
> Low-latched in leaf-light housel his too huge godhead...
> Tongue true, vaunt- and tauntless;
> Breathing bloom of a chastity in mansex fine.

The imagery of Christ as a phallus being orally given to a young man fit in quite well with the more primitive fellatio-centered religious practices of various tribal cultures around the world.

Another priest who was member of the Uranian Movement, John Francis Bolxam, also utilized religious practices in his pederastic writings. "The instant he had received, Ronald fell on his knees beside him and drained the chalice to the last drop. He set it down and threw his arms round the beautiful figure of his dearly loved acolyte. Their lips met in one last kiss of perfect love, and all was over."[25] Again, the disguised oral associations with the religious act would appeal to both readers of pederastic literature as well as those who took the poem at face value.

The works of Henry James, one of the key figures of Realism, also tended to approach the subject of sex, though once again, perhaps due to his New England background, his references tended to be heavily disguised and obscure. In the short story *The Figure in the Carpet*, James employs a number of metaphors and double entendres that could be read as references to oral sex. The character Gwendolen has published a book entitled *Deep Down*, which seems to make an erotic reference. Her fiancé, Corvick, travels to India where he learns some sexual secret he agrees to only share with her once they are married. "She had it, as I say, straight from Corvick, who had, after infinite search and to Vereker's own delight, found the very mouth of the cave. Where IS the mouth?"[26] The secret seems to have been a discovery by Corvick of how to perform cunnilingus, which he then shares with Gwendolen. His fiancée herself is told to accept both the marriage and the secret that will come with it. "'Poor dear, she may swallow the dose. In fact, you know,' she added with a laugh, 'she really MUST!'"[27]

Similar moral concerns across the Atlantic at around the same time led to the creation of a legendary breakfast cereal. John Harvey Kellogg, a Seventh Day Adventist and prominent medical officer at the Battle Creek Sanitarium, made improving the health of his fellow Americans his life's work. Ultimately he sought a spiritual cause for many ailments and argued that unnatural sex practices such as masturbation and oral sex contributed to a decline in a person's well-being. "The nervous shock accompanying the exercise of the sexual organs—either natural or unnatural—is the most profound to which the system is subject."[28] To help combat these urges, Kellogg recommended a bland diet, eventually including a cereal of his own creation, Corn Flakes. The breakfast enjoyed by millions from then to now was originally intended to cut down not on weight or cholesterol, but on the sex drive of breakfasting Americans. Kellogg interestingly represents one of the first attempts to scientifically prove a negative aspect toward oral sex.

With the advent of modern psychology, sex in its various forms became a legitimate area of study because of its pervasiveness in the human experience. Unsurprisingly, Sigmund Freud utilized oral sex in both his theories and practice of psychoanalysis. This was most likely due to a combination of the facts that it was taboo and that Freud recognized the desire for it in modern man. In the Dora case study, Freud diagnosed a young woman's aphonia as the result of an unconscious desire to fellate her father and a family friend. A similar theory was put forward by sociologists around the same time; it speculated that prostitutes suffered from raspy voices because they performed fellatio and the mouths of sodomites became deformed.[29] Oral sex also featured prominently in the Little Hans case which dealt with a child's fear of horses. Finally, in Freud's psychoanalysis of Leonardo da Vinci's childhood, he suggested fellatio as a recurring theme in both the artist's dreams and his paintings. Leonardo once wrote of a childhood experience, "It seems that it had been destined before that I should occupy myself so thoroughly with the vulture, for it comes to my mind as a very early memory, when I was still in the cradle, a vulture came down to me, he opened my mouth with his tail and struck me a few times with his tail against my lips." To Freud this represented nothing less than a homosexual fellatio fantasy. He carried his argument further with an analysis of the painting *The Virgin and Child with St. Anne*. According to his theory, the garment of the Virgin Mary hides a vulture, the tail of which connects the mouth of the infant Jesus with Mary. This represents an oral fixation that ties into Leonardo da Vinci's dream.

In fact, to Freud, dreams of fellatio and the act itself were unconscious reminders of and desires for nursing.

> Women, it seems, find no difficulty in producing this kind of wishful phantasy spontaneously. Further investigation informs us that this situation may be traced to an origin of the most innocent kind. It only repeats in a different form a situation [when] we took our mother's nipple into our mouth and sucked at it and when at a later date the child becomes familiar with the cow's udder whose function is that of a nipple, but whose shape and position under the belly make it resemble a penis, the preliminary stage has been reached which will later enable [her] to form the repellent sexual phantasy.[30]

To Freud, all homosexual acts, especially oral sex, can be explained as an unconscious desire for one's mother. When the great psychoanalyst developed his theory of the stages of sexual development, he placed the oral stage as the lowest level of maturation. Besides being in line with his view of weaning and oral desire, this low placement showed that Freud's views of fellatio and cunnilingus were actually little changed from the time of the ancient Greeks.

An interesting trend psychologically in the growth of interest in oral sex in the late 19th century was the rise of the vampire as a literary element. A number of historical personages and folk tales influenced Bram Stoker in his creation of Dracula, including Countess Elizabeth Bathory who famously bathed in the blood of young girls to maintain her youthful appearance. One of the literary precursors was the novella *Carmilla* which appeared in 1872. Written by Joseph Sheridan Le Fanu, the story follows a female vampire who seeks to seduce and drain the blood of her niece. The obvious oral and sexual implications of the story were not lost on the reader, and influenced not only Stoker but also future versions of the tale. The vast majority of vampires in literature and film were actually female.

The elements of vampirism resembled elements of cunnilingus, the succubus, and the fear of vagina dentata.

Oral sex continued to be looked at as a form of perversion by the vast majority of 19th-century thinkers. Various researchers and moralists highlighted negative examples of fellatio or cunnilingus to push their policies. In his study of human sexuality, Bernard Simon Talmey connected a desire among unmarried women for cunnilingus to the practice of bestiality in both advanced and primitive cultures.[31] He specifically mentioned cases involving the use of animals to orally pleasure women in an effort to delegitimize the practice. "Moll cites a case from the annals of the court, where the woman was accused of having abused the watchdog for sexual gratification by making the animal lick her sexual parts."[32] Elsewhere the same author blamed the isolation of boarding schools and convents for much of the same thing. "Sapphism and Lesbianism are, therefore, prevalent in boarding schools and convents for young girls…. Those of a strong sexual impulse are given to mutual masturbation and cunnilingus."[33]

The case of Victor Ardisson, the Vampire of Muy, a known grave robber and necrophiliac, became all the more scandalous when it was reported that he had abducted the corpse of a three-year-old girl to breathe life back into her through cunnilingus.[34] Ardisson early on in life was obsessed with consuming his own semen and with performing cunnilingus on young girls, details which were used during his trial to demonstrate his perverted nature. Famed German psychiatrist Richard von Krafft-Ebing referred to oral sex as "horrible sex acts [which] seem to be committed only by sensual men who have become satiated or impotent."[35] In his study of various sexual perversions published in 1894, Krafft-Ebing discussed cases that involved oral sex, almost all of which were performed on young children, further damning the act.[36] Other psychologists speculated that it was a common practice of older men who were attempting to have sex with young children and that it was necessary to prepare both themselves and their victims.[37] This view was largely in keeping with the prevailing opinion of Romans two millennia before who saw cunnilingus as a sexual act of the elderly. The medical field also frowned on the practice, with some viewing it to be fundamental to the origin of the period's most notorious disease, syphilis. "'They pushed the contempt for modesty so far,' says Rosenbaum, 'that they had no shame in serving women and girls during their menses; and this is a fact that has great importance from the standpoint of viewing the genesis of syphilis.'"[38]

While Victorian morality prevailed in England and the 2nd and 3rd Great Awakenings took place in America, much of the apparent puritanism in Europe was perhaps the result of the contemporaneous rise in nationalism across the continent. Nations like Germany and Italy wanted to reclaim a more glorious, pure, and moral past. Regardless of the nation in question, though, oral sex and other practices were viewed as foreign influences coming from decadent international cultures. The case of Leo Frank in 1913 continued this opinion, as various forces in the conservative South attempted to portray the well-known Jewish businessman as a sexual deviant. Frank was indicted on charges that he raped and murdered his 13-year-old former employee, Mary Phagan. In an attempt to establish Frank's character, the prosecution's main witness detailed the former's obsession with oral sex, particularly cunnilingus. "Mr. Frank was standing up there at the top of the steps.... His eyes were large and they looked right funny ... he asked me, 'Did you see that little girl' ... I had seen him in a position I haven't see any other man ... a lady was in his office, and she was sitting down in a chair and she had her clothes up to here, and he was down on his knees, and she had her hands on Mister Frank."[39] His sexual appetites were used to depict him as foreign, un–American, effeminate, and perhaps even homosexual, depending upon the jury's own personal understanding of the legal term "sodomy." Frank was eventually found guilty, but when his death sentence was commuted to life in prison, a local mob, infuriated by what they saw as a miscarriage of justice, seized Frank from prison and lynched him.

The time period from the French Revolution to World War I saw minor but important changes to views on oral sex in the West. A greater acceptance of the practice among the elites helped to further the softening of views toward at least fellatio. As was common, however, conservative and religious groups actively fought against any actual legal acceptance, something that would require a far greater cultural shift.

7

20th Century

World history is far from linear. Man seems to advance in fits and jumps with important events and people. Periods of normality are punctuated by moments of evolution and achievement. As has been observed, the acceptance of oral sex in Western society had advanced only slightly from the time of Moses. While various art forms continued to push the boundaries of acceptable behavior and subject material as they had since the days of ancient Greece, the Western public still bore a relatively monolithic view of the practice of oral sex. From the opening salvos of World War I until the end of the 20th century, an unprecedented revolution in oral sex took place. The catalysts for this movement appear to have paralleled those that pushed forward other liberal reforms, urbanization, the horrors of war, secularization, and a trend toward anarchic individualism.

The first proponent of this change may very well have been King Edward VII of the United Kingdom. Though his short reign from 1901 to 1910 did witness several important, transforming events in England, it was his almost 60 years as the Prince of Wales that defined his life. Maybe it was the long length of time as the dauphin or a response to the moral domination of his mother and father that led young Bertie, as he was known, to a life of renowned hedonism. In many ways his activities would put those of his more well-known son, Prince Albert Victor, to shame. He had various lovers during his life, most notably Jenny Churchill, the mother of the future prime minister Winston Churchill, and Alice Keppel, great-grandmother of Camilla Parker Bowles. In fact, Queen Victoria said her son's first sexual scandal in 1861 was a contributing factor in the death of her husband that same year. While at a military camp in Ireland, Edward's friends smuggled an Irish prostitute named Nellie Clifden into the 20-year-old's bedroom. Though Prince Albert actually died of typhoid, Victoria blamed his demise on the revelation of her son's indiscretion. Following the royal funeral, as concerns for Victoria's emotional health and fitness to rule emerged and suggestions were made for her to rule jointly with her son, Bertie was sent on a trip abroad. The future king went on a four-month tour of Egypt, spending most of the time reading novels about adultery and shooting crocodiles from a boat on the Nile. He even got a tattoo on his forearm.

Edward spent most of the 1880s in a series of French brothels, including the Moulin Rouge and Le Chabanais. Sex was not the only thing that Bertie had an appetite for, though, and his waist eventually swelled to 48 inches. Due in part to this, the great Soubrier furniture house in Paris was commissioned at some point in the 1890s to design a *fauteuil d'amour*, the most etymologically accurate loveseat. Edward himself designed it to fit at least two women specifically for an oral tryst, but the piece undoubtedly lent itself to other configurations. Though his Parisian days ended in 1901 when he ascended the throne, Edward's loveseat continued to reside in various brothels in France before being bought and sold by interested parties. The Soubrier family was eventually able to purchase it back in 1992, though they immediately "had to reupholster the *fauteuil* ... the chair was dirty, very dirty."[1]

The general sexual awakening in America came in the person of Ida Craddock. Beginning life as a Quaker, Craddock went through a series of religious experimentations before founding her own erotic theosophical assemblage called the Church of Yoga. Despite claiming to only have had sex with a spirit named Soph, she wrote a number of works on the sexual awakening of women in the time. Craddock was a staunch proponent of sex but she remained firmly opposed to the notion or oral sex. Fellatio was little more than a sexual perversion, "that widespread sexual perversion which in modern times is termed the French Method," and cunnilingus was merely the result of a man's failure to pleasure his wife in a more traditional way.[2]

Perhaps the greatest cautionary tale at the end of the last century involved French president Félix Faure. At a time when anarchists were waging war against various European and American heads of state, Faure, who famously granted blanket amnesty to all political opponents, was felled by a blow from his mistress. On February 16, 1899, President Faure telephoned his paramour, Marguerite Steinheil, and invited her to the presidential palace. Steinheil would later refer to herself as a "psychological advisor" to the president. Upon hearing screams from the drawing room, aides to the French leader rushed in, only to find Faure dying of a cerebral hemorrhage in the embrace of a partially nude Steinheil. Rumors quickly circulated as to the exact nature of his death; the most popular was that his mistress was performing oral sex on him as he died. Georges Poisson, famed art historian and curator of the Museum of the Ile-de-France, stated, "We have witness accounts from the general secretary of the Elysée at the time and the valet. The president was found with his hand clenched in her hair and the president's aides hacked her hair with such clumsiness that her skull was cut."[3] Faure, whose time in office was marred by the Dreyfus affair, was arguably not in the best of health. Far Right newspapers, though, accused Steinheil of murder and actively investigated the incident. Various sources soon began to proffer nicknames for the unfortunate lover, including *la pompe funebre*, a play on the French word for undertaker that literally means "funeral pumper." Future prime minister Georges Clemenceau, then a local newspaper editor for a rival faction, wrote, "Il voulait être César, il ne fut que Pompée." Directly translated it means "He wished to be Caesar, but ended up being Pompey." The last word was also slang for being fellated. "He wished to be Caesar, but ended up being blown."

The beginning of World War I led not only to an increase in patriotism and censorship, but also to another appearance of oral sex at the forefront of vice and scandal. A generation before Senator Joseph McCarthy led his infamous communist witch hunt in the United States Congress, Noel Pemberton Billing, a member of the British Parliament, was leading a similar crusade to root out German agents during the Great War. Billing was convinced that through various groups, the German military was utilizing homosexual liaisons, especially through oral sex, to weaken the resolve of England to fight. As part of this, he argued, a Cult of the Clitoris had developed in which women of high standing participated to aid the Germans. Billing and his followers alleged that there were 47,000 prominent British men and women whose sexual activities, particularly oral, left them open to blackmail by the Germans during the war. Among those he accused of different acts of cunnilingus were the famed *Salome* actress Maud Allan and Margot Asquith, the wife of the prime minister. One of Billing's most ardent supporters was Lord Alfred Douglas, the former gay paramour of Oscar Wilde, who during the trial described the latter as "the greatest force for evil that has appeared in Europe during the last three hundred and fifty years." Ultimately, Billing was victorious in the libel case against him, and despite the failure of a German oral sex cabal to materialize, concern for the effect that the private life of the individual would have on the larger society again came to the forefront of political discourse.

The general moral permissiveness of the 1920s among some segments of society, brought about as much by the horrors of World War I as by the ever-changing socioeconomic and technological make up of the West, allowed for increased attention to the practice of oral sex. The general population did not confine itself to merely following the clothing styles, spending habits, and lifestyles of the upper class and celebrities; in some cases it also copied their sexual permissiveness. In much the same way as the five centuries since the Renaissance, this tolerance was pushed by art, literature, and the actions of the elite.

Art and its graphic depiction of oral sex had continued to evolve in both style and frequency during the late 19th and early 20th centuries due in part to the concurrent rise of erotic pulp fiction. A prominent example of this new era of erotic art was Peter Johann Geiger. An official court painter at Vienna, Geiger made a number of erotic watercolors in the latter half of the 19th century. Though these images were most likely not meant for a larger audience, they augmented a growing trend of established artists dabbling in topics that were not suited for Romantic Era patrons.

One of the first artists to enjoy actual commercial success in erotic art was Frenchman Martin van Maele. His illustrations for the 1905 book *La Grande Danse macabre des vifs* included 44 drawings of sheer sexuality. Yet even van Maele's open embrace of oral sex and sexuality was meant for a limited audience, with perhaps 100 copies total printed. Further works by the artist including *Trilogie erotique* in 1907 and *La Sorciere* in 1911 continued the theme. Van Maele continued to publish his erotic art well into the 1920s, by which point it was becoming more acceptable in the West. His original publication even enjoyed something of a resurgence of interest in the 1970s during the Sexual Revolution.

One of the artists to follow Maele's lead was Franz von Bayros. A member of the Decadent Movement, von Bayros was active in the years leading up to World War I. His art was very erotic in nature, adopting elements of fetishism and featuring frequent modernist portrayals of oral sex in ways that would have appalled previous generations of artists who operated in the shadows behind metaphors.

The Decadent Movement itself had its origins in late 19th-century France as an erotic outgrowth of Romanticism. It is therefore not surprising to find French art keeping pace with its literature. In 1907 the French version of *De Figuris Veneris* was published, illustrated by Edouard-Henri Avril. The book had first been written almost 90 years before by German historian Friedrich Karl Forberg and was an examination of Greek and Roman erotic works. Avril's drawings closely followed classical examples from paintings and ceramics and detailed almost 100 different sexual positions, including several examples of oral sex. Shortly afterward, Avril illustrated an edition of the classical erotic work *Fanny Hill*. The 18th-century book enjoyed a resurgence of interest around the dawning of the 20th century, especially with the addition of Avril's prints.

As can be seen, the vast majority of erotic images accessible in the West at this time tended to involve classical themes and classical works. This was obviously an attempt to justify their publication but most likely tended to limit their access to the upper class.

Likewise, those on the extremes continued to incorporate ideas of oral sex into their work as they always had. Baroness Elsa von Freytag-Loringhoven, a rather eccentric Dada poet and artist who was once arrested for appearing in public wearing a man's suit and smoking a cigarette, produced a number of sexualized poems just after the end of World War I. One of these, "King Adam," is a sexualized retelling of Genesis in which von Freytag-Loringhoven invites her lover to "kiss me ... upon the gleaming hill," a reference to oral sex. Her work was published serially and was so controversial that the Society for the Suppression of Vice made sure it could not be distributed by mail.[4] The poet not only expected to have her poem censored, but in many ways even called for it herself. That particular line in "King Adam" is accompanied by the phrase "donated to the censor." Von Freytag-Loringhoven is not only acknowledging that the poem will most likely never be seen by the public, but is also symbolically exposing the continued repression of cunnilingus. Considering Jewish legends regarding Lilith's expulsion from Paradise for demanding equal oral sex from Adam, the poet's choice is all the more brilliant. So successful was the censorship of her poems, that, with her early death, her work has been mostly unknown for decades.

Shortly before the start of World War I, famed occultist Aleister Crowley published one of his more famous works, *The Book of Lies*, concerned in part with ritualistic sex and magic. Chapter 69 of the book is, not surprisingly, concerned with oral sex. Entitled "The Way to Succeed—and the Way to Suck Eggs," which itself is an allusion to fellatio ("suck seed") as well as to cunnilingus ("suck eggs"), the page-long chapter discusses time and time again the idea of mutual oral sex.

> This is the Holy Hexagram.
> Plunge from the height, O God, and interlock with Man!
> Plunge from the height, O Man, and interlock with Beast!
> The Red Triangle is the descending tongue of grace; the Blue Triangle is the ascending tongue of prayer
> This Interchange, the Double Gift of Tongues, the Word of Double Power-ABRAHADABRA!-is the sign of the GREAT WORK, for the GREAT WORK is accomplished in Silence. And behold is not that Word equal to Cheth, that is Cancer. whose Sigil is [Cancer[?
> This Work also eats up itself, accomplishes its own end, nourishes the worker, leaves no seed, is perfect in itself.
> Little children, love one another![5]

The idea of interlocking triangles with the subsequent reference to "interlocking tongues" is a clear allusion to the practice of oral sex. The final passage highlights the perfection of oral sex as it "leaves no seed." Crowley referred to it in a later commentary as "Gallic" in its fashion, a clear reference to either the practices of the priests of Cybele or the frequently mentioned French origin of the act.

The stereotype of the French as lovers of oral sex was only reinforced by the experiences of those who fought in the Great War. Soldiers returning from the Western Front to America and England brought tales of the sexual preferences of Gallic women. In keeping with these expectations, American prostitutes began to refer to fellatio as "French love" and condoms as "French letters."[6] These opinions would be supported by the next generation's experiences in Europe during World War II. Birth control advocate Margaret Sanger in her search for additional methods to prevent pregnancy in women became convinced that France's low birth rate meant that some method existed there which Americans should adopt. Apart from oral sex, she discovered little of value in Paris, yet the common push she and Freud made to legitimize the idea of sex for pleasure rather than reproduction, without the consequence of pregnancy, found common ground with the proponents of oral sex.

Shortly after Crowley began his publications on the magical powers of oral sex, numerous doctors started to examine the practice from a medical perspective. Gynecologists especially sought to investigate the usefulness of either cunnilingus or fellatio as an aid in intercourse and possibly conception. Interestingly, this was quite in keeping with Jesuit ideas put forward in the 16th century. Perhaps the most famous of these modern-day theorists during the 1920s was Dr. Theodoor van de Velde, a Dutch gynecologist who in 1926 published the early 20th century's seminal book on marriage and sexuality, *The Perfect Marriage*. Despite its controversial subject, which led it to be placed on the Vatican's list of banned books in 1931, the work went through 46 reprints and sold more than half a million copies. Van de Velde initially suggests what he terms "the genital kiss" be used as a means of vaginal lubrication. "But the most simple and obvious substitute for the lack of lubrication is the natural moisture of the salivary glands… this form of substitute must be applied to the vulva, not once, but repeatedly. And this may best, most appropriately, and most expeditiously be done without the intermediary offices of the fingers, but through what I prefer to term the kiss of genital stimulation, or genital kiss."[7]

The doctor suggests that "the genital kiss" is not only useful for lubrication, but will also "overcome frigidity and fear in hitherto inexperienced women,"[8] yet in keeping with the still-dominant thought of the time, van de Velde cautioned against the practice of cunnilingus as an end in and of itself. "But the husbands must exercise the greatest gentleness, the most delicate reverence! The old proverb says: from the sublime to the ridiculous is but a step. In the lore of love, this proverb means that supreme beauty and hideous ugliness are separated by a border-line so slight that our minds and senses may transgress it, unawares!"[9]

On the subject of fellatio, the doctor likewise saw the practice as a tool to correct sexual dysfunction. Once again, though, "is it necessary ... to emphasize the need for aesthetic delicacy and discretion here? To advise her to abstain entirely from such contacts during the early stages of married life, and only to venture on them later, and experimentally? To remind her that she runs greater risks than he does, in approaching that treacherous frontier between supreme beauty and base ugliness?"[10] According to van de Velde, young girls should avoid performing oral sex and guard against becoming addicted to it, but he assures the reader that it shouldn't be a concern because a woman "knows this intuitively" because of her inherent modesty.[11]

The Lost Generation played a significant role in the liberalization of oral sex much as it did with attitudes toward women's rights, art, music, alcohol, and drugs. Part of this certainly came from the advent of radio and cinema which helped to spread news and culture at an unprecedented level. Celebrities became heroes and cultural icons, with their sometimes depraved lifestyles becoming the focus of constant public attention. This was certainly true of Charlie Chaplin and his divorce in 1927. The 35-year-old actor had married the 16-year-old Lita Grey in November 1924 after she had become pregnant. He married her to avoid jail time, and they had little in common. The couple divorced after only two years. It was a scandalous and messy event, with Lita claiming that Charlie's insistence on oral sex and threesomes contributed to the marriage's failure.[12] That these two acts were paralleled demonstrated the continuing view of fellatio in society. As detailed in the court records of the proceedings, Chaplin "solicited, urged and demanded that the plaintiff submit to, perform and commit such acts and things for the gratification of defendant's said abnormal, unnatural, perverted and degenerate sexual desires, as to be too revolting, indecent and immoral to set forth in detail." In his defense, the actor later stated that it was his belief that all married women performed fellatio.[13]

Another celebrity scandal that piqued the public's sexual interest involved legendary actor Errol Flynn, often typecast as a romantic lead. His indiscreet offstage affairs led to a famed lawsuit in 1942. Flynn was accused of statutory rape after having had sex with two underage girls, Betty Hansen and Peggy Satterlee. The trial received tremendous publicity even though World War II was raging across Europe and the Pacific. The public hurried to Flynn's defense and the actor's lawyers were quickly able to destroy the victims' character both in court and in public. Hansen, it was said, had been encouraged to press charges to help her escape from a pending trial after she was arrested for performing fellatio.[14] Flynn's lawyer, Jerry Giesler, revealed this during a cross-examination of Betty.

> **Giesler:** Didn't you testify before the county grand jury that you committed an act of perversion?
> **Hansen:** Yes.
> **Giesler:** Do you know that this constitutes a crime in California?
> **Hansen:** Yes.
> **Giesler:** And you hope not to be prosecuted for this act?
> **Hansen:** Yes.[15]

In the end, Errol Flynn was victorious, and while his reputation was tarnished in the eyes of some, those of Hansen and Satterlee were utterly destroyed.

While Errol Flynn was hoping that his sodomy charge would not end his promising career, Steve McQueen was using oral sex to rise to stardom. While still in his late teens, the young and rebellious McQueen traveled to the Caribbean, visiting different islands and working on several ships. He tried his hand at acting in Cuba, performing in a two-person show in Havana. According to one of his biographers, McQueen's act consisted of him sitting near a beautiful woman named Rosa who demanded coffee. Once he received it she would remove his pants, fellate him, and after he had ejaculated into the coffee, she would drink the cup.[16] By 1947, McQueen was in the U.S. Marines and soon after went to New York where he started his professional acting career.

Men were not the only libertines of the pre–World War II era. Various actresses became more renowned for their drug use and sexual indulgences than they did for their performances on stage or on screen. An example was Marlene Dietrich, who carried on affairs with a number of famous male and female celebrities in Hollywood. She is alleged to have performed cunnilingus on fellow actress Tallulah Bankhead at a party. A famed bisexual, Bankhead once expressed her distaste for fellatio and cunnilingus in an oft repeated quote: "If you go down on a woman, you get a crick in your neck. If you go down on a man, you get lockjaw." According to famed film critic Rex Reed, Bankhead once used oral sex to get revenge against Joan Crawford. After being upstaged by Crawford at a party where the latter wore a luxurious dress covered in gold dust, Bankhead appeared on the balcony in the nude, with gold dust sprinkled over her pubic hair. Gaining the attention of everyone at the party, she exclaimed, "Guess who just went down on me?"

Other women of the Hollywood "sewing circle," as the informal group of bisexual actresses was called, included Judy Garland. The star of the *Wizard of Oz* continued to have flings throughout her life with both men and women, allegedly preferring oral sex to regular intercourse according to biographer Axel Madsen.[17] In the late 1930s, while married to Harmon Nelson, Bette Davis had an affair with tycoon Howard Hughes. According to Davis, she was the only woman who was able to get Hughes to climax. "She's telling everybody, all over town, that she cured Hughes of his recurring impotence with women by performing oral sex on him in a room she'd filled with glossy photographs of Hollywood's handsomest men—all shirtless."[18] When Davis' oral affair became known, Nelson quickly filed for divorce. Hughes himself eventually left Davis for a far better fellator in the form of Errol Flynn and was also noted for having received such attention from Billy Haines and Blanche Sweet.[19] In a scene that was to become legendary in Hollywood, a drunken Paulette Goddard lowered herself under a table at the restaurant Ciro's and fellated Spencer Tracy, who was then married to Katharine Hepburn. Argentine actress Mona Maris became known as the oral sex queen of Hollywood, fellating such legendary men as director John Ford.[20] When not cherry-picking the top talent of Hollywood, Maris could be found stooping to lower levels for lower class men. During the filming of *A Devil with Women*, staring Humphrey Bogart, Maris "managed to fellate most of the crew, at least the more rugged and handsome members."[21] Finally, Mae West, well known as a sex symbol in the 1930s and 1940s, had by the 1950s and 1960s largely withdrawn to more private endeavors. Among these was her young lover Paul Novak. The two spent more than two decades together until the end of her life, with West reportedly performing "daily fellatio upon him because she thought it good for her skin."[22] The increasingly relaxed attitude toward oral sex in Hollywood seems to have been an equal opportunity development.

Likewise, the infamous "casting couch" in Hollywood was reaching its height, with many future stars breaking into the business on their knees in some studio offices. Marilyn Monroe got her start fellating Joe Schenck. These trysts helped her secure her first movie with Columbia Pictures, *Ladies of the Chorus*, which was released in 1948. Following a series of successful films a few years later she finally became a star in Hollywood and is reported to have declared, "That's the last cock I'll have to suck."[23] Another famed casting couch executive was Jed Harris. Born Jacob Horowitz, Harris was responsible for a number of acclaimed Broadway productions in the 1920s and 1930s, including *Our Town*. Harris was also famous for requesting potential lead actors and actresses to perform fellatio on him to receive stage time.[24]

Not all of these directors escaped the consequences of their actions. In March 1931, F.W. Murnau, famed director of *Nosferatu*, died in a car accident on the Pacific Coast Highway. Though it was officially proclaimed an accident, rumors quickly circulated that Murnau had been fellating his 14-year-old part–Filipino driver, Garcia Stevenson. The young man lost control of the wheel at some point and slammed the car into an electrical pole. Stevenson survived but Murnau succumbed to his wounds at a hospital shortly afterward. It's unknown whether this was the exact cause of Murnau's death or simply legend, but the spread of rumors became a reality for those at the time and since.

The 1920s also saw one of the oddest political sex scandals in American history. Known as the Newport Scandal, it began in 1919 when assistant secretary of the Navy Franklin D. Roosevelt approved an undercover investigation to expose homosexual affairs in the Navy. Reports surfaced that sailors dressed as women were freely roaming the city of Newport at night offering oral sex, occasionally for money, to both residents and visiting sailors. The Navy had dealt with the issue of sodomy since its founding and had customarily handed out harsh punishments for those accused. Around the same time as the Newport Scandal, Chief Quartermaster James Ray Harwell was convicted of engaging in oral sex with another man based solely on a love letter. He was subsequently sentenced to 15 years of hard labor at Portsmouth Naval Prison. In keeping with the Navy's tough stance against sodomy, Roosevelt signed off on a plan that ordered sailors to perform oral sex on other enlisted men, officers, and even prominent residents of the city of Newport to identify homosexuals.[25] Once word of this operation, which amounted to entrapment, became public, a Congressional investigation quickly ensued, tarnishing the image of Roosevelt and others. Roosevelt resigned his position in 1920 and was promptly named the Democratic nominee for vice-president. In September of that year, various newspapers, including *The Providence Journal*, claimed that Roosevelt had "destroyed or sequestered navy records in order to shield himself."[26] Certainly this negative publicity played a role in securing the defeat of the Democratic Party that year in the presidential election. In addition to concerns over America's entrance into the League of Nations, immigration, internationalism, and progressivism, oral sex played a role in the election of the men who ushered in the Republican-dominated Roaring Twenties.

Other examples of oral sex influencing politics abound. In 1914 an undercover operation in Long Branch, California, netted 31 men for performing oral sex. Two police officers had gone undercover to expose the seedy sex clubs of the beach town, creating a state scandal, yet as fellatio or intent to commit fellatio were not within the California legal code, most of the men were acquitted and released. Angry citizens demanded action and the state quickly adopted a new law the next year including fellatio as a form of sodomy.

A similar scandal unfolded in November 1912 in Portland, Oregon. A prominent city lawyer and high ranking member of the state's Democratic Party, Edward S. J. McAllister, was arrested and indicted on what newspapers at the time referred to as an "immoral act."[27] According to the dissenting judge's opinion, "Work entered and saw Kadel wiping his penis with a handkerchief; that Work ejaculated, 'Hello, what is this?' and Kadel replied, 'McAllister and I are having a little trade,' which, in the parlance of the morally depraved, means the performance of the act defined in the indictment." After he attempted to flee the state, McAllister was arrested and tried for performing oral sex on Roy Kadel. Following a sensational trial, he was found guilty and sentenced to one to five years in prison. Fortunately for McAllister, this decision was overturned with the declaration of a mistrial. Yet, like in California, a deeper issue concerned the state assembly. Oregon's statute against sodomy did not specifically mention fellatio, leading to the strong possibility that many more convictions would soon be overturned as happened with the *Rex v. Jacobs* case of 1817. The legislature quickly passed a new bill in 1913 that officially outlawed fellatio and tripled the punishment for the crime.

The jazz music of the era had obvious connections to social rebellion and many of its performers and songs tended to be highly sexualized. As many of the performers of the time started their careers in brothels and gambling halls, the content of their songs often reflected this. Some examples include "Shave Me Dry" by Lucille Bogan, "You Can't Tell the Difference After Dark" by Alberta Hunter, and "Banana in Your Fruitbasket" by Bo Carter. Perhaps the song most associated with oral sex was Maggie Jones' "Anybody Here Want to Try My Cabbage?," a clear allusion to cunnilingus.

William Carlos Williams' poem *Portrait of a Lady*, published in August 1920, dealt with the act of oral sex. It centers on the 1767 painting *The Swing* by Jean-Honoré Fragonard. The Rococo piece is itself quite erotic, depicting a woman on a swing kicking her left leg high in the air. Below, a man hides in the bushes to the left looking and gesturing toward her open skirt. Williams' poem is less a portrait of this lady than of the narrator who is observing her. "Your thighs are appletrees whose blossoms touch the sky." The watcher then proceeds to describe his journey up and down the woman's legs ending with his lips covered in sand from the shore and petals from the appletree, allusions to oral copulation.

Art continued to push the boundaries of acceptable depictions of sex and sexual acts, especially within the Surrealist Movement. Having grown out of Dadaism in the 1920s, it came to represent the illogical worldview of many of the Lost Generation following the horrors of World War I. Meret Oppenheim's surrealist piece *Le Déjeuner en fourrure*, or *Breakfast in Fur*, consisted of a teacup, saucer, and spoon all covered in the fur of a Chinese gazelle. As with all of the art of the movement, beyond the initial sense of illogical composition, a deeper statement on sexuality emerges. Oppenheim's combination of a traditionally female object, the teacup, with fur, was meant to symbolize a woman's reproductive organ. The use of the object promoted cunnilingus.

As a visual art form, pre–Code Hollywood made movies that reflected the promiscuous habits of its actors and actresses, with the majority of the most erotic pieces being produced abroad. The oldest surviving pornographic film, *A L'Ecu d'Or ou la Bonne Auberge*, was filmed in France in 1908 and prominently featured oral sex. Hedy Lamarr stared in *Ecstasy*, a Czech-Austrian film in which she received cunnilingus from another character, in 1933. Though the action itself isn't shown, the cutaways to phallic imagery make it clear to anyone watching. Lamarr's facial expressions also represent the first portrayal of an orgasm on film. Due to this scene and the general storyline of the movie, it was never officially approved for distribution in America by the Hays board. Once Hollywood began to enforce a code of morality in its productions, oral sex all but disappeared from movies. Not until 1959 and the release of *Some Like It Hot* with Marilyn Monroe would the subject even be hinted at.

The period up to World War II saw an increase in the publication of books about oral sex. More and more these works tended to encourage or at least legitimize the practice. Famed sexologist Havelock Ellis opined that as a useful and indeed pleasurable act, oral sex should be viewed as acceptable. Several years later, in 1937, Max Exner wrote in *The Sexual Side of Marriage* that oral sex was not only the realm of men as a means by which to prepare women for sexual penetration, but also the realm of women. The decade also saw the beginning of sex education among the nation's youth, introducing both new ideas and new practices to young Americans. A quite predictable backlash followed, as many feared that discussed acts, even if shown in a negative light, could become experimented with acts. The American Sexual Health Association conducted a survey in 1933 of the frequency and types of sex acts performed by prostitutes in major cities and determined that only around 10 percent of all encounters were oral, a trend line that social conservatives at the time sought to maintain or even reduce.

While American soldiers who served in World War I were only in Europe for a brief period of time, the GIs who landed at Normandy in 1944 had already spent years in England and would now enjoy the hospitality of France for at least two years more. This meant that the often sexually inexperienced and sexually conservative American men in uniform experienced a whole new world of lovemaking. The French practice of *fumer le cigare* undoubtedly took the soldiers by surprise, giving an erotic twist to the old saying "The French made love with their mouths and war with their feet."

Sex was utilized by both sides as a means of propaganda during World War II. While the British and Americans used their blonde bombshells to entertain the troops at USO rallies and as airplane art, the Germans and Japanese took it a step further, priding themselves on social and moral traditionalism, and saw the Western allies as decadent and sexually deviant. Numerous leaflets and postcards were dropped among the encroaching armies as part of a psychological campaign. The Germans especially sought to convince the soldiers that their girlfriends back home were participating in deviant sexual practices, most notably oral sex, in an attempt to demoralize the enemy. The American OSS soon copied this tactic, employing sexual iconography to weaken the Germans' resolve to fight. Propaganda cards also ridiculed Hitler and Mussolini by showing sexual encounters between the two men. They were also frequently depicted performing oral sex on women.

Post-war American society was a curious combination of conservative and liberal elements. While the 1950s echoed the economic success of the 1920s, at the same time they were a social reaction against the excesses of that earlier decade. Family life, and in turn sexuality, was portrayed as representing the conservative ideals of traditional America. Yet just as racial and civil tensions percolated just under the surface so did a revolution in oral sex.

The title "Paul Revere of the Sexual Revolution" in America belonged to Dr. Alfred Kinsey. During the 1940s, Kinsey conducted interviews and experiments on the sexuality of Americans that would eventually be published in two volumes, *Sexual Behavior in the Human Male* (1948) and *Sexual Behavior in the Human Female* (1953). The scope of his research into the subject was unprecedented at the time, engaging broad cross-sections of the population in regard to their most intimate acts. Among other data and information in the work was an analysis of oral sex habits of adult Americans. Considering that the practice was still illegal in almost all states, what Kinsey found was quite astonishing. In the five years between the publication of the two works, Kinsey discovered that the percentage of people who had received oral sex rose from 40 percent to 62 percent.[28] This appears to be double the number who practiced the act a generation before during the Roaring Twenties. As often happens in American society, the law only changes once a majority is breaking it. Despite this, Kinsey was quick to point out that taboos with the practice still remained. In fact, "there are several instances of wives who have murdered their husbands because they insisted on mouth-genital contacts."[29] While it is impossible to know with any certainty the percentage of adults around the world who engaged in oral sex prior to the 20th century, it is safe to assume that the number was nowhere near as high as that reported by Kinsey in post-war America.

In the same year that *Sexual Behavior in the Human Male* was published, W. H. Auden, the accomplished English poet, produced one of his lesser known pieces. Entitled "The Platonic Blow (A Day for a Lay)," Auden imagined a sexual encounter between two young men that ended in fellatio. In the poem, he artfully mixes scents of spring air with the smell of male locker rooms, reminiscing about ancient Greek gymnasiums. Yet, Auden goes much further, leveling the practice of giving or receiving oral sex in a way that would have been unthinkable to the Greeks. The poem goes on in vivid detail to describe the course of lovemaking between the two young men, ending with the narrator fellating his 24-year-old mechanic companion. The poem was by far the most detailed poem yet written for a large audience on the subject of oral sex. The metaphors and obfuscated language of previous writers for 3,000 years gave way to the plain English of Auden in describing the act and its outcome.

Not to be outdone, John Updike penned his own paean to oral sex entitled "Fellatio." In the poem he describes poetically the beauty of secretaries fellating their lovers. Utilizing the natural imagery of fountains, flowers, landscapes, meadows, and silos, Updike seems to portray the act as completely in keeping with nature and therefore not unnatural. Nor does he shy away from recognizing the reproductive function of the ingested semen, carefully choosing such words as seed, baby's breath, and the entire metaphor of a fertile field. In 1984, his book *Roger's Version* featured a vividly imagined oral encounter between the narrator's wife and his rival. In fact, much of Updike's notoriety as an author arose due to his inclusion of oral sex in his seminal 1960 work, *Rabbit, Run.* The main character, Harry Angstrom, has a two-month-long affair with a prostitute named Ruth. Oral sex plays a prominent role in their relationship in both chapters seven and nine, but in keeping with traditional associations, it is used to highlight the fact that she is a sullied woman.

New attempts were also made at instruction in oral techniques. In fact, the 1950s hardly deserve the monolithic view that has been associated with it as a repressed generation of conformity. Mail order pamphlets discussed various aspects of sexuality, including oral sex. *Questions and Answers about Cunnilingus,* for instance, cost 35 cents and could be discreetly delivered to the home. In England, the mail was used to advertise Paul Ableman's highly controversial book *The Mouth & Oral Sex.*

Gershon Legman, who later worked as a researcher at the Kinsey Institute, published an entire textbook on oral sex, *Oragenitalism,* in 1940. Not surprisingly, the book was repressed, seized, and most copies destroyed under state and federal obscenity laws. Not until 1969 did the book finally see full publication. In his writing, Legman included what he claimed was a translation of a monograph by an anonymous Frenchman from around 1914. Entitled "A Practical Treatise on Fellation: Its Advantages and Inconveniences," it provided minute instructions on how to properly perform or receive oral sex. Some of the suggestions proved rather laughable, including the notion that fellatio was best when performed in a small room with dark furniture, plenty of port, and snacks that were not too phallic in shape. The work also detailed methods and tips for giving fellatio including the shapes a young woman was to draw with her tongue while she engaged in the act. Finally, the author suggests that there are more than 14,288,400 positions in which to perform cunnilingus.[30] While much of this work may have been satire, it did become popular reading during the Sexual Revolution of the 1970s and certainly inspired experimentation among those who succeeded in obtaining a copy.

The openness toward oral sex that was beginning to emerge after World War II only grew as the Baby Boomer generation became sexually-active young adults. Avant-garde artist Andy Warhol debuted a 35-minute silent film entitled *Blow Job* in 1964. Actor DeVeren Bookwalter is shown in a close up of his face as he apparently receives fellatio from an unknown person. The camera never departs from his face, leaving the rest of the action up to the imagination of the viewer. Warhol is directly addressing the ancient Greek and Roman taboo against the action by examining the passiveness of the receiver. Two years later, Warhol produced another film entitled *Blow Job #2*, or *Eating Too Fast*. This time the camera pans down for a portion of the film and reveals the back of the head of the person performing the sex act on the actor. Warhol's use of two male actors did little to detract from the ever-present notion that oral sex was limited to prostitutes and homosexuals.

This trend was also evident in the poetry of the Beat Generation and later the Hippie Movement of the 1960s. Poet Allen Ginsberg once famously quipped, "Just because I like to suck cock doesn't make me any less American than Jesse Helms." In fact, Ginsberg initially traveled to San Francisco where he wrote his most well-known poems after being kicked out of a friend's home. Carolyn Cassady discovered Ginsburg and her husband engaged in oral sex. The poet was expelled from her house and began the journey that resulted in the publication of "The Howl" a year later. The epic poem was rife with references to various sexual acts, including fellatio, celebrating those "who blew and were blown by those human seraphim, the sailors, caresses of Atlantic and Caribbean love."

Fellow poet John Wieners, who was at various points in his life institutionalized, wrote a number of poems which focused on oral sex in particular. Most notable among these was "Memories of You," which included a lengthy description of his various oral encounters with men in both Boston and New York City. As with many other 19th and 20th century poets who touched on the subject, Wieners combined natural imagery with his depictions of these erotic acts, again attempting to portray it as a natural occurrence.

Female writers also seemed willing to tackle the subject of oral sex, specifically fellatio, in late 1960s literature. Anaïs Nin, a Cuban writer, became one of the first and most prominent female writers of erotic literature after the Second World War. Her two most famous collections of short stories, *The Delta of Venus* and *Little Birds*, feature numerous scenes of sex, including one graphic depiction of a character receiving fellatio. Contained in the short story "The Woman on the Dunes," Nin writes, "She licked it softly, tenderly, lingering over the tip of it. It stirred. He looked down at the sight of her wide red mouth so beautifully curved around his penis. With one hand she touched his balls, and with the other she moved the head of the penis, enclosing it and pulling it gently."

Characteristically, another early female-authored erotic work was published in France in 1967. Written by Emmanuelle Arsan, the appropriately titled *Emmanuelle* details a variety of erotic and scandalous encounters. At one point the main character performs fellatio on a man and in the process produces one of the first written accounts of "deep throating" in modern literature. "She explored more and more intimately, searched, moved forward and back, abruptly returned to the end of his penis, pushed it to the bottom of her throat, so deeply that she nearly choked, and there, without withdrawing it, she slowly and irresistibly pumped it while her tongue enveloped and massaged it."

As in previous centuries it is the sex lives of the elite that are the best documented, and no one represented the youth of post-war

America quite like the Kennedys. While the president was known for his many lovers, according to his wife he was not insistent on oral sex. The First Lady apparently first learned how to properly perform fellatio during one of her own affairs. Actor William Holden once quipped, "I had to teach Jackie how to [have oral sex]. She told me that Jack had never insisted on that. At first she was very reluctant, but once she got the rhythm of it she couldn't get enough. If she goes back to Washington and works her magic with Kennedy, he will owe me one."[31]

One of Jack Kennedy's youngest paramours, 19-year-old intern Mimi Beardsley, provides us with another incidence of oral sex in the White House. While serving there from 1962 to 1963 she recalled that on one occasion the president asked her to "take care" of his assistant David Powers. "It was a dare, but I knew exactly what he meant. This was a challenge to give Dave Powers oral sex. I don't think the President thought I'd do it, but I'm ashamed to say that I did. It was a pathetic, sordid scene, and is very hard for me to think about today. Dave was jolly and obedient as I stood in the shallow end of the pool and performed my duties. The President silently watched."[32]

President Kennedy himself does not seem to have completely sworn off oral sex. In one of the more famous and dangerous sex scandals of his time in office, JFK became infatuated with alleged East German spy Ellen Rometsch. An aide to Lyndon Johnson named Bobby Baker was said to provide women to many government officials and helped connect Rometsch to the president. According to an interview done years later, "She really loved oral sex.... She went to the White House several times. And President Kennedy called me and said it's the best head-job he'd ever had, and he thanked me."[33] Congressman Gerald Ford seems to also have become involved with Rometsch during the Warren Commission. The head of the FBI, J. Edgar Hoover, supposedly possessed a recording of Ford receiving fellatio from the East German and threatened to blackmail him unless he revealed information about the Commission. Robert Kennedy had Rometsch deported back to Germany to avoid any investigation that would tarnish his or his family's image.

Kennedy also seems to have enjoyed fellatio during his affair with Marilyn Monroe. Famed English actor Peter Lawford, Jack's brother-in-law, arranged the tryst between the two. For several years, Kennedy and Monroe met frequently for sex. Monroe became attached to the president to the point of dangerous obsession. Lawford coordinated visits and allegedly even filmed the actress fellating Kennedy in a large marble bathtub.[34] Monroe in 1959 had starred in the first film to even hint at oral sex since the enforcement of morality codes in Hollywood movies. *Some Like It Hot* featured several jokes that referenced fellatio.

Kennedy was not the only famous man of the era who allegedly had mixed feelings about oral sex. Elvis Presley, while rumored to have had any number of lovers, seems to have preferred sexless romances. Dozens of his paramours, including June Juanico, June Wilkinson, Christina Crawford, and Dolores Hart, all claimed to have never been intimate with the King despite dating him. Cybill Shepherd remains one of the best, though debatable, sources for the oral sex life of the singer. According to her, she introduced Presley to fellatio, though the claim is denied by another of his paramours.[35] She claimed that he refused to perform cunnilingus on her: "Me and the guys talk and, well, we don't eat pussy." Elvis Presley, raised in the religious South, was apparently very much a product of his time when it came to his views on oral sex. This is contradicted, however, by Priscilla Beaulieu, who first became intimate with Elvis at the age of 14 while he was stationed in Germany. "He worked his art of foreplay without penetration. In lovemaking, as in entertaining, Elvis' outstanding talent was oral."[36]

Across the Atlantic Ocean, England was experiencing several high profile sex scandals of its own in the 1960s. The Profumo Affair broke in British newspapers in 1963 and quickly brought down Secretary of State for War John Profumo, Prime Minister Harold Macmillan, and indeed the entire Conservative Party during the 1964 general election. That same year another scandal surfaced that perhaps proved slightly more appalling and appealing. Margaret Campbell, then Duchess of Argyll, had been known in her youth for scandalous affairs with both English and American men of power and wealth. Following a failed first marriage and a number of other affairs, she married Ian Douglas Campbell, 11th Duke of Argyll, in

1951. However, her second marriage proved to be no more successful than her first. Her husband soon began to suspect that she was once again pursuing extramarital relationships and searched her room for evidence. He found locked in a cupboard a series of Polaroids which would soon become the center of both a judicial and political witch hunt. The photos depicted the Duchess, in her trademark pearls, performing fellatio on a headless man. Though a divorce was quickly granted, the quest to identify the mystery lover enthralled the government and public of England. From a potential list of seven dozen men, her husband and his investigative team eventually narrowed it down to around five individuals including a famed American actor and the brother of Nazi scientist Werner von Braun. The minister of defense even underwent a medical exam to prove his innocence before stepping down from his cabinet position. Regardless of the identity of any of Campbell's lovers, her reputation and many of theirs were ruined by the event.

Fellatio almost brought down the presidency of Lyndon B. Johnson. The Texan had assumed the office of president only 11 months before, after the assassination of Kennedy. Now, in October 1964, as he was actively campaigning against ultra-conservative Barry Goldwater of Arizona and adroitly handling the rapidly evolving Vietnam crisis, a sex scandal emerged which threatened to topple him from office. On October 7, 1964, Johnson's closest aide, Walter Jenkins, left a party at *Newsweek* headquarters in Washington, D.C. He proceeded to the local YMCA where he ended up performing oral sex on a 60-year-old Hungarian immigrant named Andy Choka in a pay bathroom stall. Undercover police arrested both men but soon released them after they paid a fine, filing no formal charges. News of the arrest leaked and by the end of the week was in the headlines of most major newspapers. Though President Johnson was able to suppress the exact crime committed by Jenkins, Americans were able to piece together the scenario. His aide quickly checked himself into a hospital for mental exhaustion and Johnson demanded his immediate resignation. White House tapes reveal a president concerned about the effects of the scandal on the election. "He's got to get out of the White House. I think the presidency is something that we've got to protect." LBJ even employed hundreds of FBI and CIA agents to investigate whether national security had been compromised or whether this was a Republican-planned encounter to embarrass him. Luckily for the president, Goldwater refused to use the scandal as political fodder and a series of subsequent belligerent moves by both the Soviets and Chinese soon distracted the attention of the media. A more forceful push by the Republican party could have drastically altered not only the election but also the history of America.

The West was not the only area afflicted by sex scandals around this time. In 1970, following a two-year affair and fearing for her life, American actress Dovie Beams held a press conference in Manila where she played secret recordings of her affairs with then-president Ferdinand Marcos. Apparently Marcos' wife, Imelda Marcos, had learned of the affair and had threatened to kill Beams before she left the Philippines.[37] The sex scandal did much to further destroy the credibility of the authoritarian president. Student protestors at the University of the Philippines, after seizing control of the local radio station, managed to obtain a copy of the recording and played the section in which Marcos begged for oral sex on a loop for hours. In response to this and other scandals and protests, Marcos declared martial law.

Nineteen sixty-nine was a good year for oral sex in Western culture. Two books were published which helped to spread its acceptance still further through American culture. Joan Garrity, under a pseudonym, wrote a book entitled *The Sensuous Woman* which quickly became a classic companion piece to *The Feminine Mystique* of a decade earlier. Garrity wrote for bored housewives, inexperienced lovers, and a new generation of girls seeking to escape from the puritanical sex views of their mothers and grandmothers. Twelve entire pages of the work were devoted to oral sex, her own experiences with it, reasons to try it, and techniques to employ.

Garrity begins by arguing that the act is not only natural but also ties into the Feminist Movement. "Does the idea of putting a man's penis in your mouth revolt you? If so you are probably a typical product of America's taboos against oral gratification. After all, we've been trained to think that one of the most natural and beautiful acts in the world, that of a mother nursing her child, is embarrassing and offensive to the eye."[38] She goes on to dismantle the other main argument against oral sex, that it is not sanitary. To the contrary, Garrity says, "kissing a man's penis is a lot less unsanitary than kissing him on the mouth."[39] The author details her own evolution, sharing how the first time a man performed oral sex on her she was revolted, but soon afterward she not only learned to enjoy receiving it but also giving it. "It was even better than caviar and champagne, both of which, come to think of it, I had disliked on first sampling."[40] Garrity provides detailed techniques for the beginner as well as the more experienced fellator. Included in these are "The Butterfly Flick" and "The Silken Swirl." Perhaps keeping with the Holly Homemaker scene of the 1950s, she finished up by suggesting a woman use "some freshly whipped cream, to which you add a dash of vanilla and a couple of teaspoons of powdered sugar."[41]

All of this was taking place within the larger context of the Sexual Revolution. The ideals of youth, feminism, and rebellion against authority and tradition all collided to produce a social uprising against order and established sexual mores. Much of this movement was aimed at women, who saw their sexuality being repressed by traditional patriarchal norms.

Even *The Godfather*, an iconic book published in 1969, aided in the normalization of oral sex in society. When even stereotypically vicious, Italian gangsters discussed their fondness for oral sex, the way was open for every American male to partake in the act. "And the other guys were always talking about blow jobs … and he really didn't enjoy that stuff so much…. He and his second wife had finally not got along, because she preferred the old sixty-nine too much to a point where she didn't want anything else and he had to fight to stick it in. She began making fun of him and calling him a square and the word got around that he made love like a kid." In the book, the character Johnny Fontaine's aversion to mutual oral sex harkens back to the concerns of Adam toward Lilith's demands for equality in sex as well as life.

The musical *Hair*, which debuted off Broadway in 1967 and was enjoying much mainstream success by 1969, also sought to challenge the traditional puritanical view of society toward oral sex. In the early part of the first act, the character Woof breaks into song, singing a bawdy verse which references sodomy, fellatio and cunnilingus as well as other acts generally viewed as depraved at the time. He finishes with an invitation to the audience to join in on the sexual acts.

On the other side of the nation, Michael McClure wrote and produced a play entitled *The Beard*. Its actors were arrested almost every night it was performed. The play was about a meeting between Billy the Kid and Jean Harlow in the afterlife. After exchanging arguments the two engage in simulated cunnilingus in front of the audience. Whether it was performed in Berkeley, San Francisco, or Los Angeles, each performance met with the same response from the authorities. Despite the more liberal leanings of Hollywood and Berkeley, simulated cunnilingus was still considered taboo.

Literature and poetry continued to reference oral sex, and emerging areas of multicultural literature presented new viewpoints on it as well. Chicana poet Gloria Anzaldua wrote a number of poems dealing with oral sex and lesbian sex as seen in Latino culture. In her poem "I Had to Go Down," published in 1987, Anzaldua addresses oral sex on a number of metaphorical levels. The poem is set in a basement, with clear positional connotations to the oral sex that follows. The narrator describes an encounter with an intruder, a possible allusion to vaginal sex, claiming that she therefore had to engage in oral sex. The notion of performing fellatio to avoid sex and the possibility of either losing honor or getting pregnant was a cultural and societal concern for many at the time. This represented a departure from the negative stereotype presented about oral sex centuries before. Further on in the poem, Anzaldua metaphorically describes a young tree growing in the center of the house. The line could be taken as a reference to the idea that the narrator had become a mature girl, with oral sex being one of the rites of passage normally associated with it then. Finally, her poem "Poets Have Strange Eating Habits" is an open homage to lesbian cunnilingus, a topic that would still have been seen as quite taboo in Latino culture at the time. Anzaldua employees much of the same straightforward and aggressive descriptions used by Auden in his poem.

While most music avoided obvious references to oral sex, musicians themselves became notorious for the practice. More so than at any other time in musical history the unrestrained morality of young fans created a haven for sexuality backstage. Cynthia Albritton became one of the most famous of these groupies with a unique goal.

Calling herself the Plaster Caster, Cynthia hoped to meet, fellate, and then cast molds of the penises of rock stars. Her first client was Jimi Hendrix and she molded many other famous members, hoping one day to open a permanent museum. Her fame even inspired two songs, "Five Short Minutes" by Jim Croce and "Plaster Caster" by KISS. Both describe the actual practice by Albritton as well as hinting at additional oral acts by the artist.

Some of the more infamous songs which spoke of oral sex during the time period included "Casino Boogie" by the Rolling Stones, "Kissing Cunt in Cannes" and "Miracles" by Jefferson Starship.

Perhaps the greatest moment for oral sex during the Sexual Revolution came in 1972. Pornographic movies were tightly restricted, producing few stars of note and relying on a select clientele who frequented darkened, dank movie theaters to make money. Despite these obstacles, there was enough money to be made in the business to lead the Italian mafia to secure the vast majority of filming operations by the 1960s. In 1972 one such producer, Louis Peraino, borrowed $22,500 from his father Anthony Peraino, one of the heads of the Colombo crime family. The film that resulted, *Deep Throat*, would revolutionize the porn industry, make Linda Lovelace a household name, vastly enrich the mafia, make fellatio a household practice, and also lead to the downfall of the Colombos.

Linda Lovelace stars in the movie as a woman seeking to take charge of her own sexual desires and satisfaction. The plot is predictably bad, focusing on her revelation that her clitoris is actually in her throat, requiring her to perform more and more oral sex to reach her own orgasm. The quality of the filming and the presence of an actual albeit bad story, though, were not the only things that grabbed the attention of the American public. Linda Boreman, who changed her name to Lovelace for filming, first got into the porn industry through her allegedly abusive boyfriend Chuck Traynor. As part of his "training" of Lovelace, Traynor supposedly had her hypnotized repeatedly until she was able to perform fellatio without a gag reflex. Her ability to "deep throat" surprised not only her co-star Harry Reems, but also the public. The film caught on in a way that the mafia, its producer, and its stars had never expected it to.

Deep Throat became such a success that it opened the porn market up to middle-class viewers. Truman Capote admitted in 1973 to having gone to see the film with "a bunch of people I thought were fun.... I thought the girl was charming."[42] Johnny Carson referenced the movie on television, the respectable *New York Times* ran an article highlighting the porno chic phenomenon in 1973, and Bob Woodward co-opted the title for his Watergate informant. The film grossed more than $30 million, with some rather incredulous estimates rising as high as $600 million.[43] Despite a major obscenity trial afterward in which Judge Joel Tyler called the film "this feast of carrion and squalor ... a nadir of decadence ... a Sodom and Gomorrah gone wild before the fire," *Deep Throat* and its depiction of fellatio became only more ingrained in the zeitgeist of the time.[44] The Supreme Court case *Stanley v. Georgia* in 1969, which legalized the private ownership of pornographic material, only furthered the distribution of these materials and the adoption of new ideas and practices. In fact, by the 1970s, an American Sexual Health Association survey showed that requests to prostitutes for oral sex had risen from 10 percent of all transactions in 1933 to nearly 90 percent by the 1970s.

The United Kingdom likewise continued a losing battle against obscene references to oral sex during the 1970s. Perhaps the most notorious example was the furor that erupted following the publication of James Kirkup's "The Love That Dares to Speak Its Name." The poem depicts the immediate aftermath of the crucifixion of Jesus. A centurion, who professes to be a former gay lover of the Messiah, narrates both his love for the man and the loss he feels. The more controversial nature of the poem occurs as the centurion proceeds to commit necrophilia with the corpse of the Savior, beginning with an act of oral sex. In the stanza, he mixes descriptions of oral sex with religious objects and acts, utilizing such words as "instrument" and "anointing." The narrator references all the other gay relationships had by the Christ as well, playing on the theme that he "loved all men." Kirkup was either consciously or unconsciously building upon the thoughts of the various heretical omophagic cults that arose in Christianity during the early days of the Church.

The shocking nature of the poem led to its being banned in the United Kingdom as well as many other nations. Suit was finally brought against the publishers under a 17th-century religious blasphemy law. The subsequent case *Whitehouse v. Lemon* in 1977 was perhaps the last in English legal history to utilize blasphemy in an attempt to censor oral sex. A telling sign of the changing nature of the English view of law and sex is that the idea of blasphemy as a crime was dropped from the common law legal code in 2008 and a group which linked to the poem on an online page, despite initial threats of prosecution, was eventually cleared of wrongdoing.

In fact, the English public became enthralled rather than appalled in 1977 by Joyce McKinney and the "Manacled Mormon." A former beauty pageant contestant and one-time Miss Wyoming, Joyce McKinney was in and out of the Church of Latter Day Saints for most of her life. A brief relationship with Kirk Anderson proved disastrous as the young man asked to be sent on mission work to repent for his sins and he was dispatched to California, Oregon, and eventually London. McKinney proceeded to follow her true love, hiring herself out as a prostitute to earn money to pay for private detectives. She relied solely on her oral sex skills, hoping to save herself for Anderson. When she tracked him to London, she drugged the young man with chloroform, took him to a deserted cottage and chained him down. According to police reports, McKinney fellated Anderson until he was aroused and then had sex with him. The episode caught the national interest for a number of reasons, not the least of which was the legal question of whether a woman could rape a man. Yet the fact that the oral sex element of the story was of little concern to English society at the time is revealing of the general trend in the nation toward the act.

In 1979, a controversial installation of art opened in Chicago before touring several major cities. Created by Judy Chicago, the work, which was hailed at the time as the first large-scale work of feminist art, was entitled *The Dinner Party*. Originally called *Twenty Five Women Who Were Eaten Alive*, it is a collection of 39 place settings of famous or mythical women in history such as Virginia Woolf and Cleopatra. Each plate contains an artistically-portrayed image of a vagina complete with unique features for its dinner guest. The exhibit generated controversy for a number of reasons among both conservative and feminist groups, not the least of which were the oral implications of combining vaginas with dinner plates.

Conservative gains in the 1980s attempted to reverse some of the more liberal social trends of the previous several decades, though often with little success. Anti–gay rights activist Anita Bryant opined in 1977, "Oral sex, where the tongue is used to stimulate the clitoris producing an orgasm, is a form of vampirism or eating of blood. Such degeneracy produces a taste and craving for the effects, as does liquor and narcotics."[45] Yet even the Reagans, the models of this return to old-fashioned American values, did not escape the taint of oral sex. Several biographies claimed that the First lady, when she was an up and coming actress in the 1940s, was a well-known fellator in Hollywood. Allegations from her former lover Peter Lawford's ex-wife as well as numerous others place Nancy in several compromising positions as she rose through the ranks in the movie industry.[46]

Shortly before Reagan was elected president, America experienced its own Félix Faure moment with the death of businessman and politician Nelson Rockefeller in 1979. Rockefeller made headlines for his scandalous divorce from his wife and subsequent marriage to a much younger woman, Margaretta "Happy" Murphy, who had only a month before divorced her husband, in 1963. With the birth of a child shortly afterward, Rockefeller proved unpalatable enough to Republican voters to lose the primaries in 1964 to Barry Goldwater. Still a prominent member of the party, he became vice-president in December 1974 following the ascension of Gerald Ford, only to be dropped during the 1976 election. Four years later, Rockefeller suffered a massive heart attack and died. Problems with the initial press reports quickly emerged as the public began to piece together the former vice-president's final moments. The 70-year-old was being fellated by his 25-year-old assistant, Megan Marshack, in his townhouse when he was killed by a massive coronary infarction. Newspapers were quick to produce a number of puns regarding his death, including "Nelson thought he was coming, but he was going" and "He died of low blood pressure, 70 over 25."

For the public, it was the rise in popularity of teen-scream horror movies that helped to keep the Sexual Revolution alive. Many of the more famous films combined the successful horror genre of the post–World War II era with the porno chic movement of the 1970s. In this environment, all forms of sex, not the least of which was oral, became more readily accepted by younger and younger audiences. In the 1981 horror movie *Halloween II*, a character named Budd sings an irreverent song about one of the nurses, "Amazing grace, come sit on my face. Don't make me cry, I need your pie." Other such scenes occurred in *Carrie, Re-Animator,* and *The Last House on the Left*. Most of the sexually-liberated characters were among the first victims in the films and references to oral sex were in the minority compared to other sexual acts and were almost never visually seen.

These cultural moves coincided with legislative moves to alter the sodomy laws that had dominated and controlled the practice since the early 19th century. Illinois became the first state to repeal its own law in 1962, thereafter allowing for the legal practice of oral sex. The only other state to follow suit in that decade was Kansas, which dumped its law in 1969. The 1970s then saw a flurry of activity with Arkansas, Alaska, California, Connecticut, Delaware, Hawaii, Indiana, Iowa, Kentucky, Maine, Massachusetts, Montana, Nebraska, New Hampshire, New Jersey, New Mexico, North Dakota, Ohio, Oregon, Pennsylvania, South Dakota, Vermont, Washington, West Virginia, and Wyoming legalizing the practice. Famous legal decisions in *Griswold v. Ct.* and *NY v. Onofre*, in 1965 and 1980, respectively, argued for a right to sexual privacy that saw a number of other statutes overturned in the 1980s, including in New York, Oklahoma, Tennessee, and Wisconsin. Thus, by the dawning of the 1990s, 32 states had removed or modified their laws to allow for the practice of oral sex.

This did not allow for the legalization of oral sex in all cases. Homosexual sodomy was still largely banned around the country. The famous Supreme Court case *Bowers v. Hardwick* from Georgia allowed for the criminalization of homosexual oral sex. Chief Justice Warren Burger cited William Blackstone's famous dictum that it was an "infamous crime against nature." As late as 2006, a 17-year-old Georgia boy was sentenced to ten years in prison for performing cunnilingus on a 15-year-old girl. Though laws were in existence in the state to allow for youths of similar age to engage in vaginal sex, these did not apply to oral encounters. Protests soon followed and the Georgia legislature quickly moved to alter its law. Genarlow Wilson was released in 2007 due to the cruel and unusual nature of his punishment.

By and large, the period from 1945 to 1990 saw a rapid evolution in the portrayal and acceptance of oral sex in both private practice and in public life. More and more cultural and artistic portrayals of fellatio and cunnilingus as well as changing social values and the rise of second-wave feminism all contributed to this shifting attitude that proceeded at an unprecedented pace. Perhaps those in government also learned that, much as with Prohibition, the power of the federal government was severely limited when it came to enforcing morality. As J. Edgar Hoover, head of the FBI once quipped, "I regret to say that we of the FBI are powerless to act in cases of oral-genital intimacy, unless it has in some way obstructed interstate commerce."

8

The Normalization
of Oral Sex

The final victory for oral sex came about after the end of the Cold War, a period of monumental change in many spheres. The overall triumph of Western liberalism occurred not only in politics and economics but in society. What began as a battle of political and economic freedom against repression grew by the 1970s to one of social freedom and individual rights against subjugation. Western culture, with its own particular views of art, literature, entertainment, and even sex, was dominant over that of the East. Thereafter, the peace dividend of the 1990s, while perhaps failing to see the political and economic growth around the world championed by Bush, Thatcher, Clinton, and others, did see an explosion in social freedoms particularly in the realm of sex.

By the 1990s sexual imagery was becoming more widely accessible due to a number of factors. The development of the VCR and the growth of the home movie rental industry allowed for the more discrete distribution of pornography. At the same time, the sexual license beginning to appear in cinema in the 1980s expanded beyond simply horror movies and into other genres. Some of the more well-known mainstream movies from the 1980s and 1990s that featured scenes of oral sex include *Boys Don't Cry*, *Two Girls and a Guy*, *American Pie*, *Basic Instinct*, *Thinner*, *What's Eating Gilbert Grape*, *The Basketball Diaries*, *Casino*, *Ace Ventura*, *Jawbreaker*, and *Boogie Nights*. The hit 1994 film *Clerks* even featured an extended discussion of the store owner's girlfriend's penchant for fellatio.

Dante: Why did you tell me you only had sex with three different guys?

Veronica: Because I did only have sex with three different guys. That doesn't mean I didn't just go with people.

Dante: Oh my God, I feel so nauseous.

Veronica: I'm sorry, Dante, I thought you understood.

Dante: I did understand! I understood that you had sex with three different guys and that's all you said!

Veronica: Please calm down.

Dante: How many?

Veronica: Dante—

Dante: How many dicks have you sucked?

Veronica: Let it go!

Dante: How many?

Veronica: All right, shut up a second and I'll tell you! Jesus! I didn't freak out like this when you told me how many girls you fucked!

Dante: This is different, this is important. How many? Well?

Veronica: Something like … 36.

Dante: What? Something like 36?

Veronica: Lower your voice.

Dante: Wait a minute, what is that anyway—something like 36? Does that include me?

Veronica: Ummm … 37.

Dante: I'm 37?

Veronica: I'm going to class.

Dante: My girlfriend has sucked 37 dicks!

Customer: In a row?

The rise in popularity of vampire films and vampire culture can also be attributed in part to this increased interest in oral sex. As previously mentioned, the vampire has always represented in its basest form contact between the mouth and bodily fluids, which certainly has erotic connotations to it. Indeed, the almost obsessive application of Freudian analysis to all forms of art and literature has transformed even Bram Stoker's classic work into a tale of repressed Victorian desire for oral sex.[1] Paglia's opinion that "there may be an element of omophagy in oral sex" would certainly hold true in this case as it does in connection with primitive cultural practices.[2] Throughout the 1990s and 2000s numerous vampire movies were produced, most of which focused on erotic elements and lesbian themes, all of which subtly referenced oral sex. The 1992 production of *Bram Stoker's Dracula* features a scene in which Jonathan Harker is fed upon by the Brides of Dracula in a heavily erotic manner, with strong visual clues suggesting that one was performing fellatio on him before the attack.

In 1995 an opera was produced and scored by Thomas Ades and Philip Hensher which took on the famous oral sex scandal of Margaret Campbell from 1963. Not only was such an unspeakable event now public entertainment, but the topic of oral sex had even invaded the lofty realm of opera. Entitled *Powder Her Face*, the show featured its lead singer performing simulated fellatio while humming an aria. More popular forms of music also touched on the broader subject, including N.W.A. with "Just Don't Bite It," "Summer of '69" by Bryan Adams, Little Wayne's "Lollipop," "Love in an Elevator" by Arrowsmith, and "Head" by Prince. Female musicians also opined on the topic, openly singing about cunnilingus throughout the 1990s. Some of the more notable examples include Lil' Kim's "Not Tonight," 20 Fingers' "Lick It," and Melissa Ferrick's "Drive." Interestingly, most of the black male-dominated rap music still tended to view cunnilingus in a negative light, a situation that would not alter until well into the 21st century.

The appearance of oral sex in movies was soon followed by its inclusion in television shows. While suggestions of sex had been part of television for decades, and portrayals of it were beginning to be seen in prime time, oral sex remained taboo for much longer. As late as 1993, not even references to it were allowed on screen. "Today, it is hard to find a form, style or configuration of sex that has not been explored on network television. But a few remain. Any actions that suggest oral sex, for example, are forbidden, and even verbal allusions are unlikely to make it on the air. 'You cannot refer to oral sex in any way,' said Marshall Herskovitz, a creator of 'Thirtysomething,' who learned this too late when such a mention was cut from an episode of the series."[3] Singular episodes and references to oral sex exist from only a few cable programs and made-for-television movies from the late 1980s. The first extended reference to the act probably occurred in an episode of *Seinfeld* in 1993. Entitled "The Mango," it features banter between characters Jerry and George referring to the latter's inability to perform cunnilingus.

George: Yep. There's one little problem.

Jerry: Sexual?

George: Yeeeaaah. Well.... I've never really felt confident in ... one particular aspect.

Jerry: Below the equator?

George: Yeah.

Jerry: Nobody does. You know, nobody knows what to do. You just close your eyes and you hope for the best. I really think they're happy if you just make an effort.

George: I don't know. Last time I got the tap.

Jerry: You got the tap?

George: You know, you're going along, you think everything's all right and all of a sudden you get that tap. (George taps his own shoulder.) You know it's like pfffff (whistling sound), all right that's enough, you're through.

Jerry: The tap is tough.

George: It's like the manager coming out and asking you for the ball.

Jerry: Well maybe she just wanted to move on to other business.

George: No, no, this wasn't moving on. I got the hook. I wish I could get a lesson in that.

Jerry: It's a very complicated area.

George: You can go crazy trying to figure that place out.

Jerry: It's a haaazy mystery.

Interestingly, George's problems seem to be solved by the end of the episode after he consumes a mango, perhaps an inadvertent reference to the use of fruit in classical art to represent sex in general and oral sex in particular. This lack of a portrayal of oral sex on network television is all the more surprising when one considers that network news was broadcasting the sordid details of President Clinton's own oral sex episodes around the same time.

By the 2000s, scenes of oral sex were still largely only implied on camera. Two well-konwn examples occurred in seasons 5 and 6 of *Buffy the Vampire Slayer*. The first suggested an episode of fellatio between two of the main characters while the second portrayed a musically-suggestive scene of lesbian cunnilingus. A periodical at the time described the second scene in the following terms: "Tara sings of her love for Willow, particularly her amazement that anyone could open her so completely to the beauty of the world; the scene ends in the couple's bedroom, with Tara gently levitating inches above the bed as Willow hovers somewhere just below the frame, one of the best metaphors for the bliss of oral sex I've seen on any screen, small or large."[4] Cable television shows, including *Blue Mountain State* and *Sex and the City*, soon broke the taboo against portraying oral sex. It was only a matter of time before network television did as well.

It would be 2010 before the first actual portrayal of oral sex occurred on network television without suggestion or metaphor. In the first episode of season two of *The Good Wife*, the title character, played by Julianna Margulies, receives cunnilingus on a bathroom sink from her husband. The studio clearly sought to emphasize the fact by both highlighting the scene in promo reels for the upcoming season and by having Margulies mention it during interviews. "I mean, I think that is the first time network television has had an oral sex scene—no?"

The Internet only hastened the normalization of oral sex. Access to an unlimited supply of pornographic material from the privacy of one's home introduced wider and wider audiences to various sexual practices in ways unthought-of in the days of limited-release movies. The Internet also provided an unparalleled resource for those who had questions about how to perform oral sex. Beginning in the 2000s, dating websites appeared that allowed individuals to find people who were strictly interested in only exchanging oral sex with each other. Phone apps in the 2010s served the same purpose.

Celebrity sex scandals were beginning to have little of the same impact or staying power of those of two decades before. British actor Hugh Grant, having achieved stardom in America with the release of *Four Weddings and a Funeral* in 1994, was arrested on June 27, 1995. He was found in a car in a residential section of Los Angeles receiving fellatio from a prostitute for an alleged $60. After a quick apology tour and a $1,100 fine, Grant was back at work. His hooker, Divine Brown, received an estimated $100,000 for her story initially and more than a million dollars in following years and became something of an instant celebrity. Grant's wife, famed actress Elizabeth Hurley, stayed with him for another five years before finally seeking a divorce.

Two years later, American sportscaster Marv Albert was arrested on assault, battery, and sodomy charges following an incident with

Vanessa Perhach. She claimed that after being called to Albert's hotel room to repair a fax machine, she found him in women's underwear and he bit her and forced her to perform oral sex. Albert, after initially denying the charges, eventually pled guilty to assault and battery. The sodomy charges were dropped, however, a legal development that would have been unheard of decades before.

Boxer Mike Tyson was not so lucky in his 1992 trial. Accused of raping Miss Black Rhode Island, Desiree Washington, Tyson was charged with one count of rape and two counts of criminal deviant behavior, specifically digital penetration and oral sodomy. After a lengthy trial and ten hours of deliberation, he was found guilty of all three charges, receiving lengthy sentences for each. As he later recounted regarding the oral sex count, "'On count three, I sentence you to ten years.' That was for using my tongue. For twenty minutes. It was probably a world record the longest [oral sex] performed during a rape."[5]

Rapper Tupac Shakur, already in legal trouble for a number of other reasons, became embroiled in a sexual assault case of his own in 1993. The incident began with a young woman providing oral sex to Tupac after meeting him a club only 30 minutes before. Four days later she showed up at the rapper's hotel room at the Parker Meridien in New York. The woman alleged that she was then sexually assaulted by three of Shakur's associates and later received threats from them should she press charges. The rapper was eventually found guilty, and during his time at Clinton Correctional Facility he met producer Suge Knight who ultimately bailed Tupac out in exchange for Tupac producing three albums with Knight's record company. This collaboration would eventually produce *All Eyez on Me* and *The Don Killuminati: The 7 Day Theory*, considered his seminal works.

Singer Rick James faced similar charges in 1993. In July 1991 James and his girlfriend Tanya Hijazi embarked on a week-long cocaine binge with a young woman named Frances Alley. Toward the end of the week James and Hijazi tied Alley to a chair and abused and tortured her. After burning her with both a knife and a crack pipe, James forced Alley to perform cunnilingus on his girlfriend. The two assailants were eventually found guilty on several charges, including forced oral copulation, for which James would serve three years in prison.

Political sex scandals, while certainly not new, seemed to not be the career death kneels they once were. Perhaps the most iconic example of oral sex in the 1990s and America's newfound impression of it came in the form of President William Jefferson Clinton. The young president was no stranger to risqué sexual encounters, having had a string of affairs and harassment lawsuits by the time he ran for the presidency in 1992. Perhaps tellingly, Nigel Hamilton's biography of Clinton compares the leader to Giacomo Casanova, yet Hamilton asserts that Clinton in fact went beyond the achievements of that famous cunnilictor. "Bill Clinton was, indeed, a New Man, in a different mold from the legendary Giacomo Casanova … oral sex, for Bill, was not simply a matter of being served but of serving the woman—and being rewarded for doing so."[6] From his early dalliances to his notorious Arkansas tryst with Gennifer Flowers, Bill Clinton had a penchant for both giving and receiving oral sex. Performer Minette Lehman even worked the president's love of oral sex into her show *The Tongue* in 1993.

Yet Clinton's most famous tryst, and the one which almost destroyed his presidency, happened toward the end of his first term in office. Monica Lewinsky worked as an intern and later as an employee at the White House for ten months from 1995 to 1996. On November 16, 1995, while the White House was largely deserted due to a government shutdown, Lewinsky had her first sexual encounter with President Clinton.

> While the President continued talking on the phone (Ms. Lewinsky understood that the caller was a Member of Congress or a Senator), she performed oral sex on him. He finished his call, and, a moment later, told Ms. Lewinsky to stop. In her recollection: "I told him that I wanted … to complete that. And he said … that he needed to wait until he trusted me more. And then I think he made a joke … that he hadn't had that in a long time."[7]

This relationship between the 49-year-old president and the 22-year-old intern continued over the next several months before becoming public knowledge. In the Starr Report that was released as part of the investigation, Lewinsky detailed their various liaisons. The second encounter occurred only a day later, after an impromptu birthday celebration.

Ms. Lewinsky testified that she and the President had a sexual encounter during this visit. They kissed, and the President touched Ms. Lewinsky's bare breasts with his hands and mouth. At some point, Ms. Currie approached the door leading to the hallway, which was ajar, and said that the President had a telephone call. Ms. Lewinsky recalled that the caller was a Member of Congress with a nickname. While the President was on the telephone, according to Ms. Lewinsky, "he unzipped his pants and exposed himself," and she performed oral sex. Again, he stopped her before he ejaculated.[8]

Six weeks later, on New Year's Eve, after President Clinton offered her a cigar, "they moved to the study. 'And then ... we were kissing and he lifted my sweater and exposed my breasts and was fondling them with his hands and with his mouth.' She performed oral sex. Once again, he stopped her before he ejaculated because, Ms. Lewinsky testified, 'he didn't know me well enough or he didn't trust me yet.'"[9]

A week later the president personally called Lewinsky to invite her to the White House for a weekend tryst. "Ms. Lewinsky testified that during this bathroom encounter, she and the President kissed, and he touched her bare breasts with his hands and his mouth. The President 'was talking about performing oral sex on me,' according to Ms. Lewinsky. But she stopped him because she was menstruating and he did not. Ms. Lewinsky did perform oral sex on him."[10]

Further incidents of oral sex followed on January 21, February 4, March 31, and April 7. At one point Lewinsky even presented the president with an online article which described the pleasurable effect of using Altoids during oral sex.[11] Following her transfer to the Pentagon, contact between the two was almost solely in the form of phone sex. According to her own testimony, Lewinsky became increasingly frustrated at the lack of intimacy. Their final sexual encounter, destined to become their most famous, appears to have occurred on March 24, 1997.

> And then I think I was touching him in his genital area through his pants, and I think I unbuttoned his shirt and was kissing his chest. And then.... I wanted to perform oral sex on him ... and so I did. And then.... I think he heard something, or he heard someone in the office. So, we moved into the bathroom.
> And I continued to perform oral sex and then he pushed me away, kind of as he always did before he came, and then I stood up and I said....

I care about you so much; … I don't understand why you won't let me … make you come; it's important to me; I mean, it just doesn't feel complete, it doesn't seem right.

Ms. Lewinsky testified that she and the President hugged, and "he said he didn't want to get addicted to me, and he didn't want me to get addicted to him." They looked at each other for a moment. Then, saying that "I don't want to disappoint you," the President consented. For the first time, she performed oral sex through completion.[12]

The stains that remained on the blue dress that Lewinsky was wearing that night became a central piece of evidence in the investigation that followed. Clinton was already involved in a sexual harassment suit involving Paula Jones when another government employee, Linda Tripp, released taped conversations with Lewinsky which detailed her similar encounters. The cover-up by the Clinton White House eventually boiled down to the president's own definition of "a sexual encounter." By claiming that oral sex was not sex, Clinton personally helped to usher in a new concept of sex for younger generations. Many at the time were not convinced by his logic and denials, however. The confusion of older generations of Americans was summed up in a famous quote attributed to either Barbara Bush or comedian Lenny Clarke: "Clinton lied. A man might forget where he parks or where he lives, but he never forgets oral sex, no matter how bad it is." Ironically, in making this statement, former First Lady Bush exposed her own now apparently antiquated view of oral sex as something so rare as to be remembered. The impeachment and trial before the Senate ended with a victory for the president. Perhaps the most telling social barometer was his approval rating, which appears to not have suffered during the scandal. In fact, his popularity rose during the lead-up to the trial in late 1998 before settling back to the 60 percent range where it had been since about January 1997. The president's pursuit of fellatio did not concern the public as much as conservatives and his political enemies had hoped.

Interestingly, during and immediately after the scandal, many of those who accused Clinton the most ardently were revealed to have had sexual affairs of their own. Many, including Helen Chenworth-Hage (R–Idaho), Robert Livingston (R–Louisiana), Dan Burton (R–Indiana), and Bob Barr (R–Georgia), resigned or lost primary challenges. It appears that while oral sex was becoming acceptable, regular old-fashioned sex scandals were not. To further buttress this claim, Speaker of the House Newt Gingrich, who was also one of Clinton's staunchest opponents, is alleged to have had his own oral sex affair back 1977. The woman behind it, Anne Manning, claimed that in a similar way to Clinton, Gingrich insisted on fellatio to be able to deny a sexual encounter. Once again, as had been true with Clinton, the scandal did little to derail his following Congressional or presidential runs.

Years later famed Pennsylvania artist Nelson Shanks was commissioned to produce the official Clinton presidential portrait. Praised and admired at the time of its unveiling, the artist later admitted that he had included a shadow of Monica Lewinsky's infamous blue dress to the president's right. Clinton's thrusting pelvis and pointing V-shaped fingers also hint toward this event. According to an interview with the artist, the Clintons were so upset upon discovering his hidden images that they continue to put pressure on the National Portrait Gallery to remove the painting.[13]

The pursuit of oral sex was becoming an integral part of dating, romance, and marriage. Barbara Cartland reported that it was Princess Diana's refusal to perform fellatio that pushed Prince Charles toward other women. "Of course, you know where it all went wrong. She wouldn't do oral sex."[14] Unlike Charlie Chaplin 70 years before, Prince Charles came through the episode relatively unscathed. Not all first ladies and princesses were opposed to the act, however. Eva Peron in fact rose to prominence largely due to her sexuality and alleged expertise at oral sex.[15]

In 1998, the case of *Powell v. Georgia* helped to finally remove that state's century-old sodomy law. In this instance a married man had been charged with performing non-consensual oral sex on his wife's 17-year-old niece. Though the initial count of non-consensual oral sex was dropped, Powell was convicted under the state's sodomy law. In his appeal, it was argued that as *Bowers v. Hardwick* had invalidated the law in terms of married heterosexual people, unmarried heterosexual people should enjoy the same rights. In the end, the Supreme Court of Georgia agreed and stripped the law of much of its power. Over the next five years, Washington, D.C., Maryland, Nevada, Arizona, Minnesota and Rhode Island followed suit. In fact, the few states that still had sodomy laws on the books really only had them for homosexual oral sex. This was finally addressed in the controversial Supreme Court case *Lawrence v. Texas* that was decided in 2003 which served to invalidate any remaining sodomy laws in the nation.

Perhaps nothing better exemplifies the cyclical nature of views on oral sex in Western history than the establishment of the Temple of Priapus. Founded in San Francisco in the late 1970s, it spread to Montreal, Philadelphia, and other cities, and described itself as a cult dedicated to the worship of the penis. Oral sex is not only part of the initiation process but also a component of worship services. In its form, function, and philosophy it is little different than analogous cults of ancient Egypt and Mesopotamia. In California in the 1980s, Mary Ellen Tracy founded the Church of the Most High Goddess, modeled after cults of Isis and Cybele. Tracy saw herself as a priestess in the tradition of more primitive sex-based religions. One of the main tenets of the faith was absolution through sexual activity. On her own website she states,

> In my calling as a priestess, I have sex with men of all sizes, shapes, colors, backgrounds, professions—an infinite variety—every day, several times a day (and even more often would be better). To date I've had vaginal sex with over 2,779 different men, oral sex with over 4,000 different men, and being bisexual, I have eaten a couple of hundred pussies along the way. Since I'm a very sexual person, I've had sex, not just in the religious rituals, but in a wide variety of places.... I've even sucked cocks through the open window of my car and through a hole in a wall.

Tracy was arrested in the late 1980s on prostitution charges, but argued in court that the state was infringing upon her freedom of religion. In the end the high priestess and her temple lost and she served five months in prison. Years later, she again petitioned the state, this time to allow a relaxing of anti-prostitution laws to allow her cult to start training temple prostitutes in the vein of the ancients. Once again, in the case of *Aset v. Garcetti* decided in 1996, Tracy's idea was struck down.

The idea in the West of oral sex as a practice of homosexuals and prostitutes had been largely destroyed. In fact, a 1993 French study suggested that more educated women were more likely to consent to fellatio than those who were less educated. A reason for this may be the fact that they are more likely to be supporters of the Feminist Movement and thus open to sexual experimentation while others may see it as a form of safe sex by which they can avoid pregnancy, ironically mirroring the possible reasons for the rise of the practice among ancient humans. At the same time a study by the University of Chicago concluded that around three-quarters of all men have engaged in oral sex, a number significantly higher than that reported by Kinsey a generation before. Among white men this number jumped to 81 percent while only 49 percent of black men reported performing cunnilingus.[16] The continued opposition of some black men to performing oral sex may have its roots in religion, traditional social views, or ideas of masculinity. This began to change in the early 2000s, however, as some male performers began to frequently boast in their songs that they performed oral sex on women. Most notable among these was Lil' Wayne, whose 2008 song "Pussy Monster" was an ode to cunnilingus. The artist employed traditional references to eating, phallic images of bowls, and even incorporated the connection between oral sex and vampires, before finishing in a refrain lifted directly from Sesame Street in which he compares his love of cunnilingus to Cookie Monster's predilection for cookies.

Since then other artists have begun including references to the act within their own songs. This stands in sharp contrast to the view of many men only a few short years before as expressed in an episode of "The Sopranos" in which the character Junior stated, "Because they think if you'll suck pussy, you'll suck anything.... It's a sign of weakness. And possibly a sign that you're a *fanook.*"

Oral sex has become a more common practice among teenagers as well in the last several decades. This may be due to sex education classes and concerns about abstinence, while attempts by the Sexual Revolution to depict it as "not-sex" certainly have also played a role. Finally, attempts by feminists to unshackle girls from what they perceive as traditional, patriarchal restrictions on a woman's inherent sexuality have eroded what were believed to be concerns of modesty. Urban legends of "rainbow parties" and Bar Mitzvah "receiving lines" have now become more fact than fiction. As stated in one periodical, "'It's like licking a lollipop,' one pretty girl from a prestigious girls' school said, flipping her hair in the ancient gesture of teenage certainty. 'It's no big deal.'"[17] A 2012 study conducted at a major southeastern university found that 62 percent of respondents agreed with President Bill Clinton, that oral sex was not actually sex.[18] Clearly the views of the more salacious politicians were becoming commonplace within the general population.

As increased promiscuity has led to a rise in the number of people around the world infected with sexually transmitted diseases including HIV, so too has the increase in oral sex. The misconception that it is a safer act may be a reason for this. Actor Michael Douglas became the face of HPV briefly in 2013 when he reported that his throat cancer had resulted from oral sex. "Because, without wanting to get too specific, this particular cancer is caused by HPV [human papillomavirus], which actually comes about from cunnilingus." He wasn't alone; the early 2000s saw a rapid increase in throat and mouth cancers among the general population, which some have attributed to the concurrent increase in oral sex.[19]

The popularity of oral sex has even led to open discussions on such topics as the health benefits of consuming sperm and whether the caloric content of semen harms one's diet. A book published in 2013 by Paul Photenhauer entitled *Semenology* purports to be the ultimate book for mixologists seeking to mix cocktails with semen while the same author published *Natural Harvest* in 2008 which worked sperm into various recipes. Practices that the medieval Church had fought hard to eliminate as esoteric forms of peasant magic are now being scientifically investigated.

Ironically, much of the same feminist ideology that pushed oral sex as part of sexual liberation in the 1960s and 1970s has now turned against fellatio. A popular debate among some feminist groups both in person and online in recent years has involved the question of whether performing oral sex on a man is degrading or returning to the fold of patriarchic expectations. *Esquire*, in an article published in 2012, claimed that fellatio was on its way out even among men, the vast majority of whom, claimed the author, preferred performing cunnilingus. While these statistics are doubtful, the idea that oral sex is still controversial and that its perceived general acceptance by the public is not yet a *fait accompli* remains. Two Italian lawmakers were expelled from Parliament in 2015 for directing rude oral sex gestures toward a female lawmaker.

As with many advancements, the perceived view of oral sex across the globe varies from nation to nation and culture to culture. France retains its centuries-old position as the most accepting of the practice. In fact, French film director Michel Hazanavicius highlighted the country's love of oral sex as one of the things that ISIS would never change. Rather tongue-in-cheek, he also informed terrorists, "One day, we may even name a plaza after Monica Lewinsky, and that will make us laugh."[20] As of 2017, plans were in place to open cafes in Sweden, Switzerland, and several other European nations to provide patrons with both coffee and fellatio. Conversely, nations such as India and Singapore that were historically more liberal toward the practice now have harsher laws in place thanks in part to years of Western occupation and influence during the 19th century. Oral sex is still a crime under Section 377 of the Indian Penal Code where it is described as "carnal intercourse against the order of nature, which does not carry the potential for procreation."

In perhaps the most bizarre example of the general acceptance of the practice, oral sex has entered the realm of political campaigns. In 2016 at the height of the presidential race between Donald Trump and Hillary Clinton, Madonna appeared at an event in New York City and offered to fellate anyone who voted for Clinton. "If you vote for Hillary Clinton, I will give you a blowjob. OK? I'm really good. I'm not a douche, and I'm not a tool. I take my time, I have a lot of eye contact, and I do swallow."[21] Both the offer and her pride in her abilities would have been unthinkable only two decades before. A month later, Italian model Paola Saulino made a similar promise to Italian men who voted no on a constitutional referendum. Unlike Madonna, however, Saulino pledged to fulfill her promise and by January 2017 had announced that the "Pompa Tour" would be filmed as a documentary complete with a list of cities and dates she would be visiting.

Conclusion

It is a truism in many things that exposure breeds familiarity and familiarity leads to acceptance. While oral sex may have been controversial and in many areas forbidden for 2,000 years, its increased representation in art and literature combined with a number of changing social and economic factors to create an oral sex revolution at the end of the 20th century. Perhaps due to the sheer enjoyment associated with it and the ability to do it in the privacy of one's own home, it was only a matter of time before oral sex became both socially and politically accepted. Likewise, when compared to other acts and habits that could be considered private, such as drug use or homosexuality, the practice of oral sex lacked the health-damaging effects of the former or the lifestyle-altering conditions of the latter.

The initial prohibitions against oral sex arose from a number of factors. Traditional arguments that the genesis of this ban was from sanitary concerns may bear some general, community level truth, but almost certainly would not have held true on an individual level. Early man most likely did not understand the concept of a menstrual cycle and therefore feared that the polluting aspect of a woman's genitals could occur at any time. The various references to blood and bleeding when discussing cunnilingus in early Greek, Jewish, Melanesian, and even Japanese texts seems to point to near universal acceptance of this. Yet at the same time, the lack of blood with regard to the male organ and the ability to control personal hygiene should not have completely disallowed the action on the individual level in both sexes.

Another factor playing into the ancient taboo against the practice of oral sex may have been a concern over population growth.

Oral sex, as a non-procreative act, could endanger the success of small tribes or centralized societies bent on expansion. Perhaps these groups feared that allowing people to satisfy their needs through oral sex, would discourage traditional intercourse and therefore lead to a decline in the birthrate. In a similar vein, oral sex may have been seen as something that would encourage adultery as it represented consequence-free extramarital sex, thus either breaking up families or preventing them from forming in the first place. Likewise, this general promiscuity would also increase the level of disease within society as opposed to monogamous marriages which tended to limit it. Interestingly, many of the same arguments were given to oppose the legalization and spread of birth control and contraceptives in the latter half of the 19th century as well.

Opposition to oral sex may have been more of the exception than the rule, with only the followers of monotheistic religions and philosophies based upon higher morality following suit. A desire to purify one's spirit and avoid the worship of bodily pleasures in exchange for spiritual ones led Judaism, Christianity, Platonists, Buddhism, Islam, and Confucianism to shy away from the practice, as they did all other forms of extreme self-indulgence. The later predominance of the belief then simply came about due to the successful spread of Christianity and Islam as well as Western cultural imperialism. Thus the return to an acceptance of oral sex was in turn a rejection of Catholicism and traditional Greco-Roman values. The Protestant Reformation clearly began this slow process, challenging ideas of celibacy and empowering the community to decide morality.

In a similar vein, the connection of the practice with homosexuality certainly also played a role in societal perceptions. This is clearly evident in both Roman epigrams where the two are often conflated as well as the common European practice of referring to all of these acts as sodomy with regards to the law for centuries. Though not specifically concerned with homosexual practices, ancient Chinese concepts of yin and yang and the proper transference of vital energy would fit into this category of argument as well.

Regardless of the origins of the opposition to oral sex, it was a curtain wall of prohibition that attempted to hold back human nature.

Especially in the West, the emergence of new religious sects and philosophical trends began to challenge what was seen as traditional, Catholic opposition to the practice. The Humanism of the Renaissance and the Protestant Reformation both began this slow process, challenging ideas of celibacy and empowering the community to decide morality. The concepts of the Enlightenment and the onset of modernity further pushed moral relativism to the fore, while art, literature, music, and movies brought oral sex to an ever wider audience and transformed counterculture into accepted culture.

At the same time the wide acceptance gap between fellatio and cunnilingus has narrowed to an almost indistinguishable point. The dream of Lilith has in effect been realized; the near equality of the sexes in sexuality. Yet part of this equality has come from the desexualization of the act itself. Oral sex has in many ways been denuded of its association with outlawed, borderline, or risky behavior and has now reached the point of being considered almost passé by the younger generation. Certainly, fears of acquiring STDs from traditional intercourse, as frequently touted by modern health instruction classes, may have inadvertently steered more young people towards the belief that oral sex is safer, or at the very least that it eliminates the possibility of pregnancy. In a similar vein, poorer but better informed people may be utilizing the practice in poverty stricken regions as a form of family planning, while those elites concerned with overcrowding of countries and the planet may be pushing it as well.

What does this drastic sea change in the view of sex in general, and oral sex in particular, hold for the modern world? An argument can be made that, when combined with the increased usage of contraceptives, the rate of teenage and unplanned pregnancies should decline. Overall, a more vigorous adoption of oral sex would decrease the birth rate of a nation, though this would negatively impact the economic and military capacity of the state in the long run. Likewise, unprotected oral sex has led to an increase in STD rates in numerous nations, with many youths mistakenly thinking the practice to be safer than sex. At the same time, there remains the age old fear of oral sex as a gateway activity which would invariably lead young people towards partaking in regular intercourse as well.

The normalization of oral sex may also be connected with the increased acceptance of homosexuality in Western society. This is most likely associated through one of two avenues of thought. As it was largely seen as an act associated with homosexuals, the general acceptance of the former would naturally lead to an increased familiarity of the latter. Likewise, it would be difficult to acknowledge one form of sexuality which was formerly viewed as unnatural and not another. The cultural movement of the West towards treating sex as an act for pleasure as opposed to solely for reproduction has ushered in the normalization of various forms of love frowned upon in many societies for thousands of years.

Oral sex as a practice has largely come full circle since the evolution of man. Paleolithic and Neolithic man, if he so desired to, freely practiced both fellatio and cunnilingus. Only the advent of religion, philosophy, and societal norms began the slow repression of his normal, anarchic sexual state. A reborn focus on the individual and his own physical interests surpassing those of society and the state in the modern world have now reversed that trend. Likewise, the slow death of religion and spirituality have also removed a strong barrier to the practice of oral sex. It is now more of a truism than ever, that everyone is doing it, though the long-term effect of this has yet to be seen.

Chapter Notes

Introduction

1. William Shakespeare, *Hamlet*, Act III, Scene II.

2. Min Tan, et al., "Fellatio by Fruit Bats Prolongs Copulation Time," *PLoS ONE* 4, no. 10 (Oct. 2009).

3. Jayabalan Maruthupandian, et al., "Cunnilingus Apparently Increases Duration of Copulation in the Indian Flying Fox, Pteropus giganteus," *PLoS ONE* 8, no. 3 (March 2013).

4. Oppian, *Cynegetica*, Book III, 139.

5. Ovid, *Metamorphosis*, Book XV, 408.

6. Kay Holekamp, "How Spotted Hyenas Mate," *New York Times*, July 19, 2011.

7. William B. Eberhard, *Female Control: Sexual Selection by Cryptic Female Choice* (Princeton: Princeton University Press, 1996), 213.

8. George Schaller, *The Mountain Gorilla: Ecology and Behavior* (American Anthropological Association, 1963).

9. Clellan Ford and Frank A. Beach, *Patterns of Sexual Behavior* (New York: Harper & Row, 1951).

10. Natalie Angier, *Woman: An Intimate Geography* (New York: Houghton Mifflin Harcourt, 1999), 68. See also Joseph H. Manson, et al., "Nonconceptive Sexual Behavior in Bonobos and Capuchins," *International Journal of Primatology* 18, no. 5 (Oct. 1997), 767–786.

11. Agnieszka Sergiel, et al., "Fellatio in Captive Brown Dears: Evidence of Long-Term Effects of Suckling Deprivation?" *Zoo Biology* 33, no. 4 (July 2014), 349–352.

12. Michael N. Pham, "Oral-Sex as Infidelity Detection," *Personality and Individual Differences* 54, no. 6 (April 2013), 792–795.

13. R.R. Baker, *Sperm Wars* (London: Fourth Estate, 1996).

14. R.R. Baker and M.A. Bellis, *Human Sperm Competition: Copulation, Masturbation, and Infidelity* (New York: Springer, 1994).

15. Sigmund Freud, "Leonardo da Vinci and a Memory of his Childhood," 1910.

16. Ada Lampert, *The Evolution of Love* (Westport, CT: Greenwood, 1997), 62.

Chapter 1

1. Rebecca Newman, "Heads You Win," *GQ*, March 29, 2012.

2. Jonathan Margolis, *O: The Intimate History of the Orgasm* (New York: Grove Press, 2005), 36.

3. Sven Sandstrom, "Images from La Marche Cave: Paleolithic Art or Recent Fakes?" *Journal of Swedish Antiquarian Research* 110 (2015), 1–9.

4. David F. Greenberg, *The Construction of Homosexuality* (Chicago: University of Chicago Press, 2008), 34.

5. Jerome Burne, "Out of Ice Age with Oral Sex," *The Observer*, Aug. 3, 1997.

6. J.C. Culberston, *Cincinnati Lancet and Clinic* 35 (1895), 354.

7. Plutarch, *Isis and Osiris*, in E.A. Wallis Budge, *Legends of the Gods* (London: Kegan Paul, Trench, and Trubner, 1912), 226.

8. See Algernon Herbert, *Nimrod: A Discourse on Certain Passages of History and Fable*, Vol. 1 (R. Priestly, 1828).

9. Book of the Dead, Chapter CXXV.

10. Robert S. Morton, "Sexual Attitudes, Preferences, and Infections in Ancient Egypt," *Genitourin Med* 71 (1995), 183.

11. Ilan Ben Zion, "4000 Year Old Erotica Depicts a Strikingly Racy Ancient Sexuality," *The Times of Israel*, Feb. 19, 2015.

12. David F. Greenberg, *The Construction of Homosexuality* (Chicago: University of Chicago Press, 1990), 97, 126.

13. Herbert Mason, trans., *Gilgamesh* from *Gilgamesh: A Verse Narrative* (New York: Houghton Mifflin Harcourt, 2003), 18.

14. Harry Benjamin and R.E.L. Masters, *Prostitution and Morality* (New York: The Julian Press, 1964), 58.

15. Diane Wolkstein and Samuel Kramer, *Inanna: Queen of Heaven and Earth: Her Stories and Hymns from Sumer* (New York: Harper & Row, 1817), 14.

16. James Neill, *The Origins and Role of Same-Sex Relations in Human Societies* (Jefferson, NC: McFarland, 2011), 97.

17. B. Alster, "Sumerian Love Songs," *Recontre Assyriologique Internationale* 79 (1985), 131.

18. Nathanael J. Andrade, *Syrian Identity in the Greco-Roman World* (Cambridge: Cambridge University Press, 2013), 257.

19. *Myths and Tales of the Chiricahua Apache* (Lincoln: University of Nebraska Press, 1942), 70.

20. Leviticus 18:19.

21. Alphabet of Ben Sirach, 23.

22. Ronald Veenker, "Forbidden Fruit: Ancient Near Eastern Sexual Metaphors," *HUCA* 70–71 (1999–2000), 57.

23. Genesis 3:2–3.

24. Daniel Chanan Matt, ed., *The Zohar*, Vol. 1, 1:66b (Stanford: Stanford University Press, 2004), 389.

25. *Ibid.*, note 366.

26. Genesis 9:20–9:25.

27. Alphabet of Ben Sirach, 18.

28. Philip Noble, "A New Hite Report—About Men," *New York Magazine*, June 15, 1981, 34.

29. Leviticus 18:3.

30. Richard W. Redding, "The Pig and the Chicken in the Middle East: Modeling Human Subsistence Behavior in the Archaeological Record Using Historical and Animal Husbandry Data," *Journal of Archaeological Research* 23, no. 4 (Dec. 2015), 325–368.

31. Genesis 19:4–7.

32. John Milton, *Samson Agonistes*, 532–552.

33. Kallah Rabbah, Chapter 1.

34. Shulchan Aruch, Orach Chaim, Section 240.4.

35. Shulchan Aruch, Even Ha-ezer, Section 25.

36. Babylonian Talmud, Nedarim 20b.

37. Maimonides, *De'ot* 5:4.

Chapter 2

1. Martin Kilmer, *Greek Erotica* (New York: Duckworth, 1993), 58, 71–72, 114, 123.

2. Aeschylus, *The Suppliant Maidens*, 17.

3. *Ibid.*, 40.

4. *Ibid.*, 531.

5. Diogenes Laertius, *The Lives of the Eminent Philosophers*, Book VII, trans. Robert Drew Hicks (Loeb, 1925), 187–188.

6. Camille Paglia, *Sexual Personae: Art and Decadence from Nefertiti to Emily Dickinson*, Vol. 1 (New York: Vintage, 1991), 95.

7. Herodotus, *Histories*, Book II, Chapter 42.

8. Ovid, *Metamorphosis*, Book X, lines 83–85, trans. A.S. Kline, 2000.

9. *Ibid.*, Book XI, lines 1–66.

10. Friedrich Karl Forberg, *Manual of Classical Erotology* (Manchester, 1884), 101–102.

11. Plato, *The Symposium*, 215.

12. Laertius, Book VIII, line 28.

13. R. B. Onians, *The Origins of European Thought* (Cambridge: Cambridge University Press, 2015), 203, and Aristotle, *Generation of Animals*, VIII, 747(a).

14. Heather White, "Notes on Palladas," *Myrtia* 13 (1998), 225–230.

15. C. Carey, "Archilochus and Lycambes," *The Classical Quarterly* 36, no. 1 (1986), 60–67. Quote from Fragment 42 of Archilochus' works.

16. Fragment 21 of Hipponax.

17. Aristophanes, *The Wasps*.

18. Aristophanes, *Ecclesiazusae*, 845–846.

19. Aristophanes, *The Knights*, 1283–1286.

20. Aeschines, *On the Embassy*, 2.23.

21. *Ibid.*, 2.88.

22. Plato, *The Symposium*, 214–215.

23. Livy, *The History of Rome*, Book I, Chapter 57, line 10.

24. Antonio Varone, *Erotica Pompeiana: Love Inscriptions on the Walls of Pompeii* (Rome: L'Erma di Bretschneider, 2002), 81.

25. Paul R. Abramson, *Sexual Nature, Sexual Culture* (Chicago: University of Chicago Press, 1995), 227.

26. Catullus, Poem 56.

27. Priapea, Poem 13.

28. *Ibid.*, Poem 30.

29. Martial, II, 47.

30. Ausonius, Epigram LXXVI.

31. Juvenal, *Apophras*, Chapter 26.

32. Juvenal, *Satires*, Number II, line 49.

33. Plautus, *Amphitryon*, lines 348–349.

34. Plautus, *Casina*, line 362.

35. Terence, *Adelphoe*, line 215.

36. Terence, *Hecyra*, lines 95–96.

37. Lucian, *Pseudologist Opera*, Chapter VIII.

38. Seneca, *Naturales quaestiones*, Book I, 16.

39. Martial, I, 94.

40. *Ibid.*, III, 81.

41. *Ibid.*, III, 88.

42. *Ibid.*, III, 96.

43. *Ibid.*, VI, 26.

44. Lucia Floridi, "The Language of Greek Skoptic Epigram of the I–II Centuries AD," in Evina Sistakou, ed., *Dialect, Diction, and Style in Greek Literary and Inscribed Epigram* (Berlin: Walter de Gruyter, 2016), 85–86.

45. Martial, IX, 67.

46. Catullus, Poem 2.

47. Horace, Epode 8.

48. Gaius Petronius, *Satyricon*, XXVI.

49. Paul Meyboom, et al., "The Meaning of Dwarfs in Nilotic Scenes," *Nile into Tiber: Egypt in the Roman World, Religions in the Greco-Roman World* 159 (2006), 170–208.

50. Apuleius, *Metamorphosis*, Book VIII, paragraph 26–27.

51. Martial, III, 81.

52. William Shakespeare, *Anthony and Cleopatra*, Act IV, Scene XV, line 40.

53. Plutach, *Lives*, XXXII.

54. Suetonius, *Twelve Caesars*, 22.2.

55. Seneca, *De Beneficiis*, II, 21.

56. Plutarch, *Life of Crassus*, 32.

57. Cicero, *On His House*, Section 25.

58. Eva Cantarella, *Bisexuality in the Ancient World* (New Haven: Yale University Press, 2002), 159.

59. Suetonius, *Tiberius*, 45.

60. *Ibid.*

61. *Ibid.*, 44.1.

62. Seneca the Younger, *On Benefits*, Book IV, Chapter 31.

63. *Ibid.*, Book I, Chapter 9.

64. Juvenal, *Satire* VI, 114–135.

65. Pliny, *Natural History*, Book X, Chapter 83.

66. Tacitius, *Annals*, Book VI.

67. *Ibid.*

68. Sulpicia, *Complaint*, 35–36.

69. Martial, VI, 91.

70. Martal references Zoilus' preference for oral sex in Book XI, Epigram 30: "Vilely smells, you say, the breath of lawyers, and of poets. But that of a fellator, Zoilus, smells worse!"

71. Martial, III, 82.

Chapter 3

1. Artemidorus of Ephesus, *Dream Analysis*, 79.14.

2. Lucretius, *De Rerum Natura*, Book IV, 1173–1175.

3. Boethius, *Consolation of Philosophy*, Prose I.

4. Epistle of Barnabas, 10:7–8.

5. Tertullian, *Apologeticum*, Chapter 9, 32.

6. Camille Paglia, *Sexual Personae: Art and Decadence from Nefertiti to Emily Dickinson*, Vol. 1 (New York: Vintage, 1991), 95.

7. St. Augustine, *Of the Good of Marriage*, Section 11.

8. St. Augustine, *Contra Faustum Manichaeum*, 22.30.

9. Epiphanius, *Panarion*, Book I, Section 25, 3.2.

10. Origen, *Contra Celsus*, Book VI, Chapter 35.

11. Epiphanius, Panarion, Book I, Section 26, 3.3

12. *Ibid.*, 3.6.

13. *Ibid.*, 4.5–5.3.

14. *Ibid.*, 5.5.

15. Penitential of Theodore, S75.04.01.

16. *Ibid.*

17. *Ibid.*

18. St. Thomas Aquinas, *Summa Theologica I*, Part II, Question 154, Article 11.

19. Quoted in W. Pinar, *Race, Religion,*

and a Curriculum of Reparation: Teacher Education for a Multicultural Society (New York: Springer, 2006), 81.

20. Thomas Balsamon, quoted in Patrick Viscuso, "Theodore Balsamon's Canonical Images of Women," *Greek, Roman, and Byzantine Studies* 45 (2005), 323.

21. Eve Levin, *Sex and Society in the World of the Orthodox Slavs* (Ithaca: Cornell University Press, 1995), 175.

22. Procopius, *Secret History*, 102–103.

23. Oswald von Wolkenstein, Kl 20.

24. Heinrich Wittenwiler, *The Ring*, line 2151.

25. Geoffrey Chaucer, *The Miller's Tale*, lines 3735–3739.

26. Nathaniel E. Dubin, *The Fabliaux* (New York: W.W. Norton, 2013), 3.

27. *Ljosavandsfolkenes Saga*, quoted in Vern L. Bullough, *Handbook of Medieval Sexuality* (New York: Taylor and Francis, 1996), 386.

28. Rosemary Ellen Guiley, *The Encyclopedia of Witches, Witchcraft, and Wicca*, 3d ed. (New York: Facts on File, 2008), 95.

29. Thomas Wright, *Worship of the Generative Powers: During the Middle Ages in Western Europe* (1865), 130–132.

Chapter 4

1. Murad Sayfuddin, *Love and Sex in Islam* (Ansar Publishing House, 2004), 42–43.

2. James A. Bellamy, "Sex and Society in Islamic Popular Literature" in Afaf Marsot, ed., *Society and the Sexes in Medieval Islam* (Malibu: Udena, 1979), 34.

3. David W. Machacek, *Sexuality and the World's Religions* (Santa Barbara: ABC-CLIO, 2003), 266

4. Dante, *Inferno*, Canto XXVIII.

5. Otfried Lieberknecht, "A Medieval Christian View of Islam: Dante's Encounter with Mohammed in Inferno XXVIII," Lecture, University of Minnesota, Minneapolis (May 14, 1997).

6. *Kama Sutra*, Part II, Chapter IX, 1.

7. *Mahabharata*, Book 3, chapters 186–187.

8. Gudrun Buhnemann, "Erotic Forms of Ganesa in Hindu and Buddhist Iconography," in Adalbert J. Gail, ed., *Script and Image: Papers on Art and Iconography* (Delhi: Motilal Publishing, 2006), 20–21.

9. Glen Alexander Hayes, *Kiss of the Yogini: "Tantric Sex" in its South Asian Context* (Chicago: University of Chicago Press, 2003).

10. Peter A. Jackson, "Non-Normative Sex/Gender Categories in the Theravada Buddhist Scriptures," *Australian Humanities Review* (April 1996).

11. *The Upaska Sutta* in Carl Olson, *Celibacy and Religious Traditions* (New York: Oxford University Press, 2007).

12. Johann Meyer, *Sexual Life in Ancient India*, Vol. 2 (New York: Routledge, 1953), 241–242.

13. Craig A. Hill, *Human Sexuality: Personality and Social Psychological Perspectives* (Los Angeles: Sage, 2008), 50.

14. Rania Huntington, "Foxes and Sex in Late Imperial Chinese Narratives," *Nan Nu* 2, no. 1 (Jan. 2000), 78–128, note 32.

15. "The Handbook of the Plain Girl," in Hsi Lai, *The Sexual Teachings of the Jade Dragon: Daoist Methods for Male Sexual Revitalization* (Rochester: Destiny Books, 2002).

16. See John Weakland, "Orality in Chinese Conceptions of Male Genital Sexuality," *Psychiatry* (1956).

17. *Book of Rites*, Book VII, Section II, line 20.

18. Allen Edwardes and R.E.L. Masters, *The Cradle of Erotica* (New York: The Julian Press, 1962).

19. Walter Edwards, *Modern Japan Through Its Weddings: Gender, Person, and Society in Ritual Portrayal* (Stanford: Stanford University Press, 1990), 111.

20. Gary Leupp, *Male Colors: The Construction of Homosexuality in Tokugawa Japan* (Berkeley: University of California Press, 1997), 109.

21. *Ibid.*, 121.

22. Gilbert Herdt, *Rituals of Manhood: Male Initiation in Papua New Guinea* (Berkeley: University of California Press, 1982), 46.

23. *Ibid.*, 61.

24. Gilbert Herdt, "Sexing Anthropology," in David N. Suggs, ed., *Culture, Biology, and Sexuality*, Southern Anthropological Society Proceedings 32 (Athens: University of Georgia Press, 1999), 20.

25. Donald Tuzin, *The Cassowary's Revenge* (Chicago: University of Chicago Press, 1997), 165.

26. James Neil, *The Origins and Role of Same-Sex Relations in Human Societies* (Jefferson, NC: Mcfarland, 2011), 41.

27. William Bligh, *Journal* (1789), II: 16–17.

28. Quoted in Douglas Oliver, *Polynesia in Early Historic Times* (Honolulu: Bess Press, 2002), 130.

29. R.J. Morris, "Aikane: Accounts of Hawaiian Same-Sex Relationships in the Journals of Captain Cook's Third Voyage," *Journal of Homosexuality* 19, no. 4 (1990), 21–54.

30. Janet Hyde, *Understanding Human Sexuality*, 9th ed. (Boston: McGraw Hill, 2006), 10–11.

31. Iwan Bloch, *Anthropological Studies on the Strange Sexual Practices of All Races and All Ages* (Honolulu: University Press of the Pacific, 2001), 62.

32. Mary Weismantel, "Moche Sex Pots: Reproduction and Temporality in Ancient South America," *American Anthropologist* 106, no. 3 (Sept. 2004), 496.

33. Iwan Bloch, *Anthropological Studies on the Strange Sexual Practices of All Races and All Ages* (Honolulu: University Press of the Pacific, 2001), 48.

34. Michael D. Jackson, *The Palm at the End of the Mind: Relatedness, Religiosity, and the Real* (Durham: Duke University Press, 2009), 220.

Chapter 5

1. Paul R. Abramson, *Sexual Nature, Sexual Culture* (Chicago: University of Chicago Press, 1995), 233.

2. Giovanni Boccaccio, *Decameron*, Day 1, Tale 10.

3. Pietro Aretino, *Lettere*, Vol. I (Rome: Salerno Press, 1997), 425.

4. Quoted in Patricia Simons, *The Sex of Men in Premodern Europe* (Cambridge: Cambridge University Press, 2011), 264.

5. Deivis de Campos, et al., "The Hidden Symbols of Female Anatomy in Michelangelo Buonarroti's Ceiling in the Sistine Chapel," *Clinical Anatomy* 29, no. 7 (Oct. 2016), 911–916.

6. *Ibid.*, 201.

7. Heinrich Kramer, *Malleus Maleficarum*, Part I, Question IV.

8. Brain P. Levack, *The Witchcraft Sourcebook*, 2d ed. (New York: Routledge, 2003)

9. *Ibid.*, and Marcus Harmes, *Supernatural and Secular Power in Early Modern England* (Farnham, England: Ashgate, 2015), 218.

10. Henry Kamen, *Inquisition and Society in Spain in the Sixteenth and Seventeenth Centuries* (Bloomington: Indiana University Press, 1985), 207–208.

11. Franco Mormando, *The Preacher's Demons* (Chicago: University of Chicago Press, 1999), 129.

12. William L. Sherman, *Forced Native Labor in 16 century Central America* (Lincoln: University of Nebraska Press, 1979), 20.

13. Luisa Sigea de Velasco, *The School of Women*, Dialogue VII quoted in Friedrich Karl Forberg, *Manual of Classic Erotology* (Manchester, 1884), 123–124.

14. *Ibid.*, 126.

15. James T. Henke, *Courtesans and Cuckolds: A Glossary of Renaissance Dramatic Bawdy* (New York: Garland, 1979), 277.

16. *Le Livre de Yconomique d'Aristotle*, critical edition of French text with English translation and introduction by Albert Douglas Menut, in Transactions of the American Philosophical Society, New Series 47, part 5 (Philadelphia, 1957), 796.

17. Judith M. Bennett, "'Lesbian-Like' and the Social History of Lesbianisms," *Journal of the History of Sexuality* 9, no. 1–2 (Jan./April 2000), 8.

18. John Witte, Jr., *Sex, Marriage, and Family in John Calvin's Geneva: Courtship, Engagement, and Marriage* (Grand Rapids: W.B. Eerdmans, 2005), 325.

19. Hans Grimmelshausen, *The Adventurous Simplicissimus* (London: William Heinemann, 1912), 51.

20. Desiderius Erasmus, *Adages*, III, VII, 70, trans. Denis Drysdall (Toronto: University of Toronto Press, 2005), 260.

21. William Shakespeare, *Venus and Adonis*.

22. William Shakespeare, *1 Henry VI*, Act II, Scene IV, line 79.

23. William Shakespeare, *2 Henry VI*, Act IV, Scene I, lines 104–111.

24. Thomas Carew, "A Rapture."

25. John Donne, "Love's Progress."

26. Wolfgang Rudat, "Milton, Freud, St. Augustine: *Paradise Lost* and the History of Human Sexuality," *Mosaic XV* (1982), 109–122, and John Savoie, "'That Fallacious Fruit': Lapsarian Lovemaking in *Paradise Lost*," *Milton Quarterly* 45, no. 3 (2011), 161–171.

27. John Milton, *Samson Agonistes*, 534–537.

28. John Wilmot, "The Imperfect Enjoyment."

29. Robert Gould, *Love Given O'er*.

30. Lindsey Davis, *Rebels and Traitors* (New York: Macmillan, 2010), 460.

31. Peter Marshall, *The Magic Circle of Rudolf II: Alchemy and Astrology in Renaissance Prague* (New York: Bloomsbury, 2009), 49.

Chapter 6

1. From *Justine* in Iwan Bloch, *Marquis de Sade: His Life and Works* (Amsterdam: Fredonia Books, 2002), 192.

2. *Ibid.*, 187.

3. Marquis de Sade, *The 120 Days of Sodom*, 93.

4. *Ibid.*, 133.

5. *Ibid.*

6. Marquis de Sade, *Philosophy in the Bedroom*, 18–19.

7. Giacomo Casanova, *History of My Life*, 299.

8. Giacomo Casanova, *The Complete Memoires* (London, 1894).

9. Legman, *The Limerick* (1969), 289.

10. John Cleland, *Fanny Hill* (1749), 80–81.

11. Letter, Napoleon Bonaparte to Josephine Bonaparte, Nov. 21, 1796.

12. Andrei Pop, *Antiquity, Theater, and the Painting of Henry Fuseli* (New York: Oxford University Press, 2015), note 90.

13. Alfred de Musset, *Gamiana* (Quebec: La Bibliothèque électronique du Québec), 50

14. Lord Byron, *Don Juan*, VI, 27.

15. Percy Bysshe Shelley, "Fragment: Supposed to be an Epithalamium of Francis Ravaillac and Charlotte Corday."

16. James Bieri, *Percy Bysshe Shelley: A Biography* (Baltimore: Johns Hopkins University Press, 2008), 126.

17. William Blake, *Milton*, 22.12.

18. *The Pearl*, Vol. I.

19. Robert Brownell, *Marriage of Inconvenience* (New York: Pallas Athene, 2013).

20. Ruth Smythers, *Marriage & Love: Instructions for Females on Courtship and Matrimony, with Tips to Discourage Sexual Advances from Husbands* (Guilford, CT: Lyons Press, 1894), 45.

21. Bruce Seymour, *Lola Montez: A Life* (New Haven: Yale University Press, 1998), 152.

22. Quoted in Jonathan Ned Katz, *Gay/Lesbian Almanac* (New York: Harper & Row, 1983), 92–93.

23. Letter, Oscar Wilde to Robert Ross, quoted in Richard Ellmann, *Oscar Wilde* (New York: Knopf, 1988), 385.

24. Transcript of Wilde,s trial, published online by University of Missouri–Kansas City Law School.

25. John Francis Bloxam, "The Priest and the Acolyte," *The Chameleon* (Dec. 1894).

26. Henry James, *The Figure in the Carpet*, Chapter XI.

27. *Ibid.*, Chapter VII.

28. John Harvey Kellogg, *Plain Facts for Old and Young* (Burlington, IA: Segner and Condit, 1881).

29. See Diane Mason, *The Secret Vice: Masturbation in Victorian Fiction and Medical Literature* (Manchester: Manchester University Press, 2008), and Oscar Wilde, *Teleny*, 45.

30. Sigmund Freud, "Leonardo da Vinci and a Memory of His Childhood," 1910.

31. Bernard Simon Talmey, *Woman: A Treatise on the Normal and Pathological Emotions of Feminine Love* (New York: Practitioner's Publishing Company, 1908), 140.

32. *Ibid.*, 158.

33. *Ibid.*, 145.

34. Katherine Ramsland, "Abuse of Corpse," *Psychology Today*, Nov. 27, 2012.

35. Julie Peakmen, *The Pleasure's All Mine: A History of Perverse Sex* (London: Reaktion Books, 2013), 368.

36. Richard Krafft-Ebing, *Psychopathia Sexualis* (London: F.A. Davis Company, 1894), 403.

37. Allan McLane Hamilton, *A System of Legal Medicine*, Vol. 1 (New York: E.B. Treat, 1894), 652.

38. J.C. Culberston, *Cincinnati Lancet and Clinic* 35 (Cincinnati, 1895), 354.

39. Found in Jeffrey Paul Melnick, *Black-Jewish Relations on Trial: Leo Frank and Jim Conley in the New South* (Jackson: University Press of Mississippi, 2012), 71.

Chapter 7

1. Tony Perrottet, "Paris for Perverts," *Slate*, May 13, 2011, http://www.slate.com/articles/life/welltraveled/features/2011/paris_for_perverts/remains_of_the_love_trade.html.

2. Quoted in Leigh Eric Schmidt, *Heaven's Bride: The Unspeakable Life of Ida Craddock* (New York: Basic Books, 2010), 162.

3. Clea Caulcutt, "Felix Faure—A Victim of Cupid in the Elysee Palace," *Radio France Internationale*, March 4, 2011.

4. Irene Gammel, *Baroness Elsa: Gender, Dada, and Everyday Modernity—A Cultural Biography* (Cambridge: MIT Press, 2003), 247.

5. Alistair Crowley, *The Book of Lies* (New York: Samuel Weiser, 1986), 147.

6. Klaus Martens, *Pioneering North America: Mediators of European Culture and Literature* (Konigshausen, 2000), 129.

7. Theodoor van de Velde, *The Perfect Marriage* (New York: Random House, 1986), 169.

8. *Ibid.*, 170.

9. *Ibid.*

10. *Ibid.*, 171.

11. *Ibid.*

12. Philip Thody, *Don't Do It! A Dictionary of the Forbidden* (New York: St. Martin's Press, 1997), 60.

13. Max Ernst, "Hands Off Love," *La Revolution Surrealiste* 9–10 (Oct. 1927), 2.

14. Irving Wallace, *The Intimate Sex Lives of Famous People* (Port Townsend: Feral Books, 2008), 68.

15. Gregory William Mank, *Hollywood's Hellfire Club* (New York: Feral House, 2007), 269.

16. Tyler S. Smith, *Whore Stories: A Revealing History of the World's Oldest Profession* (Avon, MA: Adams Media, 2012), 164.

17. Axel Madsen, *The Sewing Circle: Hollywood's Greatest Secret* (New York: Birch Lane Press, 1994).

18. Darwin Potter, *Katharine the Great: Secrets of a Lifetime Revealed* (Blood Moon Production, 2004), 347.

19. *Ibid.*

20. *Ibid.*, 243.

21. Darwin Potter, *The Secret Life of Humphrey Bogart: The Early Years* (Blood Moon Productions, 2003), 148.

22. Christopher Hawtree, "Paul Novak," *The Guardian*, July 21, 1999.

23. Wallace, 38.

24. Potter, 220.

25. Jonathan Alter, *The Defining Moment: FDR's Hundred Days and the Triumph of Hope* (New York: Simon & Schuster, 2006), 48.

26. "Challenged," *The Logan Republican*, Sept. 16, 1920, 2.

27. "McAllister Jury Retires," *Morning Oregonian*, Feb. 22, 1913, 4.

28. Alfred Kinsey, *Sexual Behavior in the Human Male* (1948), 370.

29. *Ibid.*, 578.

30. Joan Garrity, *The Sensuous Woman* (New York: Dell, 1971), 123.

31. Darwin Porter and Danforth Prince, *Jacqueline Kennedy Onassis: A Life Beyond Her Wildest Dreams* (Blood Moon Productions, 2014).

32. Mimi Alford, *Once Upon a Secret: My Affair with President John F. Kennedy and Its Aftermath* (New York: Random House, 2012), 102.

33. Todd S. Purdum, "Sex in the Senate," *Politico*, Nov. 19, 2013.

34. Michael John Sullivan, *Presidential Passions* (New York: SPI Books, 1991), 37.

35. Tracy McVeigh, "Love Me Tender," *The Guardian*, Aug. 11, 2002.

36. As quoted in Caroline Howe, "Elvis' Sex Secrets Exposed," *Daily Mail*, Nov. 17, 2014.

37. Frank Walker, "Philandering Dictator Added Hollywood Stars to Conquests," *The Sydney Morning Herald*, July 4, 2004.

38. John Garrity, *The Sensuous Woman* (New York: Dell, 1971), 116.

39. *Ibid.*

40. *Ibid.*, 119.

41. *Ibid.*, 122.

42. Elly Brinkley, "The Still Untold

Story of Linda Lovelace," *The Wall Street Journal*, Aug. 8, 2013.

43. Michael Hiltzik, "'Deep Throat' Numbers Just Don't Add Up," *Los Angeles Times*, Feb. 24, 2005.

44. Bruce Weber, "Joel J. Tyler, Judge Who Pronounced 'Deep Throat' Obscene, Dies at 90," *New York Times*, Jan. 14, 2012.

45. Quoted in Sarah Schulman, "The History of the Commie-Pinko-Faggot," *Womanews* (July/Aug. 1980), 1.

46. Tyler S. Smith, *Whore Stories: A Revealing History of the World's Oldest Profession* (Avon, MA: Adams Media, 2012), 138.

Chapter 8

1. Tanya Pikula, "Bram Stoker's *Dracula* and Late-Victorian Advertising Tactics: Earnest Men, Virtuous Ladies, and Porn," *English Literature in Translation 1880–1920* 55, no. 3 (2012), 283–302.

2. Camille Paglia, *Sexual Personae: Art and Decadence from Nefertiti to Emily Dickinson*, Vol. 1 (New York: Vintage, 1991), 95.

3. Elizabeth Kolbert, "Television; What's a Network TV Censor to Do?" *New York Times*, May 23, 1993.

4. Stephanie Zacharek, "The Hills Are Alive with the Sound of … Vampire Slaying!" *Salon*, Nov. 7, 2001.

5. Mike Tyson, "'I was ferocious': Mike Tyson Talks Candidly About His Darkest Hour," *USA Today Online*, Nov. 12, 2013.

6. Nigel Hamilton, *Bill Clinton: An American Journey: Great Expectations* (New York: Random House, 2003), 316.

7. "The Starr Report," II, B.

8. *Ibid.*, II, D.

9. *Ibid.*, II, E.

10. *Ibid.*, III, A.

11. Cullen Murphy, *God's Jury: The Inquisition and the Making of the Modern World* (Boston: Mariner Books, 2013), 62.

12. "The Starr Report," VI, D.

13. "Painter Says He Included Monica Lewinsky's Dress in Bill Clintn Portrait," Philly.com, March 2, 2015.

14. As quoted in John Lanchester, "The Naked and the Dead," *The New Yorker*, June 25, 2007.

15. Wallace, 381.

16. Felicity Barringer, "Sex Survey of American Men Find 1% are Gay," *New York Times*, April 15, 1993.

17. Caitlin Flanagan, "Are You There God? It's Me, Monica," *The Atlantic* (Jan./Feb. 2006).

18. Kylie P. Dotson-Blake, "Exploring Social Sexual Scripts Related to Oral Sex," *The Professional Counselor* 2, no. 1 (Feb. 2012), 1–11.

19. Deborah Kotz, "Throat Cancer and Oral Sex," *Boston Globe*, June 10, 2013.

20. Alex Ritman, "Paris Attacks: Michel Hazanavicius Pens Sexually Explicit Open Letter to ISIS," *Hollywood Reporter*, Nov. 18, 2015.

21. Cole Delbyck, "Madonna Opens Amy Schumer's Stand-Up Show By Offering Blow Jobs to Hillary Voters," *Huffington Post*, Oct. 19, 2016.

Bibliography

Abramson, Paul R. *Sexual Nature, Sexual Culture*. Chicago: University of Chicago Press, 1995.

Alford, Mimi. *Once Upon a Secret: My Affair with President John F. Kennedy and Its Aftermath*. New York: Random House, 2012.

Alster, B. "Sumerian Love Songs." *Recontre Assyriologique Internationale* 79 (1985), 131.

Alter, Jonathan. *The Defining Moment: FDR's Hundred Days and the Triumph of Hope*. New York: Simon & Schuster, 2006.

Andrade, Nathanael J. *Syrian Identity in the Greco-Roman World*. Cambridge: Cambridge University Press, 2013.

Angier, Natalie. *Woman: An Intimate Geography*. New York: Houghton Mifflin Harcourt, 1999.

Bagemihl, Bruce. *Biological Exuberance: Animal Homosexuality and Natural Diversity*. New York: St. Martin's Press, 2000.

Baker, Robin. *Sperm Wars*. London: Fourth Estate, 1996.

Baker, R.R., and M.A. Bellis. "Human Sperm Competition: Ejaculate Manipulation by Females and a Function for the Female Orgasm." *Animal Behaviour* 46, no. 5 (1993), 887–909.

Benjamin, Harry, and R.E.L. Masters. *Prostitution and Morality*. New York: The Julian Press, 1964.

Bieri, James. *Percy Bysshe Shelley: A Biography*. Baltimore: Johns Hopkins University Press, 2008.

Bloch, Iwan. *Anthropological Studies on the Strange Sexual Practices of All Races and All Ages*. Honolulu: University Press of the Pacific, 2001.

Bloch, Iwan. *Marquis de Sade: His Life and Works*. Amsterdam: Fredonia Books, 2002.

Brownell, Robert. *Marriage of Inconvenience*. New York: Pallas Athene, 2013.

Bullough, Vern L. *Handbook of Medieval Sexuality*. New York: Taylor and Francis, 1996.

Cantarella, Eva. *Bisexuality in the Ancient World*. New Haven: Yale University Press, 2002.

Carey, C. "Archilochus and Lycambes." *The Classical Quarterly* 36, no. 1 (1986), 60–67.

Crowley, Alistair. *The Book of Lies*. New York: Samuel Weiser Press, 1986.

Culberston, J.C. *Cincinnati Lancet and Clinic* 35. Cincinnati, 1895.

Dotson-Blake, Kylie P. "Exploring Social Sexual Scripts Related to Oral Sex." *The Professional Counselor* 2, no. 1 (Feb. 2012), 1–11.

Dubin, Nathaniel E. *The Fabliaux* New York: W.W. Norton, 2013.

Eberhard, William B. *Female Control: Sexual Selection by Cryptic Female Choice*. Princeton: Princeton University Press, 1996.

Edwardes, Allen, and R.E.L. Masters. *The Cradle of Erotica*. New York: The Julian Press, 1962.

Ernst, Max. "Hands Off Love." *La Revolution Surrealiste* 9–10 (Oct. 1927).

Forberg, F. Karl. *Manuel of Classical Erotology*. Manchester, 1884.

Ford, Clellan, and Frank A. Beach. *Patterns of Sexual Behavior*. New York: Harper & Row, 1951.

Gammel, Irene. *Baroness Elsa: Gender, Dada, and Everyday Modernity—A Cul-*

tural Biography. Cambridge: MIT Press, 2003.

Garrity, Joan. *The Sensuous Woman.* New York: Dell, 1982.

Glazebrook, Allison. *Greek Prostitutes in the Ancient Mediterranean.* Madison: University of Wisconsin Press, 2011.

Greenberg, David F. *The Construction of Homosexuality.* Chicago: University of Chicago Press, 1990.

Griffiths, John Gwyn. *The Origins of Osiris and His Cult.* Amsterdam: Brill, 1980.

Grimmelshausen, Hans. *The Adventurous Simplicissimus.* London: William Heinemann, 1912.

Guiley, Rosemary Ellen. *The Encyclopedia of Witches, Witchcraft, and Wicca,* 3d ed. New York: Facts on File, 2008.

Hamilton, Allan McLane. *A System of Legal Medicine,* Vol. 1. New York: E.B. Treat, 1894.

Harmes, Marcus. *Supernatural and Secular Power in Early Modern England.* Farnham, England: Ashgate, 2015.

Harper, April, ed., *Medieval Sexuality: A Casebook.* New York: Routledge, 2008.

Henderson, Jeffrey. *The Maculate Muse: Obscene Language in Attic Comedy.* Oxford: Oxford University Press, 1991.

Henke, James T. *Courtesans and Cuckolds: A Glossary of Renaissance Dramatic Bawdy.* New York: Garland, 1979.

Herbert, Algernon. *Nimrod: A Discourse on Certain Passages of History and Fable,* Vol. 1. R. Priestly, 1828.

Herdt, Gilbert. *Rituals of Manhood: Male Initiation in Papua New Guinea.* Berkeley: University of California Press, 1982.

Hill, Craig A. *Human Sexuality: Personality and Social Psychological Perspectives.* Los Angeles: Sage, 2008.

Huntington, Rania. "Foxes and Sex in Late Imperial Chinese Narratives." *Nan Nu* 2, no. 1 (Jan. 2000), 78–128.

Hyde, Janet. *Understanding Human Sexuality,* 9th ed. Boston: McGraw-Hill, 2006.

Jackson, Michael D. *The Palm at the End of the Mind: Relatedness, Religiosity, and the Real.* Durham: Duke University Press, 2009.

Jackson, Peter A. "Non-Normative Sex/Gender Categories in the Theravada Buddhist Scriptures." *Australian Humanities Review* (April 1996).

Kamen, Henry. *Inquisition and Society in Spain in the Sixteenth and Seventeenth Centuries.* Bloomington: Indiana University Press, 1985.

Keuls, Eva. *The Reign of the Phallus.* Berkeley: University of California Press, 1993.

Kilmer, Martin. *Greek Erotica.* New York: Duckworth, 1993.

Kinsey, Alfred. *Sexual Behavior in the Human Male.* New York: W.B. Saunders, 1948.

Krafft-Ebing, Richard. *Psychopathia Sexualis.* London: F.A. Davis Company, 1894.

Lai, His. *The Sexual Teachings of the Jade Dragon: Daoist Methods for Male Sexual Revitalization.* Rochester: Destiny Books, 2002.

Lampert, Ada. *The Evolution of Love.* Westport, CT: Greenwood, 1997.

Leick, Gwendolyn. *Sex and Eroticism in Mesopotamian Literature.* New York: Routledge, 1994.

Leupp, Gary. *Male Colors: The Construction of Homosexuality in Tokugawa Japan.* Berkeley: University of California Press, 1997

Levack, Brain P. *The Witchcraft Sourcebook,* 2d ed. New York: Routledge, 2003.

Levin, Eve. *Sex and Society in the World of the Orthodox Slavs* Ithaca: Cornell University Press, 1995.

Lewis, Sian. *The Athenian Woman: An Iconographic Handbook.* New York: Routledge, 2013.

Mank, Gregory William. *Hollywood's Hellfire Club.* New York: Feral House, 2007.

Marsot, Afaf. *Society and the Sexes in Medieval Islam.* Malibu: Udena, 1979

Martens, Klaus. *Pioneering North America: Mediators of European Culture and Literature.* Konigshausen, 2000.

Maruthupandian, Jayabalan, et al. "Cunnilingus Apparently Increases Duration of Copulation in the Indian Flying Fox, Pteropus giganteus," *PLoS One* 8, no. 3 (March 2013).

Mason, Diane. *The Secret Vice: Masturbation in Victorian Fiction and Medical Literature.* Manchester: Manchester University Press, 2008.

Masterson, Mark. *Sex in Antiquity: Exploring Gender and Sexuality in the Ancient World.* New York: Routledge, 2014.

McGreal, Scott A. "Does Oral Sex Have an

Evolutionary Purpose?" *Psychology Today*, Feb. 28, 2013.

Melnick, Jeffrey Paul. *Black-Jewish Relations on Trial: Leo Frank and Jim Conley in the New South*. Jackson: University Press of Mississippi, 2012.

Meyer, Johann. *Sexual Life in Ancient India*, Vol. 2. New York: Routledge, 1953.

Mormando, Franco. *The Preacher's Demons*. Chicago: University of Chicago Press, 1999.

Morris, R.J. "Aikane: Accounts of Hawaiian Same-Sex Relationships in the Journals of Captain Cook's Third Voyage." *Journal of Homosexuality* 19, no. 4 (1990), 21–54.

Murphy, Cullen. *God's Jury: The Inquisition and the Making of the Modern World*. Boston: Mariner Books, 2013.

Neill, James. *The Origins and Role of Same-Sex Relations in Human Societies*. Jefferson, NC: McFarland, 2011.

Nobile, Philip. "A New Hite Report—About Men." *New York Magazine*, June 15, 1981, 32–34.

Oliver, Douglas. *Polynesia in Early Historic Times*. Honolulu: Bess Press, 2002.

Olson, Carl. *Celibacy and Religious Traditions*. New York: Oxford University Press, 2007.

Onians, R.B. *The Origins of European Thought*. Cambridge: Cambridge University Press, 2015.

Paglia, Camille. *Sexual Personae: Art and Decadence from Nefertiti to Emily Dickinson*, Vol. 1. New York: Vintage, 1991.

Peakmen, Julie. *The Pleasures All Mine: A History of Perverse Sex*. London: Reaktion Books, 2013

Pham, Michael N. "Oral Sex as Infidelity-Detection," *Personality and Individual Differences* 54, no. 6 (April 2013), 792–795.

Pikula, Tanya. "Bram Stoker's *Dracula* and Late-Victorian Advertising Tactics: Earnest Men, Virtuous Ladies, and Porn." *English Literature in Translation 1880–1920* 55, no. 3 (2012), 283–302.

Pop, Andrei. *Antiquity, Theater, and the Painting of Henry Fuseli*. New York: Oxford University Press, 2015

Porter, Roy. *Sexual Knowledge, Sexual Science*. CUP Archive, 1994.

Ramsland, Katherine. "Abuse of Corpse." *Psychology Today*, Nov. 27, 2012.

Rudat, Wolfgang. "Milton, Freud, St. Augustine: *Paradise Lost* and the History of Human Sexuality." *Mosaic XV* (1982), 109–122.

Savoie, John. "'That Fallacious Fruit': Lapsarian Lovemaking in *Paradise Lost*." *Milton Quarterly* 45, no. 3 (2011), 161–171.

Sayfuddin, Murad. *Love and Sex in Islam*. Ansar Publishing House, 2004.

Schaller, George. *The Mountain Gorilla: Ecology and Behavior*. American Anthropological Association, 1963.

Schmidt, Leigh Eric. *Heaven's Bride: The Unspeakable Life of Ida Craddock*. New York: Basic Books, 2010.

Sherman, William L. *Forced Native Labor in 16 century Central America*. Lincoln: University of Nebraska Press, 1979

Simons, Patricia. *The Sex of Men in Premodern Europe*. New York: Cambridge University Press, 2011.

Skinner, Marilyn B. *Sexuality in Greek and Roman Culture*. New York: John Wiley & Sons, 2013.

Smith, Tyler S. *Whore Stories: A Revealing History of the World's Oldest Profession*. Adams Media, 2012.

Smythers, Ruth. *Marriage & Love: Instructions for Females on Courtship and Matrimony, with Tips to Discourage Sexual Advances from Husbands*. Guilford, CT: Lyons Press, 1894.

Stevens, John. *Tantra of the Tachikawa Ryu*. New York: Stone Bridge Press, 2010.

Talmey, Bernard Simon. *Woman: A Treatise on the Normal and Pathological Emotions of Feminine Love*. New York: Practitioner's Publishing Company, 1908.

Tan, Min, et al. "Fellatio by Fruit Bats Prolongs Copulation Time." *PLoS ONE* 4, no. 10 (Oct. 2009).

Taylor, Timothy. *The Prehistory of Sex*. New York: Bantam, 1997.

Thody, Philip. *Don't Do It! A Dictionary of the Forbidden*. New York: St. Martin's Press, 1997.

van de Velde, Theodoor. *The Ideal Marriage*. New York: Random House, 1986.

Varone, Antonio. *Erotica Pompeiana: Love Inscriptions on the Walls of Pompeii*. Rome: L'Erma di Bretschneider, 2002

Veenker, Ronald. "Forbidden Fruit: Ancient

Near Eastern Sexual Metaphors." *HUCA* 70–71 (1999–2000), 57.

Viscuso, Patrick. "Theodore Balsamon's Canonical Images of Women." *Greek, Roman, and Byzantine Studies* 45 (2005).

Wallace, Irving. *The Intimate Sex Lives of Famous People*. Port Townsend: Feral Books, 2008.

Wright, Thomas. *Worship of the Generative Powers: During the Middle Ages in Western Europe*. 1865.

Index